DOWNSIZING

DOWNSIZING

Confronting
Our Possessions
in Later Life

DAVID J. EKERDT

COLUMBIA UNIVERSITY PRESS
NEW YORK

COLUMBIA
UNIVERSITY
PRESS

Columbia University Press gratefully acknowledges the generous support
for this book provided by Publisher's Circle member Bruno A. Quinson.

Columbia University Press
Publishers Since 1893
New York   Chichester, West Sussex
cup.columbia.edu

Library of Congress Cataloging-in-Publication Data

Names: Ekerdt, David J. (David Joseph), 1949– author.
Title: Downsizing : confronting our possessions in later life / David J. Ekerdt.
Description: New York : Columbia University Press, [2020] |
Includes bibliographical references and index.
Identifiers: LCCN 2019050913 (print) | LCCN 2019050914 (ebook) |
ISBN 9780231189804 (cloth) | ISBN 9780231189811 (trade paperback) |
ISBN 9780231548557 (ebook)
Subjects: LCSH: House cleaning. | Orderliness. | Older people—Conduct of life.
Classification: LCC TX324 .E34 2020 (print) | LCC TX324 (ebook) |
DDC 648/.5—dc23
LC record available at https://lccn.loc.gov/2019050913
LC ebook record available at https://lccn.loc.gov/2019050914
♾

Columbia University Press books are printed on
permanent and durable acid-free paper.

Printed in the United States of America

Cover design: Lisa Hamm

FOR PEGGY, WITH WHOM I HAVE ACCUMULATED MUCH

CONTENTS

Introduction: Not Forever 1

1 A Convoy of Possessions Across the Life Course 20

2 With Aging, How Large a Convoy? 42

3 Moving Calls the Question 69

4 Contours of Household Disbandment 92

5 Gifts to Others 128

6 Selling Possessions 150

7 Donations and Discards 169

8 Emotion and Evaluation 189

9 Advice 210

Appendix 223
Notes 227
References 247
Index 261

DOWNSIZING

INTRODUCTION

Not Forever

C lare Twomey is a British ceramics artist whose exhibits invite members of the public to interact with her work. One such exhibit, titled *Forever,* was displayed at the Nelson-Atkins Museum of Art in Kansas City, my hometown, in 2010–2011. The artist had earlier visited the museum to view a famous antique pottery collection consisting of 1,345 items that the museum is required to keep "in trust" and intact "forever." The collection gave her an idea.

Twomey selected one item in the collection, a two-handled cup dating to 1720, and had it reproduced 1,345 times. She created an installation at the museum in which the cups were placed in rows on long tables, with numbers beside them. Museum patrons were invited to view the identical cups, select one that they would like to own, and write down the number of that cup to submit in a weekly drawing. Through these drawings, the cups were gradually assigned to people. The exhibit was extremely popular.

If you were assigned a cup, you were notified, and your name was put beside it. You were required to sign a "deed" in which you pledged to care for the cup, value it, and display it "forever," just like the pottery in the museum's collection. The entire encounter among artist, objects, and the public was, according to Clare Twomey's website, meant to explore "ideas of permanence, responsibility, memory, desirability, and value."[1]

At the time of *Forever*, I had been conducting research on older people, possessions, and downsizing for several years. This exhibition encapsulated the problem: people think that they must keep certain things forever. The consumption of mass-produced goods is an astonishing phenomenon. Fifty identical sets of fine china came out of some factory one day. One set came to be owned by my grandmother, and one set came to be owned by your grandmother, and each grandmother took the china home and made it *hers*. Today we can never separate the china from the family because it was *hers*, and our family's set is not at all the same as the set that your family has.

I wanted to win one of the museum's cups and smash it on a YouTube video: "Take that, Clare Twomey. It's only a cup!" I kept submitting my name for a cup, but I never won. When distribution day came at end of the three-month exhibit, people came in to get their cups and sign the deed promising to care for the cup "forever." Thirty of the cups were not claimed, so the exhibit went into a second round. People were now invited to write and submit a full formal museum label of the kind that could be displayed beside a cup. Among the hundreds of submissions, thirty label writers would be chosen to get a cup. So I wrote a label, and finally I got a cup.

To conclude this exhibit, the director of the museum and the artist herself each picked a contributed label to feature on the museum's website. The director's pick for the label read in part:

> This *Cup* is a reflection of my dedication of support to our museum and to the ideas of permanence, responsibility, memory, desirability and value as they relate to art and its preservation in our beautiful city. The *Cup* is displayed here in my home, enclosed in this dedicated cabinet shelf, as a daily reminder of my pledge from 2010, *Forever.*[2]

Such sentiment was perfectly consistent with the stated intention for the exhibit: to highlight responsibility for the protection and conservation of objects. For her part, Clare Twomey selected my label. I had given the artwork a title and wrote, in part:

"Not *Forever*. For a while." The title for this cup gently disputes the impossible promise of "forever." Material goods such as ceramics can endure, but human frailty and mortality put a bound on the commitments of individual lives. "For a while" is all we can promise.[3]

After I had argued with the entire premise of the exhibit, Clare Twomey picked my label. For this choice, I have to admire the artist, because she knows that I know that she knows exactly what she is up to. She is inducing 1,345 people to behave as though mass-produced goods are entirely special, personal, singular, and inalienable to them. And that is genius!

As for my cup, I do care for it. I display it in a glass case, with the label, because there is a heck of a good story to tell when anyone expresses any passing interest in my piece of salt-glazed stoneware.

THINGS IN MOTION

This is a book about possessing things both cherished and ordinary. The possessing and the things themselves can be rolled into a term—*material convoy*—in order to convey the idea that belongings accompany our lives across time. This book takes a special interest in the material convoy as it crests in size at midlife and its fate begins to become an issue for oneself and others—especially in later life when, in relocating from larger to smaller quarters, getting rid of possessions becomes necessary. I report findings from research among older Americans who have recently relocated and divested themselves of possessions and among others who are aware that they may someday need to move. This research has taken two directions that diverge from most other approaches to the question of aging and possessions, which tend to concentrate on static and single things.

First, during this experience—potential or actual relocation in later life—possessions are metaphorically "in motion," on their way to new places and to being viewed in new ways. When things reside or stay with people, when they are kept, they have meaning as part of a human-material bond. Taking things out of their accustomed places to move them creates what Nicky Gregson calls a "gap in accommodation." In that gap the human-material bond is exposed to scrutiny.[4] Things-in-motion can be revelatory.[5] They prompt questions: Why do I have this or keep this? Should I continue to do so?

Second, the approach taken here addresses the possessions of later life in their totality. Much has been learned from studies of one kind of thing—for example, older people's experience with clothing or gardens or entire houses. Studies of self-identified, selected "cherished possessions" have built a body of knowledge about the meaning of things. At the same time, the "convoy" metaphor shifts our focus to consider the body of possessions in their entirety, from the heirloom to the trivial, as a dynamic aggregate, the whole of which demands attention to Clare Twomey's "ideas of permanence, responsibility, memory, desirability, and value."

Although this is a report about things, it is even more an exploration of what people do with things. Some consequences result from the shift in focus from viewing possessions as static things to viewing them as dynamic and from seeing them as single pieces to seeing them as a whole. If things are part of the "extended self," as Russell Belk has put it, when the status of those things changes, the self may need to change, too.[6] Or perhaps it is the other way around. If the person changes, as happens with advancing age, then there may be implications for the status of the material convoy. If things are "in motion," then they will have their meaning tested. An owner might assume that some possessions are necessary to happiness, or wanted by others, or at least worth some money. Divestment activities will test these assumptions. Finally, as long as possessions reside in the same place, they are mainly the business of that household—private property. But bring them to the attention or into the view of others, and the private becomes public, the personal becomes communal. Like a dollhouse with one wall removed, one's things are exposed to scrutiny.

I have written this book not only to develop this set of ideas but also to turn readers' minds in several directions. I want to *focus at-*

tention on the inevitable reckoning that awaits anyone growing older in a consumer society in which accumulation of mass-produced goods is a given. The time comes when households can no longer easily accommodate and care for the thousands of belongings that the inhabitants have taken in to maintain daily life. As this happens, people's vague self-consciousness about "their stuff" rises to the level of a potential or actual predicament. This reckoning now faces tens of millions of Americans as the baby boom cohort passes into retirement and beyond. If this book leaves anyone feeling uneasy—for oneself or others—about household possession practices, that is all to the good.

I want to *kindle admiration* for those who accomplish household downsizing. What they manage to do in two or three months' time is hard and really quite remarkable. Not only do they divest great quantities of material, they adapt, reconcile themselves to age-related limitations, and solve a problem that most others put off to another day. They change themselves in the process. I bring the voices of our research participants forward so that readers can benefit from their stories of how they did it and how they reflect on the episode. I want to *encourage less sentimentality* about the material convoys and homes of older adults. People do indeed have possession and place attachments, but we need more clear-eyed thinking about *all* of the household's contents and, with advancing age, the continued suitability of present housing. One thing that downsizers discover is that the accustomed meaning of many, many things eventually fades. I want to *mute scolding* about any overfull households in later life. People facing a confrontation with their things already know that there is a problem and it puzzles them: "It's just incredible the stuff you collect. Sheesh!" Let's allow that people had good reasons for furnishing themselves to be competent adults, parents, workers, and more. We can suspend judgment that they may have been foolish consumers in favor of respect and support for their initiatives to manage the future.

Finally, for people who study later life, I want to *elevate the material dimension of the life course*, possessions in particular. More than incidental, possessions are a partner in the process of aging. These are the mundane things that people see, touch, and move among all day long; these things help and they comfort, but they can also bother and threaten, all with real behavioral effects. They are the material enactment, past and present, of age-related economic, family, and cultural roles. They are a record of human development, aspiration, and regret. When asking what it is to grow older, answers await within the interiors of the home.

TERMS

Because the subject of this book is things-in-motion, especially as older adults relocate, it is worth saying something about two sets of terms. First, there are terms for the physical items: possessions, belongings, property, things, objects, and stuff. *Possession* is based on the Latin word "to sit," and it seems appropriate to think of possessions as those things that reside long enough to require some attention, even if only to be put somewhere. In a similar sense, *long* is the word embedded in *belonging*. To belong is to be in some relation to a person. *Possession* and *belonging* are good synonyms; both words signal items that have settled in with us, that have duration. *Property* is a term to be used sparingly because it is rooted in the idea of ownership, and not all possessions may be owned by an individual. Some possessions are owned in common, and an individual or keeper is not actually free to unilaterally decide their fate. Following the convention of "thing theory," an *object* is mere materiality, whereas a *thing* is something invested with a relationship to a person.[7] Things have a bearing on me, whereas objects do not necessarily have such standing. *Stuff*, according to Daniel Miller, is hard to define because it is hopeless to think of anything that would be excluded from this all-encompassing term.[8] I forgo the use of the word *stuff* as a catch-all synonym for possessions or things, reserving it to designate a special status of material that I shall explain in chapter 4. So possessions, belongings, and things are more than objects, and any of it sometimes has the unique characteristic of being stuff.

Second, various verbs can describe the reduction of the material convoy: dispose, divest, disband, downsize, and dispossess. It is no coincidence that some of these words share the prefix *dis-*, which indicates undoing or negation. To *dispose* means to un-place or to replace in the sense of re-settling an object, putting it somewhere else. Disposition covers many activities, as when there is a gift disposition or waste disposal. *Divest* is somewhat narrower in scope; the word literally means to undress but also extends to the removal of any property. To *disband* is to break up. In later life relocations, the object of disbandment is the household and its contents. Jean-Sébastien Marcoux used this exact concept to describe the behavior of older movers in Montreal, calling it (in French) *casser maison*, breaking up the house.[9] Likewise, the older women interviewed by Donald Redfoot and Kurt Back called their moves "breaking up housekeeping."[10] *Downsize* came into common parlance in the mid-1970s. The term was applied to describe the redesign of automobiles but soon came to describe the refashioning of companies, eventually becoming a euphemism for dismissals and layoffs. Now the term commonly extends to the reduction of the volume of possessions and the size of the dwelling. Finally, *dispossession*, as I see it, has a psychological slant, reserved for the parting of persons from possessions. One may dispose or divest as a behavior, but dispossession is an experience. In the chapters ahead, I have made an effort to police the rigor of these behavioral descriptors: disposal and divestment are what one does with possessions at any point in life, disbandment and downsizing apply to households, and dispossession is a matter of one's feelings.

A SHELF FOR THIS BOOK

Because this is a book about possessions—kept things—I have suggestions about the (imaginary) shelf on which it might be placed. What else would one see there? To begin, a file bulging with topical clippings from magazines and newspapers, blog posts, and website pages—all drawn from the constant river of lifestyle commentary and all bearing some optimal perspective on possessions that promise a better, richer life. Some writers meditate on the meaning and emotional content of certain significant objects. Other writers speak to readers' uneasiness about the less-than-ideal management of their homes and how their consumption of goods is out of control, from which flows advice about taming clutter and disorganization. Other articles address readers' alarm about the homes and habits of others and how to maneuver them toward better domestic order. The steady supply of such articles is no accident. They serve an industry that stands ready to offer goods, services, and counsel for possession anxiety. In addition to short pieces, these themes get bundled comprehensively into advice manuals and how-to books that can guide adults toward mastery of messy material convoys.

Next, this book could be shelved with the scholarly literature on the relation between people and possessions. Here would be studies of material culture, as in anthropology and museum studies; studies of consumers and consumption, as in sociology and marketing science; and studies of the ways that self and identity are constituted and expressed by things, a longstanding focus in social psychology and in cultural and humanistic studies. This book could also be shelved compatibly among the research on place and relocation in later life. In this category, the foremost thinking proceeds from environmental psychologists and gerontologists and their concern with the fit between persons and the places where they live. The quality and arrangement of these places, homes, and housing is a particular focus of architecture and design. Movement between places—relocation, migration—is a specialty of demographers and geographers, and this book is aligned with their interest in why people move and do not move.

Finally, this book could sit somewhere near the big shelf of sweeping frameworks that organize thinking about life-span human development and that orient scholars to the life course perspective. Themes from the human development literature certainly find their way into research on household disbandment in later life: loss versus gain, adaptation, selection, coping, resilience, stress, and control. Themes from the life course perspective, such as transitions, life stages, and lifelong processes, can also readily inform the problem of aging and possessions. The life course principle of "linked lives" encompasses the family dimensions of household disbandment, including parenting, caregiving, intergenerational decision-making, solidarity, and support. Human development and life course frameworks also attend to the key reality of health and functioning in later life—how advancing age raises the risk of vulnerability and with it the significant residential question: Where is the best place for me to live?

How older people divest and downsize is a singular topic that is not only newsworthy and practical in its own right but also rooted in big narratives about human development and the life course. This topic can be approached from many disciplinary angles. It lies at the intersection of people, possessions, place, and time. There are some matters at that intersection that this book will cover only tangentially or hardly at all.

Most important, I have not attempted a full account of residential relocation as a story about housing, which is an individual-level transition that encompasses decisions about housing, the search for it, negotiations, financial and legal arrangements, the immediate moving experience, and setting up in the new place. In project interviews, people offered many details about these steps and about the emotions involved; however, the research was organized to focus specifically on possession management across this process. In particular, for homeowners, the interviews did not directly pursue the "real estate story" and the disposition of the most obvious possession: the residential property itself. Over time, the dwelling is likely to have been developed, modified, or shaped to the needs of its occupants.[11] Participants who lived in houses told us about the work that they had put into the place and their feelings about the way that it had been sold or valued. The home as a "thing" and leave-taking from it are topics that deserve full study in their own right. At the same time, the relationship between relocation and downsizing is a nice chicken-and-egg question and is taken up in chapter 3.

Hoarding behavior is outside the scope of this book. Compulsive hoarding—the acquisition of large quantities of things and the inability to remove them—is conduct that is best assessed and handled by mental health professionals.[12] In the popular imagination, hoarding lies on a continuum with minimalism at one end and hoarding at the other as an extreme form of possession acquisition with lax clutter management. Reality television shows have built a voyeuristic, public fascination with the behavior; people will casually call themselves and others hoarders (and pack rats) when they see what they think is overaccumulation. Compulsive hoarding, however, lies outside the bounds of normal possession management, and we did not encounter it in the households we visited. Hoarding tends to begin early in life. It is hard to classify as a psychiatric disorder, resists treatment, and confounds public health and safety officials, social service agencies, and property managers.[13] There is active research on hoarding, and resources are available to help people cope with it.[14]

With a focus on people's management and divestment of their own things, the book also passes over two additional situations of later life: moves to residential care and posthumous clean-outs by others. Moves to residential care, if the stay is extended, will radically concentrate personal possessions in the new setting. The material convoy is typically reduced to selected photos and decorative items, personal care supplies, and perhaps minimal furniture. This topic, too, has received research attention, especially as to the meanings of such residual holdings.[15] After such moves, the disposition of the household contents that one has left behind falls to others, as does the dismantling of a home after its occupants have died.[16] The experience registers powerful emotions among those who undertake these clean-outs.

SOURCES OF INFORMATION

My observations at the intersection of older people, possessions, place, and time come from a program of research that has encompassed four data collection efforts. I describe them in a general way here, with more technical detail about samples included in the key references. I also name and credit my collaborators on these projects. I am indebted to their creative thinking about how to conduct this research and their reflection and insight about people's responses to our questions. These are the colleagues to whom I refer when I use the collective *we* and *our* to talk about findings and conclusions.

Elder and Family Study

This initial project was undertaken to explore the feasibility of research on elders and household downsizing. We wanted to find out, for example, which interview techniques and lines of inquiry would be most productive and make the best use of participants' time. The project was supported by the National Institute on Aging under the title, "Strategies for Household Disbandment" (AG19978). The collaborators on this project were Mary Elizabeth Bowen, Molly Dingel, Jaber Gubrium, and Julie Sergeant.

In 2002–2003 we interviewed thirty-eight older adults in thirty households who had moved in the previous year either within or to the region around Lawrence, Kansas, and Kansas City, Missouri. We located these volunteers by posting flyers at congregate housing sites, by soliciting the community generally, and by word-of-mouth referrals. We screened for volunteers over the age of 60 who had moved to a smaller household, who had not moved to a nursing home, and who had been able to functionally participate in the move. The interviewees ranged in age from 60 to 87. If a couple resided in the household, we interviewed both together.

The interviews centered on participants' recollection of activities from the period of time when the participants knew that they would move until they did move. We asked how they came to make decisions about what they would and would not take to the new place, about methods of disposition, about the help the participants received, and about their feelings throughout. Also in this project, we asked elders to identify someone who had helped with the transition so that we could "get some additional perspective" on the move. Sixteen households gave us referrals, all to family members, and we completed interviews with fourteen. These sessions followed the same format as those with elders and focused on the disbandment period—the breaking up of the household in the months and weeks prior to the move. Additional details are available in key project publications.[17]

Midwest Study

Similar in conception to the first study of elders, this project was fielded with a more comprehensive set of questions in a two-site, unitary design.[18] Funding under the title "Downsizing Possessions for Residential Moves in Later Life" likewise came from the National Institute on Aging (AG30477). In order to meet the objection that household disbandment is mainly a problem of affluence, we aimed to interview a sample of elders who were economically diverse. We recruited in the same region as the first study and in the area of Detroit, Michigan. The two research teams ultimately spoke with ninety-eight persons in seventy-nine households between 2008 and 2013. The participants were recruited and screened using methods similar to the first study. We sought participants out through health fairs, retirement communities, and community newspapers, as well as by word of mouth. In all cases, people said that they had less space in the new place and had been required to dispose of things. For a subset of households, we also attempted to secure pre-move interviews, but the chaotic U.S. housing market during this period made it very difficult for people to project moving dates. Almost all interviews took place in participants' homes.

The collaborators on this project were Mark Luborsky and Catherine Lysack, co–principal investigators at Wayne State University, and their colleagues Cathy Cross and Jennifer Van Nuil. The University of Kansas team included Aislinn Addington, Ben Hayter, and Gabriella Smith. Rebecca Swinburne Romine compiled economic data about the impact of the recession in the study's locales. Jaber Gubrium at University of Missouri was a project consultant.

National Survey

In 2010, we were able to place some questions about possessions and relocation into a national survey. The University of Michigan Health and Retirement Study (HRS) is a longitudinal panel study that surveys a representative sample of approximately twenty thousand people in America, supported by the National Institute on Aging (U01AG009740) and the Social Security Administration. The HRS collects economic, health, and psychosocial information from persons aged 50 and older. Panel members have been resurveyed every two years since 1992, with new birth cohorts added over time. Each wave of the HRS includes ten experimental question modules, one of which is randomly assigned to a 10 percent sample of respondents who also answered the core survey. Experimental modules are strictly limited to a few minutes in length. The collaborators in the Midwest Study composed a twelve-item module on possessions that was fielded with the 2010 wave of the HRS. The module was completed by 1,898 persons, of whom 1,814 were 50 and older (a 90 percent response rate). These data have since been made available to the public and are linked to the full archive of data on HRS respondents, available at hrsonline.isr.umich.edu. Lindsey Baker joined us in the analysis of these new questions.[19]

Ageing as Future Project

Older adults' views on residential planning come from the project Altern als Zukunft/Ageing as Future, a collaborative, multimethod, multisample study of perceptions of time in later life being carried out in the Czech Republic, China, Germany, Taiwan, and the United States. Funding for this project has come from the Volkswagen Foundation in Germany (Az 86 758/86 759/86 760). The material here is drawn from interviews that Catheryn Koss and I conducted in 2013 and 2014 with thirty community-dwelling individuals in the midwestern United States. The individuals were recruited in the community using age and sex quotas to reflect a range of experience with retirement and later life. Interview content centered on daily life in retirement and preparations and expectations for the future.[20] On the latter theme, we specifically asked whether participants had plans for where they would live in the future and when they felt was the right time to deal with this issue. These conversations helped us to derive the conclusions about "residential reasoning" that are included in chapter 3.

The insights gained from these four projects were available to us only thanks to the time, generosity, and hospitality of our research participants. With enormous goodwill, they patiently, playfully, reflectively, and sometimes wearily endured our questions. On a number of occasions, they thanked us for the opportunity to discuss what happened when they downsized and moved. "Believe it or not, it's very refreshing to talk about it [the downsizing] sometimes, the way we did today, because I can see it clearer." In *Learning from Strangers*, Robert Weiss writes that it is a privilege to be "admitted to someone else's private experience."[21] Our participants admitted us into their lives and homes, sometimes with a full tour of both.

In the chapters ahead, some of these persons will be named (with pseudonyms). An appendix lists the 134 participants in the 109 households of the Elder and Family Study and the Midwest Study, along with age and marital status. Whether named or not in the pages ahead, all of these people have richly informed this book.

Other sources of information deserve acknowledgement. Julie Sergeant and Erin Smith, each conducting separate doctoral research on residential relocation, helped establish a demographic frame for the particular stories emerging from our interviews. Dennis Domer and Keith Diaz Moore, professors of architecture at the University of Kansas, each in his own way introduced me to the importance of places and dwellings in later life. Keith has been my tutor in environmental gerontology. Dennis, along with Erin Smith, challenged me to imagine innovative forms of community housing for later life. In recruiting volunteers for interviews, I am in debt to facility directors and housing managers who gave us entrée to their residents in order to make our pitch and who also dropped practical comments along the way about "people's stuff." Mary Kay Buysse welcomed me to attend annual conferences of the National Association of Senior Move Managers, putting me among professionals whose business is divestment and downsizing services for older adults and their families. Senior move managers have stories. One local move manager, Gerre Wade, was an early sounding board for our research ideas, and checking in with her has always been time well spent. Finally, Erin Adamson lent editorial assistance for the writing of this book, and Stephen Wesley of Columbia University Press and three anonymous reviewers helped guide it to its final form.

There is important, inadvertent historical context for our research: the Great Recession. A housing bubble—years in the making and inflated by risky mortgages—burst in 2007, leading to a full-blown crisis in 2008 that cascaded through the global financial system. Stocks plummeted, unemployment rose, and spending on durable and nondurable goods declined dramatically. By the end of 2009, U.S. housing prices had dropped 28 percent from their peak in 2006.[22] By one estimate, "on average, households lost one-quarter of their wealth between the middle of 2007 and early 2009, and a third of those losses were in home equity."[23] The widespread job and wealth losses also had an emotional toll. Survey data showed sharp declines in life satisfaction and positive affect, and sharp increases in worry and stress.[24] The Midwest Study and the 2010 wave of the HRS were fielded in the midst of these events.

In the two standard metropolitan statistical areas of the Midwest Study, both Kansas City and Detroit had experienced less of a pre-recession housing bubble than was seen nationally. In Kansas City, housing price data drawn from the Federal Housing Finance Agency shows low but positive growth rates in home prices from 2005 to 2007, followed by a more moderate decline in prices (relative to the national trend) from mid-2007 on. In the Detroit metro market, home prices turned negative in 2006 and saw much greater decreases compared to the national average. Price declines later moderated in both regions, but home values still had not resumed growing by the end of 2011. The bad news on unemployment was a mirror image of home prices. According to the U.S. Bureau of Labor Statistics, the national unemployment rate in 2007 was 4.6 percent, rising to 9.6 percent in 2010. Kansas City area statistics tracked the national numbers, with unemployment rising to 8.9 percent in 2010. The Detroit area saw a similar trend, but at higher levels. Joblessness already stood at 8.6 percent in 2007, rising to 16 percent in 2009 and decreasing to just under 15 percent in 2010. In these two regions of the United States, the effects of the downturn lingered into the second decade of the century.

The financial crisis was not the focus of our studies; we did not ask direct questions about it. Being mostly retired, the people in our interview and survey studies would have mainly felt the recession's hit on their retirement savings and home values. We heard participants voice concern for family members and neighbors who faced the same circumstances and were also at risk for job and income losses. Recessionary effects also must have weighed on the complete strangers who were the ones making decisions to buy the participating elders' houses and personal property. It is difficult to specify how the national mood affected the responses of our research participants. If conducted in another period, accounts of moves and downsizing might well have been somewhat less fraught. As we talked to people, the economic downturn was a background motif, a taken-for-granted situation expressed in observations that "things are not selling," "nobody is buying," and "the economy's not so good."

The three interview studies were conducted in similar ways. Guided conversations with single participants typically lasted sixty to ninety minutes; interviews involving couples tended to last longer, because both contributed answers. None of the interviewers (myself included) knew the participants prior to interviews. Sessions were recorded and transcribed; interviewers' notes were generated for project records. In the excerpts cited in this book, I have masked or changed some details to preserve confidentiality, including the use of pseudonyms. All ethical requirements of informed consent, confidentiality, and protection from harm were met in accordance with U.S. standards for research. Project collaborators used thematic analysis to identify common patterns that emerged as important to participants' descriptions of their possession management and relocation experiences.[25] Concurrent with the selection and condensation of themes, we were alert to disconfirming instances and negative cases so as to guard against interpretive bias.[26]

From these interview studies, conducted on regional samples of limited size, we could not claim to have sampled the universe of U.S. experience with aging, relocation, and possessions. However, I can confidently claim that we found regularities and patterns, gathering similar narratives across households about, for example, the sequence of disbandment activities, the gendered hierarchy of family giveaways, the bottom line on possession sales, and the weight of deadline stress as a move draws near. This narrative consonance is no coincidence. For one thing, even though downsizing is typically a nonroutine, do-it-yourself task, people do not need to make it up as they go along. There is enough communal and biographical experience with relocation to generate common repertoires of behavior for the project of relocation. Everybody makes a floor map of the new place; everybody goes on the hunt for boxes. Another reason for converging stories is this: social rehearsal. Our project's interviewers were probably not the first persons to have heard the account of the move: its triumphs, its missteps, and its details about what went where and who did what. By the time we caught up with people—at some months' remove from the actual transition—they were likely to have become quite practiced at talking about it. Moving is a big event, and is enormously topical in one's social circle as it approaches, happens, and recedes into the recent past. Conversationally, the movers have figured out what other people want to know, what may catch their interest, and what may bore them. Participants said pithy things in our interviews that almost certainly they had tried out on others or had adopted from others. In the end, we do not really know what happened day by day over the disbandment process—we weren't there—but we do know what people tell stories about.

PLAN OF THE BOOK

Chapters 1 through 4 build on one another in a progression of ideas: the concept of a material convoy, its intersection with aging, how relocation demands a confrontation with the convoy, and some major dimensions of that encounter. Chapter 1 introduces the metaphor of the convoy to frame in a comprehensive way how people enact multiple life stages with multiple material goods. Material convoys are dynamic across changing lives, begging explanations for keeping and not keeping, both of which entail labor on their behalf. Chapter 2 takes up the composition of material convoys, their size, and the moral judgments that the convoys may provoke. Advancing age is likely to cause an accumulation of goods and shift the meaning of things, which in turn contributes to nagging feelings that convoys grow too large to be manageable in later life.

The predicament of possessions is accentuated by residential relocation, the topic of chapter 3. Older adults tend to move to smaller quarters, crossing a threshold to a more limited life. Of necessity, the stock and store of one's belongings must likewise be reduced. The chapter outlines temporal scenarios for the intertwined processes of relocation and possession downsizing. Now the work gets underway. Chapter 4 describes major dimensions of the disbandment project: how it is a cognitive task that involves planning, sorting, and decision-making; how the meanings of things and self are now up for review; the sequence of disbandment strategies; and important contexts within which the work proceeds.

Chapters 5 through 7 explore the major divestment strategies in more detail. These chapters can be read in any order. Gifts to others are the subject of chapter 5. Intentional placements seem an obvious strategy, and they are often governed by gender and kinship norms. Gifts, however, can meet with mixed success. Compared with direct gifts, open-ended offers ("Come get what you want") are less likely to test one's ties to family and friends. Sales (chapter 6) likewise seem an obvious strategy, and most downsizers try them. Their success depends on competence with sales procedure and pricing and on the ability to drain sentiment from possessions. Neither gifts nor sales, however, remove large quantities of goods. What does not leave by these means moves on to donations and discarding (chapter 7). In this strategy, the materiality of things begins to eclipse their meanings. Both of these outlets are apparently convenient but nevertheless prove to be laborious. Still, there is some intentionality to these divestments even as batch thinking now denominates things in truckloads, carloads, and bagfuls of mere stuff.

Chapter 8 summarizes the emotions of household disbandment: deadline stress, fatigue, regrets, and loss of control, as well as feelings of empowerment and optimism for life to be lived on a new footing. Such experience is also colored by the household's level of affluence. Chapter 9 carries lessons and conclusions, closing the book with our participants' advice to others, to which I add my own suggestions for elders, family members and friends, and professionals and researchers.

Even as the chapters ahead discuss regularities and common patterns in household downsizing, people's practical ability to accomplish the project diverges along lines of gender and social class. In this, possession management reflects processes of inequality that cumulate and shape experience across the entire course of life.[27] The contents of the separate chapters will bring out certain points about such social differences, and chapter conclusions will underline them.

Like one of Clare Twomey's cups, the contents of the material convoy will easily outlast the length of human life. If you can't take it with you—to the great beyond or just the next home—it's got to go somewhere. How people manage that is the story of this book.

1

A CONVOY OF POSSESSIONS
ACROSS THE LIFE COURSE

In thinking about the relationship between aging and possessions, we confront two different part-whole questions. First, should we focus on single possessions or particular kinds of possessions, or should we address the whole lot at once? Carving out selected possessions or types of things, such as clothing or collections, has been the more common route in social science research. However, in this chapter I want to develop a metaphor—the "convoy"—that can help us attend to things in their totality.

The second part-whole question is whether the management of possessions is something unique in later life or simply one stage of a lifelong encounter with the material world. As with the question about possessions, I favor the more encompassing view. Whole-life explanatory frameworks are now the established way to understand the temporal sweep of experience from birth to death. From such quarters as the biology of aging and its theory of evolutionary selection or from life span developmental psychology, explanations for human progression offer coherent logics for the understanding of human lives.[1] One such framework is the life course perspective in sociology, a "theoretical orientation" that encourages a long view of the varied circumstances of social life.[2] The life "course," that is, the way that life "goes," can be viewed objectively, as when demographers describe the usual patterns and regularities of social roles, such as the average age of marriage. As compared to the way that life typically goes, we can examine life histories, the way that lives have actually gone for individuals, for what reasons and with what outcomes. Yet another course for life is the way that it *should* go, the idealized scripts or maps for life's events to which individuals are socialized and which they then act to create.[3] The objects of life course thinking are careers, trajectories, sequences, and pathways that consist of roles and situations whose timings and durations vary in the context of history and place. These are lives in motion, on their way to the next stage, transition, or turning point. And because these are social lives, the trajectories and transitions of a single individual are linked and interdependent with those of others.

All possessions and *whole* lives are therefore the starting points for this inquiry into the particular challenges posed by belongings in later life.

A MATERIAL CONVOY

Scholarship about the life course is overwhelmingly focused on intangibles, principally age-patterned social roles, relationships, and health. These themes meet up in the influential convoy model of social relations. Robert Kahn and Toni Antonucci applied the convoy metaphor to describe a changeable structure of social ties that accompanies a person from birth to death:[4] "Individuals are conceptualized as part of a dynamic network or convoy that moves with them through time, space, and the life course."[5] The convoy of social relations—family, friends, colleagues, acquaintances—can protect and gratify individuals but also put them at risk. Social scientists who study the social convoy have methods for measuring it, and they have established both the antecedents and health consequences of convoy characteristics. Potentially, the social convoy can provision the life course with support, stress, or both.[6]

With a nod to this previous work, my colleagues and I have proposed that life course studies can take a "material turn." In this we join others in a shift of perspective, moving materialities—objects, bodies, spaces, technologies—forward from the background of real life to be instead tangible footings for subjective experience and change.[7] The discussion that follows is about possessions, but it is worth noting that the life course is also and importantly accomplished by material culture that is not personally owned, by affordances such as clean water, electricity, transportation corridors, public spaces, landscapes, and works of art.

Akin to the social convoy, the body of one's possessions at any one time and as borne through time is a *convoy of material support*.[8] Like the social convoy, the material convoy has members that are more important and less important (some even forgotten), members that endure and are transient, and members that also populate the convoys of others. The material convoy undergoes predictable age-linked changes (e.g., expansion in early adulthood). People develop affective and affirmative relations with their things: they want to give them a good home, or they can't stand to look at them. Like the social convoy, parts of the material convoy are maintained for their actual or potential supportiveness, but a larger convoy does not necessarily guarantee more benefit. Social networks and material convoys share one other feature: the person at their center may regard the constituents with ambivalence.[9] The stock and store of one's belongings can be a resource, an achievement, a delight, and a comfort, yes, but they may also by turns be a burden.

Possessions are more than mere adjuncts to the roles and transitions of the life course. They are the means by which successive social roles are embodied and conducted (imagine a child without toys, an adult without keys). Possessions furnish life course careers as workers, partners, parents, property owners, and cultural participants. People understand their place and progress in the life course in relation to goods, using them to fulfill age-related norms, expectations, and roles. Changing bodies receive grooming from self-care products and are mediated by clothing as people stage and re-stage their appearance. Living areas and properties are stocked and re-stocked when the household expands to include partners and children, who then entrain their own material convoys over time. Successive jobs require specialized clothing, equipment, and even

means of transportation. Away from work, possessions provision leisure time with entertainment, recreation, and flights of self-
development. Things received as gifts, often given to mark the passage of time or big life events, add to the convoy even as they create
future ties to others. Residential stability and maturity may also position one to accept custody and responsibility for heirlooms and
"family things."

Possessions have communicative value for presenting and telling
stories about oneself. Possessions are a way to evaluate in oneself
and others how well life is going and where it might go next.[10] Just
as they can signal conformity to age expectations and scripts, possessions can also be deployed for rebellion and resistance to age.
Thus, an ongoing career of consumption actualizes and expresses
the life course. The goal is not merely to have or use things but also
to *be* someone—a homeowner, a hunter, a host.

In later life, three additional dimensions attend the material convoy.[11] First, some belongings have been layered into the household
and endured for a long time, making them biographically meaningful and even more prone to be kept.[12] Things can get stickier as the
years go by. Second, with advancing age, the manageability and
future disposition of belongings come into question. Older adults are
well aware of their mortality, and many feel a responsibility not to
burden others with their things. Third and following from this second
dimension, the social convoy of family and friends takes an increasing
interest in the safety and security of elders, and this concern can extend to their material convoys. What is to become of it all?

It is not difficult to envision a sovereign individual surrounded
by a dynamic constellation of possessions, a person at their center
who animates them, gives them meaning, and uses them today or
lays them by for tomorrow. We are the conductors of our convoys.
At the same time, the very materiality of the convoy—its being
there—can have its own effects. The convoy can, unbidden and
mirror-like, prompt reflection about oneself and the ways that life
has progressed. Another potential effect of convoy contents in later
life is to "age" the possessors. If household occupants live among
quantities of objects that are disused and abeyant with their future

accommodation in doubt, the juxtaposition creates an impression of mutual obsolescence.

The convoy's many parts may have been assembled for all sorts of reasons, but its complete materiality and its volume can come to seem threatening and beyond control. In one of our interview studies, we asked a married woman in her early seventies how she spends her time. Her reply was about possessions and bristled with frustration about the sheer bulk of her household's contents:

> Lately I've been trying to get rid of some of the clutter around here because we've got so much crap. If we ever get a chance to sell this house, we got to get rid of it. And it's just junk! It's not— We've sold everything that's worth anything, you know, already. It's just stuff we've accumulated. And [she sighs] you don't know what to do with it.

To carry off a competent life course, one needs a material convoy. This fact is never clearer than when encountering a human being who literally has nothing. Where I live, when a baby is born and put up for adoption, the law requires a waiting period during which the consent of the birth mother and birth father are secured. During that period, which could last a few weeks, the baby is placed with a foster family until the adoption is finalized. Some years ago, my wife and I were the temporary foster placement for a number of babies. The social worker would call to alert us about a newborn and, on very short notice, arrive with the child.

And that baby had nothing. It arrived with only the hospital-issued nightgown and blanket, along with a plastic bag of free diapers, some formula, and some lotion that local merchants donated to all new infants. The baby had no name. Nothing. But waiting somewhere was a new, adoptive family (always unknown to us) that had a name ready and a dedicated nursery area of the home that included furniture, clothing, toys, personal care supplies—a ready-made material convoy that would ratify the baby's passage into the social convoy of a new family. Placement with a family would likewise be placement in *one's own* material convoy, which had an entire lifetime ahead of it.

The material convoy, then, is a wide frame for considering the question of aging and possessions: a persistent but dynamic body of possessions that accompanies people across their changing lives. Things may come and go, but there is always a convoy.

KEEPING

Why do people have things *at all*? According to the convoy concept, people have possessions in order to actualize the life course. But why do people have in their convoys *this particular thing or that*? The question is answerable in two ways. One way is to look into the acquisition of objects, and another way is to look into their keeping.

Possessions are acquired by various means. People find possessions, are given them by others, create them, or buy them. In the scholarly field of consumer and consumption studies, the buying of possessions gets the lion's share of attention. Even so, there are multiple phases in the life cycle of material goods, and each of these are of interest: the initial production of commodities and the social relations around that activity; the way that commodities are marketed and consumers are induced to purchase them; the possession of things over time; and their eventual recycling or disposal.[13] The moral and political dimensions of such material stages have been closely examined, yet the dominant emphasis on consumers' acquisition of goods in the marketplace has left a gap. The back end of the consumption cycle, "what consumers actually do with the things they acquire, how they appropriate things and, indeed, divest them, has remained by comparison relatively unconsidered."[14] Shopping is an important topic, but this book focuses on what happens to the things at home.

The reasons for acquiring things—consumers' motivations—may well also be the reasons for retaining them (I need a working vacuum cleaner; that painting is so beautiful), but it is also possible for the function and meaning of a thing to shift over time. Tim Dant points out that material objects, once possessed, have an afterlife wherein they are "lived with" and can attain quasi-social relationships with their owners.[15] This living-with or living-into has been called many things: cultivation, accommodation, habituation, cathexis, appropriation, attachment, endowment, singularization, and decommoditization.[16] Basically, the thing is made over as mine, and in that process it may take on other values—a first hint that the meaning of things is slippery.

Our interviews suggested nine reasons why people keep things in their material convoys, understanding that single belongings may carry more than one meaning or function.[17]

Things Seem Useful

People maintain some belongings because they satisfy a need or help manage everyday life—if not today, then on some probable occasion. Everyday utility, now or to come, tops any list of possession motives, lay or scholarly. From our research, one could believe that beds are the most eminently practical thing in the house, given how quickly people mentioned that they had kept this or that bed when they moved. Dining tables ran a close second in the hierarchy of retention. At the same time, respondents tagged the disposal of many objects with the valedictory rationale, "I had no use for it." Even when giving such things away, they were happy to report that their former possessions were now useful to others. One woman said of her crochet hooks: "Why keep 'em? Don't use 'em anymore, why keep 'em? I gave them away. [Interviewer: Oh, to the thrift store?] Yeah. Somebody could use them." This is also the occasion to say that things have meaning not just in themselves but likewise in relation to one another.[18] So one shoehorn is occasionally useful, but what is the use of a second shoehorn?

Things Are Worth Money

Objects might be kept for no other reason but that they could be recommodified, converted into cash. A number of our respondents held on to sets of china, crystal, and silverware that these people thought were valuable, even though they had not made much use of these objects and family members did not want them. Collections were also held because they were "worth something":

> I had got a collection of unicorns. My daughter is kind of responsible for the collection. She kept adding things to it, but she doesn't want them now. They are worth something, but I don't know as if I could ever sell them for what they are worth.

The statement reveals a challenge that divestment brings to the fore: how to realize the value of such holdings in the marketplace (see chapter 6). The worth of things is entirely hypothetical pending an actual test of their monetary value at the yard sale, the auction, or the antiques shop.

Things Give Pleasure

People judged some belongings to be beautiful or delightful in their own right—for example, flowering plants. Possessions also served as prompts to the imagination.[19] Books, in particular, seemed to fulfill this purpose for the elders whom we studied. One man exclaimed, "I would not have left my books. Those are treasure." Another woman, an American history buff, delighted in a rock that she said came from Lake Superior when the Mackinac Bridge was built. The hedonic value of things begs for further probing. Is beauty all in the eye of the beholder—idiosyncratic—or are consumers trained to certain tastes? Do individual items have the charm that they do because they are lodged in a larger arrangement, say, the decor of an entire room?

Things Represent Us

Belongings, singly but also as composed into sets or ensembles, express our meanings or feelings, encode our values, and reinforce our conformity or uniqueness. Our things remind us who we are and tell our story to others.[20] In our interviews, we asked whether some things were harder to deal with than others, assuming these would be the more cherished objects. One woman, a musician who refused to part with her most prized possession, responded:

> I don't think there was anything I felt too strongly about, except the piano. That was so much part of my life because I taught for so many years—not only the way I earned my living but because music's part of my life.

Things can also be retained as material biography, memorializing personal occasions, relationships, achievements, ways of engagement in the world, and past selves. Life's souvenirs might include "a lot of bowling trophies, a whole basement full of bowling trophies," or "eighteen plaques of different kinds . . . from the volunteer work." At least three women had kept their wedding dresses from long ago. Another man rued the relinquishment of his LP record collection, which had been a reminder of his onetime cultural currency. One woman had a tablecloth that was so stained she could no longer use it, but she could not throw it away because it reminded her of a trip she and her husband had taken to Europe. It was a mnemonic cue—in Grant McCracken's words, "a site of important personal information."[21]

It bears restating that some possessions represent our conformity to social conventions and norms. They are not prized or cherished but simply necessary to a frictionless performance of one's stage or station in life.

Things Conjure the Future

People keep things that they have not fully explored, used, or incorporated. Such objects include unread books, underused gadgets, and clothes that are presently a size too small. We asked a 78-year-old widow our standard question about having any hobbies, and she said:

> Painting—I painted. So I had a lot of paint equipment: oils, watercolors. I guess you name it, and I had it.
> [Interviewer: Did you hold on to the painting stuff?]

I still have that. They have an art class here [in the retirement community], so I'm hoping to get involved in that, but I still haven't done it yet.

When people face the disposal of unused possessions in disbandment, they are conceding that possible futures or possible selves will not come about.[22] Said one woman: "I had a lot of hobby stuff. I went through that and put a lot of it in the garage sale. And a lot of things that I had hoped to do sometime [laughs]." There will be more to say about possible selves in chapter 4.

Social Reciprocity to Gift Givers

Things received as gifts remind their keepers of past occasions or emotions, but some gifts can carry an obligation to conserve the gift and so perpetuate a bond with the giver. Keeping things is keeping ties, a feature of the social order long observed by anthropologists.[23] One woman, who had recently moved to an assisted living facility, not only kept the gifts of others but also devised a way to memorialize her benefactors even after her death. Asked whether she collected anything, she said:

No, I'm not too much of a collector except what I got from foreign students. I was in the host family program at the college, and I have also visited them in other countries. Japan and China and Malaysia. They'd call me "Mom." There are things I picked up overseas, or they gave them to me. They're not terribly valuable, but I'm proud of this collection. And I wouldn't know where I got all these things, but I have a book that says either who gave them to me or where I picked them up when. So that if anybody's interested after I'm gone, they'll have a little history.

Responsibility to Forebears

This motive is most complex, because family and ancestry are layered onto whatever utility, monetary value, or delight might already adhere to the thing. The conservation of heirlooms immortalizes forebears and ensures the continuity of family history. These are the things that outlive their keepers, durable and inalienable things whose disposal is unthinkable.[24] These are so well-seated in the convoy as to be "enclaved," literally, locked up.[25] One couple took pride in their antiques and was insistent about holding on to family furniture. The wife said, "We kept it all. The dining room furniture belonged to his parents when he was little." Her husband added, "If we couldn't have kept the buffet, we wouldn't have moved." The proper disposition of "family things" occupies a place in downsizing accounts seemingly out of all proportion to their volume. The paradox of heirlooms is that the longer a thing endures in the hands of kin, it has more family "past" to perpetuate, but the forebears who originated it grow less familiar to the current owners.

Conservation Is a Virtue

That some people "never throw things away" is an exaggeration, but we noted a strong moral compulsion to retain things that might be useful, if not to the saver, then to someone else. People suggest that such saving among current elders is a habit of frugality born of the scarcities of the Great Depression and war, but our study is unable to confirm that suggestion. What we can confirm is a strong reluctance to discard functional objects, even if not foreseeably useful. "We're keepers," people said. "I kept a lot of clothes," said one woman, "My closets are just full. I don't know when I'm going to wear them, but I hate to give them away. If you keep them long enough, they come back in style again."

We Keep Because We Can

Finally, to round out an understanding of retention, there is one more reason why people keep and perhaps accumulate things across the life course: because they can. One man recalled that he kept things just because he had the space:

When you live in a house for 48 years with the kind of room we had, you might say, "Oh, I might need that some day." Clothes, for one thing, but other stuff, kitchen stuff. You know, even flower vases and all kinds of things.

Americans dwell in ever larger containers wherein the convenience of storage exceeds the inconvenience of disposition. For example, the average size of new single-family homes sold in the United States grew from about 1,000 square feet in 1950 to 1,500 square feet in 1970 to 2,687 square feet in 2015.[26] At the beginning of that sixty-five-year period, 66 percent of new homes had two or fewer bedrooms, and 53 percent had no garage; at the end of that time frame, 89 percent of new homes had three bedrooms or more, and 85 percent had a two-car, three-car, or larger garage. If one's house is not big enough, the U.S. self-storage industry in 2018 offered 82.5 square miles of rentable, roofed storage space in approximately fifty thousand facilities nationwide.[27]

This list of nine ways that people value things (and hypothetically motives for keeping them) could be subdivided more finely or collapsed into fewer reasons. Mihaly Csikszentmihalyi and Eugene Rochberg-Halton generated eleven categories of meaning from their influential research on people's feelings about important household objects. From a survey of 192 adults, Marsha Richins distilled six reasons for valuing important possessions. Robert Rubinstein reported seven categories of meaning for special things among a sample of eighty-eight adults, and Laura Kamptner found six functions of possessions when asking seventy-two older adults about their most important things.[28] These authors' method—asking about significant or important possessions—is an occasion to keep in mind that the material convoy also holds many belongings that are not special or that people have actually forgotten about.

Across all of the scholarship on the meaning of possessions, the two most generic motives for having things appear to be (1) instrumental control of one's environment and (2) the symbolization of self and others.[29] Things are useful, and things symbolize. As to the latter, possession research almost always circles back to the idea that possessions are an important means for expressing self or identity.[30] Both Lita Furby and Russell Belk have strongly contended that possessions are extensions of the self: "A key to understanding what possessions mean is recognizing that, knowingly or unknowingly, intentionally or unintentionally, we regard possessions as parts of ourselves."[31]

Behavioral economists have identified an "endowment effect" as a general motive for keeping things.[32] People are constitutionally loath to give up things that they own and intend to use or enjoy, even when there is a corresponding gain. The argument about "loss aversion" is made in monetary terms, but one could equally well imagine reluctance to lose the skill, admiration, memory, self, and hope that have been invested in possessions. This bias in favor of keeping, however, does not mean that divestment is out of the question.

Jean-Paul Sartre, in his philosophical tome *Being and Nothingness*, distilled the motives for possession to a unity when he observed that *having* is essentially (a way of) *being* in the world: "The totality of my possessions reflects the totality of my being. I *am* what I have."[33] So, my father's war medals are me remembering; my sunglasses are me managing my comfort. If I am what I have, this portends an important question about divestment or dispossession. Erich Fromm posed the problem this way: "If I am what I have, and what I have is lost, who then am I?"[34] Fromm had his own answer (an anti-consumerist answer) but at the very least the question suggests that divestment will expose one to a new way of being.

NOT KEEPING

Just as there are reasons why particular things might be kept in the convoy, there are likewise reasons why they might be shed. (And this is quite apart from the effort it would take to shift them in or out—a topic for the next section.) The divestment of possessions is a regular feature of everyday life. From her studies of the way the people occupy houses and live with belongings, Nicky Gregson concludes that "acts of ridding things are centrally implicated in the fabrication of homes and are integral to the various practices of habitation and inhabitation that occur therein." Acts of ridding, she writes, "are always just going on."[35]

Consider three general circumstances under which the material convoy loses items.[36] First, there are outside threats to possession that arise from natural and social sources. Things can rot, crumble, rust, wear down, or die, thus ruining their practical or emotional value. Things can be devastated by fire or smoke, violent breakage, water or mold, or vermin. Theft can remove possessions, and not only by burglary. We have met adult children who, believing that their parents have excess belongings, will take it upon themselves to trash things behind the elder's back. Items are also removed when possession is contested: for example, when property is divided during a divorce or when goods enjoy familial ownership and another kin member claims a turn at possession. Divestment by all of these outside means is involuntary and irretrievable. The things simply become functionally unavailable.

The second circumstance that makes possessions vulnerable is some sort of failure with their capacity for social mediation. Goods, according to Mary Douglas and Baron Isherwood, are the visible part of culture, vehicles of communication and membership.[37] Yet they may someday fail to supply the information that we need for daily social commerce or the sentiment that sustains group or kin membership. When goods don't "work," we feel that they no longer represent our interests, identity, or rank, or they invite negative social judgments.[38] We maintain clothing, utensils, machinery, furnishings, leisure goods, decorations, rooms, buildings, and yards. We may not have acquired all these things purely for purposes of strategic display, but display they do. They put us forward, packaging a presentation of our persons for regard by others.[39] And if we sense that these things tell our story in an adverse way (e.g., we are out of fashion by some standard), we find that our possession motives are up for review. In my household, we have stopped entertaining with our smallish, crystal wine glasses in favor of new flute- and globe-shaped stemware that is the current standard for serving white, red, and sparkling wine. Those old glasses—once wonderful wedding gifts—are no longer "us."

Social judgment about *excess* possessions—materialism—is a prompt for adults' periodic, voluntary campaigns of clutter reduction. The moral charge of "too much" is directed more at volume rather than specific objects. The downsizing imperative—a staple of popular media—has given rise to an entire industry that, ironically, supplies another form of consumption. According to one report, U.S. sales of home organization products stood at $9.7 billion in 2017 and were headed to nearly $12 billion by 2021. This category includes containers, shelving, and accessories that organize storage in closets and garages, as well as outdoor sheds that take the overflow from the rest of the house.[40] The ability of capitalism to commoditize anything—in this case, overspread commodities—should never be doubted.

Life course change is the third circumstance inviting divestment. Because we acquire and keep goods in order to fulfill social roles, it follows that role relinquishment might be the occasion to revisit possession motives. For example, work roles compel the acquisition of specialized clothing, tools, transportation, and self-care materials. Upon changing jobs, these materials may need an overhaul. The successive stages of child-rearing lead to the relinquishment of goods and furnishings used to support infancy, then childhood, then youth. My home was once ankle-deep in toys and playthings, of which only a residual few remain in a box in the closet, for visitors. Role change and moving on can leave some possessions not only functionally irrelevant but also negatively charged if former stages of life are now seen as undesirable. Disposition of belongings, though usually portrayed as a difficult process of detachment from self, can in some circumstances be a welcome occasion to push away possessions that are extensions of an undesired self.[41]

Concurrent with another kind of life course change, motives for possession can become untenable with disability or increasing limitations in later life. Sometimes the shedding of possessions occurs in conjunction with a move to smaller quarters. Sometimes downsizing is undertaken to anticipate a life change, such as a move to residential care or even death.[42] We know elders who have thinned their things in order to free adult children from any posthumous burden of excess possessions or to protect the elders' legacy from the judgment that they had been carelessly acquisitive. Though downsizing in later life appears as a surrender to age-related vulnerability, such "selection" of more manageable household contents can be a positive, gratifying step.[43] In our interviews, we asked participants about possessions that had been difficult to divest. Lorraine Morse, aged 74, replied that it was "probably some of the crystal things, dishes, things like that 'cause I really liked them and I appreciate them." We asked if that was family crystal. "Some of it was mine, some of it was family." But the surrender of the crystal was adaptive:

> I had bridge here yesterday and I used—I got these real cheap plastic pitchers. Now five years ago you wouldn't have caught me dead using those. I mean I wouldn't have. Oh, I wouldn't have thought of it. Well, the crystal ones, first of all they're too heavy empty, and you put something in it and you can't hardly lift it. So I got rid of all the crystal pitchers. Well, then I bought these plastic ones. They work fine and the people who play bridge do not care. And, they can't lift the heavy stuff either. We're all older and ya just have to get realistic.

All of these circumstances—loss of functionality, loss of communicative capacity, life course change—bring possessions to a point of devaluation wherein "certain things that mattered once come not to matter."[44] The objects can then be divested, but that is easier said than done.

THE LABOR OF CONVOY MAINTENANCE

The composition of the material convoy is not driven wholly by the meaning of things. The preceding discussion about keeping (or not) may have left two impressions that are oversimplified: about the control of convoy contents and the effort it takes to manage them.

It is convenient to talk about an "individual" who "has" possessions and meanings for them, but the fact is that the possession of many things is shared. One of the principles of the life course perspective is "linked lives."[45] Lives are lived interdependently: events and transitions in one person's life can entail change in the lives of others. Just so, parts of any one person's material convoy can be mixed with the convoys of others, making boundaries of ownership "porous."[46] Spouses own things in common, although the control of those things may be an arrangement in the marital division of labor. Parents supply their children with such goods as clothing and furniture, but children may feel the emotions of ownership about these items and contest who has the right to dispose of them. For example, when an older child lives elsewhere for a time (college, military service), can parents appropriate the child's room, furniture, and appointments for another purpose? How free is a widow to dispose her late husband's effects? Dena Shenk and colleagues recount the story of Mrs. Wilson, whose late husband was "a great garage person" and "loved working with wood":

> The navy blue jacket that he wore when doing woodwork still hangs on a hook in the garage. Shortly after his death, she mentioned to her children that she was thinking of donating the jacket. She had already given some of his clothes to her sons. To her great surprise they gave her a staring look and responded, "Mom, leave that there." Although it didn't hold special meaning for her, she left the jacket hanging in the garage as they requested. She also told her sons to take nails and some other things from the garage but, again, they responded, "Leave them there."[47]

Finally, there are the possessions that symbolize the kinship line, whose keeping in any one place is provisional, and whose loss to the family is hard to conceive.[48] Holders of these "family things" accept the responsibility for taking care of them, but this does not extend to any unilateral authority to purge them.

Along with authority, the ability to manage convoy contents depends on one's capacity for the labor of both possession and divestment. Kept things are far more than inert lumps of matter. They are accommodated by being placed, stored, arranged, contained, tidied, maintained, cleaned, secured, insured, and provided for. Some belongings are emotionally invested and even attributed with an inner life toward which one must act with respect. "Upkeep" is a most fitting word for these efforts. Every object that joins the convoy comes with a quantum of required labor, even if that is only to set it somewhere. Collectively, however, the care of the convoy, the agency in its keeping, is not trivial.

It seems straightforward to predict that people will release a thing from their convoy when the motives for its possession—utility, symbolization—have been extinguished, perhaps brought on by the item's functional failure or incapacity for social mediation or life course obsolescence. In this case the labor of possession is not worth the effort. The thing is no longer valuable or delightful, or no longer carries the past. Alternatively, reasons for keeping may remain intact but the labor of possession becomes unsustainable—too costly in terms of time, money, or effort. Thus, possessions endure as such so long as motives for possession match or exceed the labor of possession—that is, motive is greater than or equal to labor. When the balance tips, the thing is a candidate for dismissal.[49]

But it is only a candidate. The suddenly problematic status of "not worth keeping" may lead to a reimagination of motive—that is, the accentuation of yet another reason for keeping the thing. Of the nine possession motives disclosed in our studies, two of them—the second (the thing is worth money) and the eighth (someone could use this)—appear as residual, last-resort rationales for hanging on to something that has lost all other purpose. I have long kept my late father's coin collection out of loyalty to his memory and an affirmation of our common boyhood occupation as newspaper carriers. But the coins' safekeeping gives me anxiety, and I presently think that I keep them mainly for their value (which I plan to explore). Alternatively, the "not worth keeping" status could lead to the search for more possession resources—more space, help with maintenance, a lockbox for those coins—which is yet more labor of possession.

The unbalanced relation between motive and labor is only the occasion for parting with material. Next comes the act itself and what might be called the labor of divestment. The work of keeping is now weighed against the work of not keeping, which has several dimensions.

The work is *cognitive*. One must conceive or choose a strategy for the outplacement: sell, give, trash, and so on. There may be procedural steps to plan or an appropriate timing to await. The work is *physical*. Objects will need to be located, retrieved from their places, hauled about, and readied for presentation (e.g., cleaned for sale, bagged for the trash). The work is *emotional*. One needs to finds ways to bear parting with things that carry the memories of self and others. One may also have to bear disconfirmations of residual possession motives (this is worth money; my children will want that). The work is *social*. Various divestment strategies involve consulting others, recruiting them to help, or paying them to undertake cognitive and physical tasks. In the end, it may all be too much bother, in which case the last of the nine possession motives—we keep because we can—flickers anew as things enter storage within or outside the property.

Finally, the work of possession and divestment will be harder given the press of other life course situations that compete for time, such as employment and parenting. This sort of housekeeping will not be easier when there are financial limitations and social isolation, and when in later life there is waning strength and stamina. Reflecting the effort devoted to its management, the material convoy might be an intentional and orderly assemblage of possessions, or something less disciplined.

MATERIAL AGENCY OF THE CONVOY

Returning to a point made earlier, the very materiality of the convoy can have its own effects.[50] One's belongings are gathered over time for all sorts of practical, expressive, and symbolic purposes. The standard view is that all these things cohere around a person or household of persons, and these persons' subjectivity endows the objects with meaning. Possessions *are* what they are thought to be by their owners or holders, who vivify the objects and grant them their place in the material convoy. Possessions are thus constituted by human agency. Indeed, the centrality of human consciousness to all the things that furnish life is difficult to doubt.

At the same time, it is possible to maintain that things have a "material agency" that shapes behavior and action in ways unintended by human subjectivity.[51] Matter as matter "generates effects ... makes things happen."[52] The source of this view is actor-network theory, which holds that human and nonhuman agents are in relation, entangled, and evolve in networks and assemblages and that neither the human nor the material can be reduced to the other.[53] Material things thus can exert an independent agency. In the case of household contents, the notion of "infrastructure" is helpful.[54] Objects visibly populate walls, surfaces, floors; they are contained in cabinets, closets, drawers and other storage places. Collectively, they face us with weight, mass, shape, color and volume, they occupy space. A latent infrastructure of objects may have been unintended, but it is there now, presenting itself as something grown larger than the separate things that compose it.

In a way, the agency of material forces has been recognized in environmental gerontology, which has long maintained that places can, by turns, comfort and also threaten older people.[55] Physical settings can form a "hidden program" that regulates behavior in a place such as a residential care facility.[56] The infrastructure of possessions, too, can morph into something that its single elements are not. In our interviews, people sat in their homes and characterized current or former contents. In the telling, large portions of the entire lot could quickly congeal into the sheer materiality of being "stuff." Belongings cease to be individual things and aggregate into an almost alien mass that is spoken of with surprise and dismay: "Why do we have so much stuff?" "I couldn't *believe* all the things I had in there." "Stuff is a lot of trouble."

When it comes to relocation in later life, household contents can function as a player in the question of moving or staying, exerting a spatial drag. The infrastructure of the household can generate an awareness of the (probably considerable) effort it would take to move it. Contained, it is no threat at all. But things held dear or useful can collectively emerge as something else, as a reality that would compel considerable labor. "There is a latent hostility—or, at least, a resistance—in objects," Noelle Oxenhandler has written. "This resistance is never more apparent than when we set about the task of moving, and, though I've moved many times, it always takes me by surprise."[57] At one remove from the subjectivity of the possessor, for family members the looming material agency of the convoy will seem even stronger. To relocation professionals and decluttering advisers, it is all a chore.[58]

Possessions are a crucial context for the business of daily life—they are there, standing by, awaiting our use, attention, or care. But they can present as something else. The invocation of their material agency is an alternative to the dominant view that belongings are primarily extensions of the self. They can flip over into being "things in the way." From the perspective of actor-network theory, the infrastructure of possessions as obstacle *emerges* in concert with their possibility of relocation. Those books on the shelf—I chose them, they are mine; but, goodness, they sure would be heavy. The material convoy equips and furnishes life, but, in another light, the convoy is also mere baggage and potentially troublesome.

CONCLUSION

The possessions of a person or household, in their entirety, constitute a convoy of material support that accompanies people from cradle to grave. Analogous to the social convoy of friends and acquaintances, the material convoy is a dynamic composition, a changeable envelope of things that is a partner to human function at all stages of life. There are all sorts of reasons for keeping things in the convoy and for discarding them, and these reasons can combine and shift over time, especially as the irreducible labor of upkeep calls the value of belongings into question. Now that I have posited the general metaphor of the convoy, there should be some caution in casting it as a neat package of items hosted and curated by a conscientious self. Paradoxically, "my" convoy contents can elude control, ownership, and even awareness of their existence. Like the social convoy of family and friends, one's things can prove to be an unruly bunch.

2

WITH AGING, HOW LARGE A CONVOY?

Hear the rueful lament of the lifelong consumer:

- "When you go through stuff, you don't realize how much you had." (Female, age 66)
- "You know, you collect stuff over the years. It's just incredible the stuff you collect. Sheesh!" (Male, aged 79)
- "It just accumulates. It's too much." (Female, aged 73)
- "Ohhhh—I couldn't BELIEVE all the things I had in there, that there was no use keeping them! And I don't even know why I kept them! I don't even know why I kept them, but I guess I did." (Female, aged 76)
- "You don't realize how much stuff there was there. You never know. Are you married? Wait until you wake up one day when you're 80 and see how much you got stored, gal!" (Male, aged 87)
- "Have you ever known anyone to have an empty closet?" (Female, aged 66)
- "You know that old saying: If you build it they will come? If you have space, you will fill it!" (Male, aged 88)
- "Like my wife says, if there's room for it, you're supposed to put something there to fill it up. [Wife:] That's what I thought drawers and cupboards are for." (Male and female, aged 82 and 84)
- "Never have an attic or a basement!" (Female, aged 66)
- "Why do we have so much stuff?" (Female, aged 71)

TO SCOLD OR NOT

The love-hate relationship with consumer culture thrives in the academic as well as the public mind. Across this pro- and anti-consumerism divide, Yiannis Gabriel and Tim Lang see a plurality of images about consumers:

> Everywhere it seems, the consumer is triumphant. Consumers are said to dictate production; to fuel innovation; to be creating new service sectors in advanced economies; to be driving modern politics to have it in their power to save the environment and protect the future of the planet. Consumers embody a simple modern logic, the right to choose. . . . And yet the consumer is also seen as a weak and malleable creature, easily manipulated, dependent, passive and foolish. Immersed in illusions, addicted to joyless pursuits of ever-increasing living standards, the consumer, far from being god, is a pawn, in games played in invisible boardrooms.[1]

In scholarly writing about consumption, Daniel Miller has identified an anti-materialist prejudice that is historically deep: "The perception of consumption as an evil or antisocial activity is rather more profound and existed long before modern mass consumption."[2] World religions traditionally viewed asceticism as virtuous and conducive to enlightenment compared to the negative consequences of wealth, luxury, and profligacy.[3] In contemporary debates, the critique of mass consumption is a proxy for a wider critique of capitalism and environmental depredation. Weighing the rhetorics of anti-consumerism critics and pro-consumer apologists, the former always seem louder.[4]

Whether we are dupes or heroes of consumption, victims or creative appropriators, the debate eventually comes to the home with observations about housekeeping. These judgements tend to fall more strongly on women.[5] Although some would defend the comforts of cozy messiness, anxiety about excess possessions is a media staple.[6] An anti-materialism movement, nurtured by online blogs, advocates simple lives freed of the burden of unneeded possessions.

In some versions, the "minimalist" lifestyle offers the benefit of more time, environmental care, affordability, emotional well-being, and higher consciousness. In some versions, upper limits on the number of possessions or size of the house are suggested: less is more. The pose of material detachment would show up in our interviews when people said, as Sheira Engel did repeatedly, "Like I say, things aren't that important to me. I mean, I like nice things and that, but they're just things."

The critique of consumption arrives in the home with the word "clutter"—scolding about overstocked and teeming households that are out of control, hand in hand with lives that are out of control.[7] There is a genre of do-it-yourself, clutter-control books and manuals that draws from the more general self-help discourse of contemporary life.[8] In the self-help framework, the issues at hand may have an institutional or societal basis but they are presented as "individually generated and solvable" obstacles.[9] Authors enjoin help-seekers to achieve personal mastery, to seek fulfillment, and to find their authentic identity and lifestyle through self-governance.[10]

The general literature on possession reduction partakes of these motifs—individual problems and self-mastery—to lay out why and how one should discipline the household's material excess. The core problem complex is this: overactive consumption clutters the household and diminishes quality of life. Authors urge readers to limit their purchasing, purge their belongings, and restrain the sheer volume of possessions. A survey of homemaking texts in the United Kingdom distills the message as one that links the organization of space with personal therapy: "if people can clear their homes of the detritus and junk that continually invade them, then they will be happier and healthier."[11] The underlying assessment of this clutter problem is that we are what we own, and if our belongings are a mess, then, by extension, so are we. The solutions are storage or disposal.

As a point of clarification, the problem of clutter and the problem of excess possessions are not the same things, though both are subjective judgments. Clutter can happen without excess possessions; excess possessions can be perfectly tidy. Yet in reality the two tend to co-occur, and so advice about one is advice about the other.

Among the household management manuals is a subgenre intended to guide the downsizing of the belongings of older adults. Although the issue here is the volume of objects rather than messy clutter, the thrust is the same. Gabriella Smith and I examined eleven such sources, about half of them pitched to family members (presumably adult children) and half addressed to elders themselves. The six books written for family members were closer in tone to mainstream decluttering literature (but without the suggestion that disposal will make room for future consumption). The familiar message is that overfull households threaten well-being and must be tamed. The interesting twist is that these are other people's (elders') households that threaten the well-being of both generations. This twining of interests in elders' belongings plays understandably to families' increasing concern for the welfare and living environments of their older relatives. With urgent, imperative tones, the problem to be addressed is twofold. One issue is the sheer volume of possessions that elders have amassed, and the other is the possibility that this convoy will visit you, overwhelm you, and become your responsibility. Elders and their family members need to master their unhealthy emotional attachments to mere stuff—no matter the sentimental or heirloom value—because this is the only way to tame the elder's material convoy and stop it from becoming a transgenerational burden.

By contrast, the advice books addressed to elders take a gentler tone, with an emphasis on the positive aspects of downsizing and relocation and the ways that later life can be more enjoyable when unburdened by the excess possessions that need constant management and care. Along with a streamlined household comes the added psychological benefit of making decisions on one's own behalf and the feeling of being in control. Unlike the literature for family, these manuals do not convey a "time is short" urgency about downsizing. What they do feature is an outright deference toward long-held possessions that are personally meaningful. The meaning of things merits considerable respect, as do the values that elders may hold, such as frugality. At the same time, overzealous saving and sentimental attachment to items are gently discouraged because they inhibit downsizing of the material convoy, which in turn hinders seniors from living their "best" lives today. As for other rationales, downsizing is also framed as a parental responsibility to avoid passing undue burdens to loved ones. And ultimately, a sifted and slimmed material convoy is a way to control one's posthumous memory and legacy.

These, then, are the arguments for the downsizing imperative at any stage of adulthood and especially in later life: achievement of a serene, fully actualized life; security; intergenerational comity; and a feeling of empowerment. There seems to be little question about urging everyone to get started.

Yet this can be done without scolding people for their indiscipline. In interviewing elders and family members about household contents, and in countless conversations with middle-aged adults about the topic of this research, people overwhelmingly tend to be sheepish, apologetic, and somewhat mystified about how they have come to have what they have. They shrug and say, as Sandra Graves did, "When you move, you have more stuff than you thought you had, you really do. I don't know where all this stuff come from, oh my goodness." Tam Perry reported that the older adults in her study, when moving, found the contents of their homes to be a "source of surprise, shame, and frustration."[12]

People voluntarily and unselfconsciously tell stories on themselves about their predicament with possessions. Harold Jones confessed, "I brought too many of my own clothes [here] that I probably shouldn't have owned to begin with." I was once discussing my research with a colleague at another university, and he told me that the findings could be helpful to him. He asked, "Do you know what a Shopsmith is?" (It's a combination machine for woodworking—quite expensive.) "Well," he said, "I have two of them." His manner was as if he had said, "Isn't that silly of me?" My experience over a dozen years now is that people literally cannot be stopped from talking about their homes and the excess things that they are keeping there, even if the excess embarrasses them.

One person's clutter is another person's comfort. If people want to go to their graves with every stick of furniture and scrap of clothing intact, I cannot try to persuade them otherwise. I assume that people know what they needed in the past and know what they need now. So although this book is not a work of advocacy, it will not shy away from pointing what others (including our interviewees) see as the advantages of a smaller material convoy. There is no possession shaming here, however. Elders already perceive a problem—no need to pile on.

ALTOGETHER, WHAT'S IN A HOME?

It is hard to get the mind around the whole stock and store of objects that people contain in a home. Perhaps it would help to see all of it in one place. This was exactly the object of Peter Menzel's photography for *Material World: A Global Family Portrait*.[13] The project was designed to illustrate the world's common humanity while documenting its great differences in material goods. Menzel and his colleagues persuaded thirty families around the world to bring all of their household objects into the yard or street for a "big picture" of the inhabitants amid their things. The photos are fascinating and beautiful. In places where homes have limited possessions, the family members are in the foreground. In affluent settings, the people appear as tiny figures in a crowded, colorful field of goods. Sannah Kvist took a similar approach in her 2012 photo series, *All I Own*, posing Swedish students with their things. Turning the camera on himself, the British artist Michael Landy gathered all 7,227 of his possessions for a project that featured their public destruction.[14]

Another comprehensive photo project, this time of possessions *in place*, was conducted by anthropologists in Los Angeles for the book *Life at Home in the Twenty-first Century*. This was a four-year study of domestic American life whose goal was to systematically document how people use their homes and situate their possessions. The research team spent a week each in the homes of thirty-two nuclear families (two parents, two children). Photographs of rooms (the book has many) were later used to catalog the *visible* posses-sions in these spaces. The authors were not shy about saying what comes of rampant consumerism: "Material Saturation: Mountains of Possessions" (the title of one early chapter). Taking just one home, the researchers found the following:

> The first household assemblage we analyzed, of Family 27, resulted in a tally of 2,260 visible possessions in the first three rooms coded (two bedrooms and the living room). To be counted, an object must be in plain sight on a table, shelf, wall, floor, closet hanger, etc.; tal-lies do not include untold numbers of items tucked into dresser draw-ers, boxes, and cabinets or items positioned behind other items. So the counts we derive are quite conservative figures compared to actual objects owned.[15]

In this way, the team generated average counts per household for some types of objects. They report averages of 3.1 televisions, 438 books and magazines, 212 music CDs, 139 toys, ninety DVDs and VHS tapes, thirty-nine pairs of shoes, and fifty-two objects affixed to the sides of refrigerators. Garages were observed predominantly to function as storage spaces, not places for parking cars. The book concludes that "while material affluence signals personal pleasure and economic success, it also entails hidden costs, including the comfort lost if possessions overly crowd a home."[16]

Leaving the whole house aside, listing the volume of possessions in even one room is a daunting task. Samuel Gosling and colleagues, conducting research in environmental psychology, devised a check-list that can itemize and classify the objects in a space. Applying this technique to the dorm or sleeping rooms of college students, it took the research team the equivalent of one person-hour to document the contents (in four hundred categories) of each single room. And, as in the Los Angeles study, these were only the *visible* objects—not those contained in drawers, wardrobes, or boxes, which would in-clude, for example, multiple items of clothing or jewelry. These au-thors sum up: "Given the sheer diversity of personal living spaces and the enormous number and variety of potential items to be found in them, we suspect that no workable coding scheme could ever be absolutely comprehensive."[17]

Trying this on myself, I inventoried the contents of my small bedside table, which has a shelf and two drawers. Its unruliness had begun to bother me, so I decided to declutter it. It literally held hundreds of possessions (the following text box contains the full list), including twenty books, twenty-one magazines, seventeen pens and pencils, two shoehorns, a pair of my late mother's red leather gloves, a bag of old coins, and my father's medals from World War II. Some of these things I cannot imagine parting with, but for some I cannot tell you why I have them or where they came from. Some items I relocated to other parts of the house. It took more than two hours to review the lot and make selected decisions about their arrangement or disposition. However, most of the things eventually went right back into the drawers they came from. The table remained unruly, but I was reconciled to its disorder.

The volume and density of possessions in a household (or one room or one nightstand) frustrate research efforts to characterize the material convoy as a whole and inquire about its collective meaning. Researchers who study the social convoy of individuals have devised methods for measuring it: counting its members and rating their supportiveness and emotional ties to the individual.[18] This task is made somewhat easier because the individuals at the center of a social convoy usually do not have thousands of others in their social circles; and, although social convoys share members between them, this kind of sharing is unlike the joint possession of many things in a marriage or family. The difference raises an issue about the proper unit of measurement for a convoy—the individual or the household.

The challenge of the material convoy is that the multitude of possessions in a place are, as Gosling's team concluded, probably uncountable in a reliable way. Although it is possible to self-report or enumerate large, singular objects (cars, televisions), other categories of belongings appear in sets and multiples (tools, jewelry, tax

THE CONTENTS OF A BEDSIDE TABLE

Small lamp
Clock radio
Desk bell
Statuette
Letter holder
Product manuals (2)
Framed Shakespeare sonnet
Book matches (3)
Rocks (4)
Political buttons (2)
Medicine bottle
Books (20)
Magazines (21)
Pens (10)
Pencils (7)
Concert program
Opera glasses (2)
Reprints (3)
Miscellaneous jewelry, cuff links
Dice
Flashlight
Guitar pick
Bottle opener
Pocket knives (3)
Old eyeglasses (2 pair)
Glasses straps (4)
Miscellaneous small hardware
Glasses repair kit
Watch
Package of earplugs
Miscellaneous greeting cards
Videocassettes (2)
Audiocassette
Shoehorns (2)
Nail clipper
Ladies' restroom sign
Windup alarm clocks (2)

Hairbrush
Shoe bags
Red leather gloves
Whistle on lanyard
Package of swizzle sticks
Business card wallet
Money clip
Sewing kit
Sand dollar
Colored stickers
Handkerchief
Carabineer
Shoe pads
Shoe laces
Auto decal
Cases for glasses (4)
Sunglasses (2 pair)
Miscellaneous buttons
Screwdriver
Cell phone chargers (2)
Bag of old coins
Coin books (2)
Father's WWII medals
....

records, cleaning supplies) of which people may not even be aware. As a result, it is difficult by objective and economical means to compare convoys between individuals or households, between age groups or any demographic groups, or to track convoys over time to understand their evolution across the life course. Not only is the size of the convoy unknown, so is its relative composition and the attachments and meanings it holds for its keepers. Perhaps the only feasible way to quantify the whole lot is to use estimates of volume and weight such as moving companies rely on when bidding relocations, but even this measure leaves the composition of the convoy opaque. The square footage of the dwelling or an indicator such as number of bedrooms might give some clue, but the density of items in the space would be unknown. Given the uncountable thousands of things that compose one's worldly goods, the research solution to date has been to conduct possession studies of selected items.

ACCUMULATION: THINGS STICK

Possession volume and clutter are qualities of a household at a given moment, but it is the *endurance* of things over time that sustains a material convoy. If things endure, if others are added, and if there not compensating divestment, the convoy enlarges. Chapter 1 began to explain how. Throughout adulthood, people typically assemble a growing volume of belongings—more kitchen implements, personal records, books, furniture, and decorations. Multiplying possessions result from marital and family roles that require the maintenance of stable residential households and from work roles that require quantities of clothing and equipment. Expansion occurs as we undertake sustained or successive projects to develop ourselves or satisfy culturally induced desires. Consumption does not need to be exuberant or intemperate for this to happen. Accumulation also grows from the lifelong reception of gifts and from the custody of shared possessions. These things are kept if they retain some value or another; if there are no outside, social, or life course threats to their possession; and if the household can accommodate them or household members are unable or unwilling to undertake the labor to dispose of them. So time goes by and things stick. Wilma Farrell concluded this about the house that she and her late husband had for thirty-six years: "All it did—that house—was collect things through the years."

There is another, very mundane reason for accumulation—neglect. It arises from the housekeeping practice of putting things away in "backstage" areas of the home.[19] And home storage is on the rise. For example, the 2010 catalog of the furniture retailer IKEA greatly expanded its pages of "smart storage technologies" relative to the catalog of 1969.[20]

Homes have public and private spaces, visible and hidden spaces, and one kind of space actually makes the other possible. According to Perla Korosec-Serfaty, "the visible spaces of dwelling draw their qualities, status, and meaning from their relationships with the cupboards, closets, drawers, balconies, garages, attics, and cellars which comprise the hidden spaces of dwelling."[21] People "stage" their homes to be presentable for themselves and others by tidying up and putting things away into the recesses. People also store things that they intend to transfer to others (eventually) or dispose of (eventually). Habits of replacement consumption without disposal (e.g., appliances) contribute to the crowding of cellars, garages, and sheds. And in these places that occupy the margins or edges of living spaces, things can be forgotten. "Things are there but they are not visible. They can be retrieved at any moment, but also forgotten at will, without any regrets or remorse as long as they are not thrown away."[22] Sophie Woodward calls these the "dormant" things; Brigitte Cluver calls them "inactive inventory."[23] Of course, things can be retrieved from the limbo of storage, but until then they will go unscrutinized for divestment or reuse. In writing about children's clothing, Nicky Gregson says that "once the wardrobe doors are open, clothing becomes open to potential release." And she concludes this about household contents in general: "Moving things and handling things bring people and things together, and things into a heightened zone of scrutiny. In being moved, touched, and handled, things are positioned to be looked at, felt, smelt, considered and thought about."[24]

So putting things away, out of sight, would ordinarily be deemed a good habit for the home. But out of sight is out of mind, and so the convoy grows. The backstage areas of the house were exactly the places where LeNora Russel felt overwhelmed during her move:

> Really it was purely the attic, basement, and garage. It was those places where you stuff stuff and you don't have to look at it everyday. You're not even reminded that it's there until you walk in and see it. That's the stuff that was hard, not emotionally hard but just hard to get done.

AGING AND THE MEANING OF THINGS

Advancing age lays down a residue of belongings acquired for successive roles, for bodily care, for self-development, for amusement, and as gifts. Advancing age also furnishes the time durations within which things are cultivated or fall out of favor. Over time, therefore, does aging also shift the value and meaning of things? Perhaps different things come to matter more. Perhaps useful things are of less interest than symbolic ones. Perhaps things that promise future pleasure or action give way to objects that embody the past. If age changes the appreciation of material goods, this would be something of no little interest to companies that seek to market products to older consumers.[25] For this reason, a good number of studies about aging and possessions have appeared in consumer marketing journals.

Over the past forty years, at least three dozen publications have appeared (including those from our research) that report primary research focused on older adults and their possessions. Most of these studies were undertaken to illuminate person-object relations for things that stay put in the dwelling. Some studies have also addressed the strategies and emotions of divestment, either as it actually happened or hypothetically could happen. From all these studies, it is hard to say whether advancing age shifts the value and meaning of things because of two limitations of research technique, both quite understandable.

First, only very small samples of anyone's material convoy typically come under scrutiny. Because the items in any modern household are nearly innumerable, in order to make possession research tractable, investigators commonly ask people to identify and discuss their most cherished, special, or important things. Among the three dozen studies, two-thirds have used this cherished-object method. For example, Mihaly Csikszentmihalyi and Eugene Rochberg-Halton asked a sample of people of all ages, "What are the things in your home which are special to you?" and then probed to determine why the object was special, what it would mean to be without it, where it was kept, and how it was acquired.[26] Studies of later life have followed this lead, asking people to identify the possessions that "you value most" and why.

This is a productive technique that yields the stories behind selected things and also discloses aspects of elders' values, identities, and significant relationships. Having specifically asked about special things, investigators reap content about the specialness of things or their special disposition. The symbolic features of selected possessions come to the fore, while the everyday utility of other household contents (or their inutility) is eclipsed. Thus, techniques of possession research among older adults tend to accentuate the prizing and preciousness of things.

One of the earliest cherished-object studies interviewed nearly one hundred elders, some of them in nursing homes. When it came to describing the meaning of possessions, the authors found it "nearly impossible to give the full range, richness, and poignancy of the responses."[27] Subsequent inquiries into the contours of cherishing (some cited in chapter 1) have attempted to distill categories of meaning that attach to belongings. In what is probably the most comprehensive report about "special things"—their possession and potential disposition—Linda Price and colleagues point to three basic reasons for valuing these belongings. Things are special because they encode memories of past associations and particular times, places, and people; things serve as symbols of the skills, competence, and achievements of self and others; and things are cherished as emblems of kinship and genealogy.[28]

Authors interpret such investment in cherished objects as the means by which older people manage the developmental challenges of their stage of life. Special possessions can maintain a sense of identity in the face of losses (such as widowhood or a move to residential care), physical limitations, and a rising awareness of finitude. These possessions can sustain and comfort people by evoking the past, promoting reminiscence, and providing assurance about important relationships. Such things have the potential, when passed on to others, to perpetuate one's self, values, and memory into the future. Altogether, research on the meaning of important possessions leaves an impression that older people have a heightened attachment to things. Elders' households are stocked with accumulated symbols of their lives, achievements, loved ones, and ancestors—the objects becoming a "kind of archive of personal history."[29] With increasing age, people cling to the comforting continuity of these material memories or else try to press them on others. Again, however, these are conclusions about a fraction of the material convoy.

The second research limitation—one common in all developmental and life course studies—is that it takes a lot of resources and commitment to follow human lives over time. In the case of aging and possessions, people would need revisiting over the years to check on their continued valuing of the same possessions or their engagement with completely other things. Because of this feasibility problem, all of the previous studies among the three dozen have been cross-sectional in design, onetime snapshots of people's views. From these reports we can be pretty sure that people do change their minds about possessions because people say they do; they say that they cast things out of the convoy and start to describe as "junk" and "crap" things that were formerly worth keeping. Yet, without successive interviews, surveys, or observations of the same people, it is difficult to demonstrate, specify, and verify a changing relationship to possessions.

If not a longitudinal study, the next best approach would be a cross-sectional study of multiple generations whose outlooks and behaviors could be compared, with differences between them being then inferred as effects of aging. This was the design of that early, much-imitated study of the meaning of things by Csikszentmihalyi and Rochberg-Halton. The researchers interviewed 315 people in eighty-two households who fell into three age groups or generations: children (aged 8 to 30), parents, and grandparents. The top three "special" objects mentioned at least once by the young were stereos, televisions, and furniture; the parent group's top three were furniture, visual art, and sculpture; the elders' top mentions were photos, furniture, and books.[30] To the authors, such patterns indicated that young selves want enjoyment and action (that is, utility) from things, and older selves prize the contemplative and symbolic.

Age group comparisons in relation to goods have been a feature of an entirely separate stream of research in social psychology and marketing. This research involves tests and applications of socioemotional selectivity theory.[31] This influential life-span theory of motivation posits that people, to the extent that they perceive time as limited, will prefer present over future satisfactions. Seeing life time as expansive, younger adults will therefore favor knowledge acquisition and novelty. Older adults, seeing life as limited, will increasingly seek emotionally positive experiences. In marketing, this has implications for age-related responses to advertisements and products.[32] The suggestion that the emotional eclipses the rational has a certain consonance with research on possessions, which finds that the cherished objects of elders are cherished for the assurance and memories they furnish. Another tenet of socioemotional selectivity theory is that older adults will withdraw to a smaller, more intimate social network.[33] One could speculate that this emotion-seeking motive also extends to the material convoy, so that awareness of mortality will move older people toward engagement with fewer but more meaningful things. So elders may want a more manageable batch of belongings, but will they act on this inclination? Will they downsize?

There is the possibility that age group differences in the style and valuing of possessions could reflect not advancing age but the cohort membership of consumers. A cohort (an age group, birth group, or colloquially a "generation") encounters the market for consumer goods at a certain historical moment. The things available at that time, such as books, recorded music, or furniture, can "date" the household if they are not later replaced with new fashions. At the aggregate level, cohorts of (aging) consumers are moving through the life course, replacing one another at various stages of life, thus layering the community with the material holdings from their unique historical experience. In all, the store of possessions, no less than the lives of their keepers, is the unique intersection of two dynamisms: individual aging and historical change.[34] The things that cohorts value and the way that they connect to possessions may be unique to the cohort. Young adults' appreciation of stereos, as reported in 1981, would not be found today—it would be some other category of object. In our interviews, we have heard this generational disconnect about household items associated with fine dining, which the older generation prizes but the children do not want, thus complicating the transfer of these things within the family.[35]

Disentangling age and cohort differences in possession attachment would be possible if we had survey and interview techniques that could answer basic questions about age-related changes in possession attachment, about the valuing of goods, and about cohort differences in possession attachment and practices. Whereas research on the social convoy has such techniques and methods, the material convoy remains largely unmeasured.

Finally, about generational differences in possession management and meaning, there is a firm conviction—often heard in casual conversation—that people now in their eighties and nineties, having come through the Great Depression and a world war, are frugal, waste nothing, and keep everything. Yet this cohort may not be so unique in the keeping of their convoys. The oncoming elders of the baby boom, by contrast, grew up in an economy of relative abundance when consumer goods became key to the construction of identity.[36] They, too, will have overprovisioned homes in later life. At any rate, there is at present no reliable technique for measuring multifaceted possession attachment (in multiple possessions at that), and so speculation about cohort differences in possession rationales has yet to be tested.[37]

A LATER LIFE PREDICAMENT

This section pulls back from a focus on the meaning of selected possessions in order to consider the material convoy as a totality. Techniques for quantifying the convoy—its size, contents—so far elude us, but it is still possible to survey people's attitudes about their belongings as a whole. Such survey responses are at hand and can be marshaled to address questions already posed in this chapter:

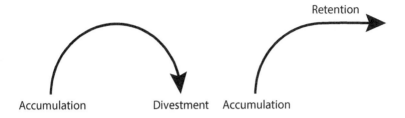

Figure 2.1 Arcs of possession accumulation.

What is the accumulation pattern for possessions in later life? And does this pattern seem to pose a problem?[38]

We might expect that the totality of one's possessions follows a temporal arc of more and then less, an iconic form in use in the West since at least the sixteenth century to depict a rising and falling trajectory of vigor and health.[39] In the case of possessions, their expansion and contraction (the left side of figure 2.1) would hypothetically match other life course patterns, such as the density of social relationships and the availability of financial resources.[40]

At some point later in adulthood, de-accumulation could be expected because the conditions for middle-age consumption typically lose force. Indeed, research on consumer expenditures in American households shows that spending on durable goods and clothing tends to peak around age 50 and then declines.[41] People are no longer housing and furnishing growing children and, after retirement, do not require work-related apparel or equipment. Widowhood leaves batches of personal possessions orphaned and candidates for disposal. Social connectedness is multifaceted, but age tends to see a reduction in network size, thus reducing the need for cultural signifiers and goods that support sociality and hospitality (e.g., entertaining).[42] Health and functional decline limit one's ability to manage the further accommodation and care of possessions. Residential relocation, if it occurs, will commonly entail a smaller place, making possession downsizing necessary.[43] Finally, gathering awareness of shorter time horizons for accomplishing personal goals may prompt the distribution of possessions to others as a way to protect the things or project the self.[44] Although there are many exceptions to these several patterns, older people hypothetically should release quantities of the possessions that equipped the daily lives that they no longer have.

During one of our interviews, Todd Koenig drew this exact rising-and-falling arc in the air with his hand as he said, "If you grasped what we had, it started down here when we moved in to Shoreham [forty-five years earlier]. And then it rose before we moved over here, then it dropped, and now it's stable."

Alternatively, a case can also be made for retention of the material convoy (right side of figure 2.1). Some people's affluence can compensate for any physical inability to care for possessions and property; what was once do-it-yourself labor, such as cleaning or yard work, can be hired out. If there is no residential relocation, the dwelling can continue to contain the possessions of middle age. The ongoing collection of belongings can secure continuity of the self in the face of aging and vulnerability. Finally, even if one wanted to downsize and divest, waiting too long may compromise the intention if diminished ability limits the capacity to undertake the labor of dispossession or if shrinking social networks limit supportive assistance, how-to information, or actual human "conduits" for divestment and disposal.[45] These are all reasons for retaining the convoy of middle age, but doing nothing—inertia—in fact requires no explanation at all given the behavioral tendency to remain in the status quo.[46] So the stock and store of possessions could trend either way with advancing age: toward divestment consistent with reduced role involvements, relationships, and capacity to accommodate things, or toward retention.

We were able to place questions about possessions into the 2010 wave of the Health and Retirement Study (HRS), a nationally representative panel survey of Americans aged 50 and older that collects economic, health, and psychosocial information (Introduction). A short, experimental set of questions about possessions was completed by a 10 percent sample of HRS respondents in 2010 ($N = 1,814$). From these responses, three patterns of age-related results are relevant to convoy dynamics.

Possession Volume

First, there was a survey question about the volume of possessions: "Thinking of the belongings that you own or are keeping at your home, do you feel that you have more things than you need, fewer things than you need, or just the right amount?" Note that people were asked to appraise possession volume in relation to their "need," not some external standard. The responses by age decade, beginning with 50 through 59, are shown in the top part of table 2.1. In these cross-sectional data, the decade-by-decade composition of the population varies and should be kept in mind. The age groups are likely to have fairly different life circumstances and therefore the "need" of things. People in their 50s probably still have jobs and families; in their 70s they are almost all likely to be retired; in their 80s only a minority (37 percent) are married. Alas, the HRS sample does not include persons in their 30s and 40s, and so a full life course picture is not possible.

In table 2.1, the pattern across age is fairly similar, with more than half, 53 percent to 62 percent, responding "more things than I need," about one-third claiming "Just the right amount," and small numbers having "fewer things than I need." We had no prior expectations about the distributions of responses among the three choices, but were surprised by the majority responding that they had more things than they needed, which suggests to us some definite level of unease with convoy size. This response was most moderate in those aged 80 and older. Perhaps by these ages some de-accumulation has occurred.

What are the correlates of feeling overprovisioned? Not gender—men and women answer this almost identically. Not personality to any significant extent (e.g., neuroticism, conscientiousness, openness to experience). It stands to reason that the bigger the household, the more the press of possessions, and that supposition is borne out. Married people, with two occupants of the household and someone else to blame, are more likely to say that they have more than they need. So are homeowners (as compared with renters) and people in dwellings with more rooms. By asset quintiles,

Table 2.1

Possession Volume, Possession Management, and Obstacle to Relocation, by Age Decade

	Age 50–59 (N=635)	Age 60–69 (N=501)	Age 70–79 (N=461)	Age 80+ (N=213)
Possession volume				
Thinking of the belongings that you own or are keeping at your home, do you feel that you have				
• More things than you need?	56	61	62	53
• Fewer things than you need?	7	6	4	4
• Just the right amount?	37	33	34	42
Possession management				
In the last year, how often have you gone through your home or other storage areas to **clean out or reduce** the number of things that you have?				
• Not at all	18	20	28	37
• A few times	59	63	62	50
• Many times	23	17	10	13
In the last year, how many of your belongings have you **sold** in a year, garage, or estate sale, a community sale, on consignment, or on the Internet?				
• None	76	77	81	85
• A few things	19	19	17	14
• Many things	5	4	2	1
In the last year, how many of your belongings have you **given away** to family or friends?				
• None	29	31	35	39
• A few things	50	52	54	47
• Many things	21	17	11	14
In the last year, how many of your belongings have you **donated** to charity, a church, or a community group?				
• None	27	22	31	32
• A few things	42	49	48	49
• Many things	31	29	21	19
Obstacle to relocation				
Think about the effort that it would take to move your belongings to another home. How reluctant to move does that make you feel?				
• Very reluctant	37	48	45	51
• Somewhat reluctant	32	29	32	27
• Not reluctant at all	31	23	23	22

Note: Possession management items show percentage responses within age decade. All items drawn from the 2010 Health and Retirement Study, 1,810 respondents.

wealthier people are more likely to admit to having too many things, with 75 percent saying so among the top quintile. The response about excess possessions, however, is sharply lower among persons who have moved in the previous two years, probably because these relocations entailed the downsizing that is typical of moves in later life.

Possession Management

Second, although the life course arc of possessions cannot be quantified, we can assess activity on their behalf from the HRS questions.[47] Activity toward possessions (in the past year) was surveyed by four questions with responses on a 1–3 scale. A general question asked about the frequency of activity "to clean out or reduce the number of things that you have" (not at all, a few times, many times). Three further questions asked about how many things had been sold by various means, given to family or friends, or donated to organizations (none, a few things, many things).

The middle portion of table 2.1 again presents the responses by age decade. Of general efforts to "clean out or reduce" belongings *in the past year*, claims to have done so "many times" decline across age decades (from 23 percent to 13 percent), whereas claims to have done this "not at all" are higher at older ages. Over age 70, the prevalence of inactivity (not at all) compared with frequent activity (many times) is nearly three to one. The pattern of showing less activity at older ages can also be seen for the three divestment strategies—selling, giving, and donating *in the past year*. Among the three specific strategies of divestment, donating is the most common, followed by gifts to family and friends, with sales being far less frequent. The hierarchy of strategies—apparent in all decades—is not surprising. Selling things requires skills, know-how, and special effort.[48] Gifts to family and friends often require an occasion, premise, transition, or acknowledged turning point in the elder's life.[49] Donating to charities and agencies is easier, however, because these outlets have regular hours and the organizations generally accept most goods.

Once again, compositional differences between the age groups can complicate any cross-age comparisons. So we conducted a logistic regression analysis to control for possible group differences.[50] We divided responses on the four questions into "any activity"—cleaning out "a few times" or "many times," disposing of "a few things" or "many things"—versus no activity. In predicting age group differences in these binary outcomes, we adjusted for factors that might account for diminished possession activity across age. These included the "possession volume" response, having moved in the past two years, marital status, number of persons in the household, sex, and especially health.

The age pattern was confirmed in these analyses: less activity at older ages. Although health affects activity in expected ways (worse health means less activity) as does homeownership and being female (more activity), the age pattern remains. To illustrate this, we calculated the predicted probabilities of activity at ages 55, 65, 75, and 85 at mean values or population proportions of the covariates. The results (shown in figure 2.2) depict lower levels of activity across age. After age 75, more than one-quarter of the respondents were predicted to do nothing to clean out, give, or donate things; after age 75, four-fifths of the respondents sold nothing over the preceding year.

There is the chance that married persons respond to such questions on behalf of their spouse. The survey items asked respondents what "you" did with "your" belongings. It is possible, even likely, that married people answered collectively—on behalf of the household—thinking about what "we" did with "our" things. Because spouses hold most possessions jointly, such replies are nonetheless valid and true to the experience of possession management. We tested for a marital effect on responses by running our analysis on single people only (41 percent of the sample), but the age pattern was nearly identical.

Our findings support the view that some proportion of older people habitually divest "many things" in later life, but larger numbers do not, suggesting a tendency to maintain collections of possessions across later life. But, absent some way to quantify possessions, it is hard to be sure. It could happen that divestment is a

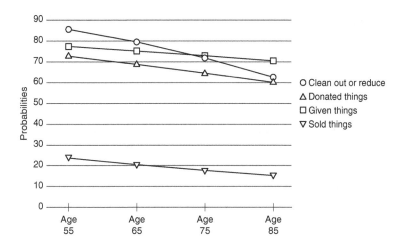

Figure 2.2 Predicted probabilities of possession activity "in the last year," at selected ages. *Source*: Reprinted from "The Material Convoy after Age 50," by D. J. Ekerdt & L. Baker, 2014, *The Journals of Gerontology Series B: Psychological Sciences and Social Sciences, 69*, p. 447. Reprinted with permission.

periodic activity, occurring in bursts rather than as a routine chore and, via these episodes, the convoy depopulates over the course of years. At the same time, our findings about divestment inertia are consistent with anecdotal evidence about the overfull homes of older adults. The inertia that we infer was directly reported by Åsa Ranada and Jan-Erik Hagberg in a study of older people (with a median age of 87) in Sweden. Nearly all of these elders had considered—but few had started—a *process of sorting out objects*. They "mainly just talked and thought about downsizing; they did not do anything substantial about it."[51]

Obstacle to Relocation

Does a tendency to have excess possessions and inertia toward their management make any practical difference? The third piece of evidence from the HRS survey concerns possessions as an obstacle to relocation, exerting a "material agency" toward aging in place. The survey question was: "Think about the effort that it would take to move your belongings to another home. How reluctant to move does that make you feel? Very reluctant, or somewhat reluctant, or not reluctant at all?" The distribution of responses by age decade is shown in the bottom part of table 2.1. Looking at the row of responses for "very reluctant," people in their 50s were most amenable to moving their things (only 37 percent very reluctant). After age 60, the percentage who were very reluctant rises to approximately half of the sample. If we bundle together the percentages for "very" and "somewhat reluctant" to indicate *any reluctance*, then the figures across the four age groups were 69 percent, 77 percent, 77 percent, and 78 percent. Thus, a substantial majority in all age groups expressed some level of reluctance. Again, we had no prior expectation about these responses but were surprised at the relatively strong reservations about moving one's belongings. People commonly voice these reservations, and the HRS replies confirm it.

In further analyses, people who had already moved in the last two years were just as unlikely, on account of their things, to want to do it again. In addition, people were more reluctant to move if they felt they had more things than they needed; if they were homeowners and thus, we infer, curating bigger convoys but also living in a larger dwelling with more space for material; and if they had more functional limitations that would affect the effort of relocation. On the other hand, people had less reluctance about moving things if they had more living children with whom they were in contact and who presumably could help. We know from other surveys that the vast majority of older Americans would like to remain in their current homes.[52] The HRS findings would support a contention that the materiality of household contents is a factor in the preference to age in place.

It is fair to conclude, from these national survey data, that older Americans have a predicament with possessions. They tend to have, by their own opinions, more things than they need, their divestment of things tapers off across age, and the effort of moving belongings contributes to a reluctance to move. Extrapolating these findings to the older population of the United States yields large numbers of people who may be looking for help with the material convoy. If there are 65.6 million Americans aged 60 and older (U.S. census figures for 2015) and, according to table 2.1, 60 percent of that age group has "more things than I need," that translates to 39 million people who feel that they have excess possessions.[53] And if, over age 60, 77 percent of people are somewhat or very reluctant to move their belongings, that is an estimated 51 million people. That is an impressive potential market for advice and services, and it helps explain adults' perennial interest in the topic of possession downsizing. With the aging baby boom, that market will yet be one-quarter larger by 2025.[54]

CONCLUSION

The critique of modern consumerism visits people's homes with scolding about housekeeping in general and clutter in particular. Messy dwellings betoken messy lives, and in the popular advice about decluttering, older adults have come in for special attention. The downsizing imperative for later life, however, poses a challenge about the right moral tone to adopt—the default stance (people have too much stuff) versus somewhat more sympathy about the personal value of possessions. The volume and density of possessions in a household are nearly impossible to characterize in a way that would facilitate research on the life course arc of the material convoy. Time predictably deposits an accumulation of things onto the convoy, in part because people acquire things without also divesting, but in part because people neglect things. Whether advancing age affects the appreciation of things is a question that has been addressed by research on cherished objects and their meanings. These selected objects are seen as maintaining identity and positive memories in the midst of narrowing lives. Despite the difficulties in characterizing the totality of possessions over the life course, there are national survey data on the attitudes of middle-aged and older adults toward the body of their possessions. Survey respondents tend to agree that their homes are overprovisioned, that processes of divestment slow across age, and that the thought of moving belongings makes older adults want to stay put. Homeowners and wealthier respondents are more likely to acknowledge encumbrance from their possessions.

This picture about age, households, and possessions leaves out one rising theme about aging and material goods. This chapter has a focus on the understandable if problematic accumulation of things that can be at odds with the reduced roles and the narrowing time horizon of later life. However, one of the primary teachings in the catechism of gerontology is the diversity of the older population. Among the tens of millions of people aged 60 and over, there is also to be found an expansive view of people's lifestyles—of individuals embarked on projects of self-development and self-expression that will involve fresh consumption of goods, services, and experiences.[55] The advice literature that advocates possession reduction in later life coexists with another genre of pro-consumerist messages for the "mature market."[56] Such lifestyle manuals and magazines promote products and experiences that risk an enlargement of the material convoy, even as the clutter police counsel the opposite.

Finally, there is one more thing to note in table 2.1. The consideration of aging and possessions bends strongly toward the judgment that households are overfull. Yet the second row of the table reports a detail to the contrary: about 5 percent of older Americans said that they have "fewer things" than they need. Exactly what this response means is difficult to know. Perhaps some people have yet-unslaked consumer thirsts. More likely, however, it is a reminder that some elders lack the material support and capacity for a certain level of well-being and security. They stand in need of more, not less, consumption.

3

MOVING CALLS THE QUESTION

Moving to a new residence calls the question on the entirety of one's things—from A to Z, from soup to nuts, the whole kit and caboodle. In contrast to the voluntary campaigns that adults undertake to thin belongings or even the occasional purges of selected items, a move is a whole-house affair. From all of the home's recesses, the status of every object is poised for evaluation Because older adults typically move from larger to smaller quarters, the material convoy will need pruning, setting in motion the physical, cognitive, emotional, and social tasks of divestment. If one wants to study the relationship between aging and possessions, there is no better opportunity to do so than during residential relocations, with their concentrated episodes of possession management. And if some elders would be better off living in housing that is more suited to their capabilities—where they could better manage their daily lives and well-being and continue to live independently—then this cannot be achieved without some encounter with the material convoy.

It is possible that older adults could move without undertaking this encounter. Yet even if the new place is the same size or larger, the body of possessions will nevertheless "flutter"—as a flock of birds flies up from and resettles onto a field—and thus generate some decision-making about particular items' continued place in the household. Another circumstance that avoids the downsizing of possessions is a move to care in the home of a relative or in a residential care facility, in which case it is left to others to disassemble the household. All of our research has involved elders' participation in the tasks of moving residence from one community setting to another. Downsizings by others or post-mortem clean-outs of the household are a kind of research that we did not conduct, yet the participants in these events have interesting experiences to report about the intergenerational valuing of things.[1]

This chapter will touch on the population frequency of moves and downsizings, people's motives for moving and not moving, the unpredictability of these transitions, the onset of disbandment episodes in relation to relocation, and the duration of such episodes.

AN UNCOMMON ACT WITH A COMMON FEATURE

Rates of residential mobility among older Americans are harder to pinpoint than one would imagine, but suffice to say that only a small proportion moves in a given year. Reviewing population reports between 1992 and 2005, Julie Sergeant found a great range of estimates.[2] Counts are affected by research design decisions and data set characteristics. For example, does one count moves by individuals or households? Do samples include persons in institutions? Do multiple moves within a time period get counted? Does mortality during the counting period lead to undercounts? Abstracting from published reports in our review, one could say that in any given year 4–5 percent of people aged 60 and older will move, with rates lower for studies with older samples.

Erin Smith tracked moves among respondents to the national Health and Retirement Study (HRS) between 2006 and 2010 and confirmed a 4.5 percent annual mobility rate across this period that also coincided with the Great Recession.[3] As in other reports, older respondents moved less often: 5.6 percent annually among those initially aged 50–62, 4.3 percent annually among those aged 63–70, and 3.4 percent annually among those aged 71–84. Following HRS respondents over the longer term, Kelly Haverstick and Natalia Zhi-van tracked a cohort from ages 51–61 (in 1992) to ages 63–73 (in 2004). The average two-year move rate for these retirement-age adults was 10 percent, or 5 percent annually. Renters were three times more likely to move than homeowners. Though a small proportion moved in any one year, over the twelve-year period 30 percent of the cohort moved at least once.[4]

So the reports cited here converge on a 4 percent or 5 percent annual mobility rate among older adults, but that experience cumulates over time in the older population.[5] Still, given a ten- or twelve-year interval, about two-thirds of people do not move. A tabulation of 2015 data for the United States shows that at ages 65–69, 49 percent of homeowners had lived in their current home for more than 20 years, a share that rises to 58 percent at ages 75–79 and to 72 percent at ages 85 and older.[6] Moving is thus a nonnormative transition of later life, not common or frequent enough for many people to become skilled and knowledgeable about how to accomplish it. And because many elders have probably not moved lately, there is every chance that things have accumulated in the household.

What is common about moves in later life is that people relocate to smaller dwellings. Such reductions are predictable because households lose members with widowhood and the departure of children, because people cash out the equity in their homes or trim rental expenses in order to fund retirement, and because the physical demands and upkeep of larger spaces may be compromised by advancing age. The alternative, upsizing the home, should be predictable when a household gains members—for example, as a result of marriage or the accommodation of kin. As a motive for moving, however, upsizing falls off across age. A tabulation of the reasons why older households chose to move, based on the 2009 American Housing Survey, found that "want a larger place" evaporates as a motive for moving after age 75.[7]

Dwelling size is measured in large national data sets by counts of the number of rooms. A comprehensive analysis of multiple U.S. sources over the period 1968–2002 shows that when individuals over the age of 50 relocate, there is an average reduction in the number of rooms occupied.[8] Owning a home is the key piece here. Home ownership is high in the older population, exceeding 75 percent at ages 65 and older.[9] When moving, the average reduction in rooms is greater if people switch from owning to renting (and such switches are more likely at older ages), but there is also a reduction even when people move from one owned home to another.[10] The drop in the number of rooms for movers was found to accelerate after age 65 and into the 80s. If smaller places are the common destination of older movers, then the reduction of possessions is imperative.

In our Midwest Study, we intentionally recruited people who had, by their own account, moved to a smaller place. As an illustration of the divestment task that these seventy-nine households faced, we can cross-classify the dwellings at origin and destination, using the self-reported number of bedrooms as an indicator of dwelling size (table 3.1). Places with more bedrooms also tend to have larger areas in the living room, kitchen, dining area, and family rooms, all of which can accommodate more possessions. More bedrooms require extra bathrooms and their contents. And more bedrooms betoken other spaces in the dwelling, such as basements, attics, and garages. Thus, every bedroom surrendered in a move signals a constriction in living space generally, and the specific need to deal with its major furniture, the things stored in that furniture, and the things in closets and hung on walls.

Reading the margin totals of table 3.1, the most frequent starting places (right margin) were three- and four-bedroom homes, and the most common destinations (bottom margin) were one- and two-bedroom dwellings. Reading on down the diagonal from the upper left, seventeen households $(1 + 2 + 6 + 8)$ had the same number of bedrooms at the start and finish, but in all cases these people claimed that they needed to divest possessions in order to fit themselves into less space overall. The biggest apparent task was that faced by those who went from three or more bedrooms down to one (twenty-one households). These were typically moves from a single-family home to apartment settings. Maureen Sable talked about the space constriction in her move to a two-bedroom apartment: "You know, when

Table 3.1
Number of Bedrooms at Origin and Destination

Bedrooms at origin home	Bedrooms at destination home				
	Four	Three	Two	One	Total
Five or six	1	1	—	2	4
Four	1	3	9	5	18
Three	—	2	17	14	33
Two	—	—	6	10	16
One	—	—	—	8	8
Total	2	6	32	39	79

Source: Midwest Study, $N = 79$.

you have three bedrooms and a family room and a basement storage room you get rid of a lot of stuff to move, basically, to a two-room house." Altogether, the participants in our Midwest Study encompassed a range of experience. Twenty-two households started out in places with four or more bedrooms and all the ancillary space and property (and larger material convoy) that that amount of space implies, but twenty-four households had a somewhat more modest move from one- or two-bedroom places. Yet in the latter households, the density, concentration, and burden of possessions may have been no less.

WHY OLDER ADULTS MOVE

Residential relocation is the behavior of 1 out of 20 or 25 older adults annually (the incidence), but there may be a one in three chance of moving at least once over any ten-year postretirement interval (prevalence). If asked, staying put generally suits older Americans just fine. In our questions about possessions in the 2010 wave of the Health and Retirement Study, we included an item that has been periodically fielded by AARP since 1989: "Do you think your current residence is where you will always live?" Of respondents aged 50 and older, 77 percent said "yes"—a result exactly in line with earlier

AARP reports. Another of our questions asked about "the chances that you will move in the next two years." Similar result: 80 percent saw no chance or a small chance of moving in the near term. In another of AARP's surveys, people were presented with the statement, "What I'd really like to do is stay in my current residence as long as possible." There was a "strongly agree" response by 72 percent of those aged 50–64 and by 78 percent over the age of 65. If combined with a "somewhat agree" response, then 85 percent altogether wanted to stay put. Shifting the focus of the question from "stay in my current residence" to "remain in my local community," the replies had only a little less intensity.[11]

This persistent pattern is commonly referred to as a preference for "aging in place," a demonstrated aspiration of the public but also increasingly a focus of research and a policy goal.[12] At a minimum, aging in place means the avoidance of institutionalized care and continued community residence. Optimally, as stated on the Centers for Disease Control's web list of "Healthy Places Terminology," aging in place is "the ability to live in one's own home and community safely, independently, and comfortably, regardless of age, income, or ability level."[13] Although people in the surveys prefer their current dwelling, in a wider sense, aging in place could also be secured by moving. By overwhelming percentages, older adults want to stay put, but this desire does not mean that they have closed their minds to the possibility of moving. Quite the contrary, as the next section will argue.

Why older adults move (or don't move) can be explained in a way that is similar to the explanation of other significant life events and transitions, such as educational endeavors, marital and childbearing choices, employment decisions, and retirement. Life course turns like these are a mix of structure and agency: structure in the roles, institutional arrangements, and personal biography that enable or constrain an individual's present options; and agency in the individual's exercise of preferences and behavior toward some end. One has the capacity to act freely, but within certain boundaries. For example, workers can choose to retire over a range of ages, but only if there is pension income available to make the transition economically feasible. Or workers can choose to continue working into their late sixties or seventies, but only if they are employable.

In accounting for residential choices in later life, there have been two basic approaches, both of which recognize elements of structure and agency.[14] One approach comes from demography. To explain why people live where they do, researchers observe characteristics of movers or migrants—their age, family situations, health, finances—as well as the characteristics of places with higher concentrations of older adults—amenities, climate, available care. These characteristics then allow inferences about motives or decision processes for relocation that also extend to explanations for not moving. The demographic approach, observing age, family, and other personal characteristics alongside place characteristics, has led to the formulation of developmental models for moves in later life identifying motivations for moves that might typify the evolving experience of later life.[15] For example, Eugene Litwak and Charles Longino drew an idealized sequence of three moves: toward amenities in the early retirement years, toward supportive kin in later years, and toward institutionalized care when health fails.[16] Such schemas have inspired considerable research.[17]

The other approach comes from environmental gerontology. With Powell Lawton and Lucille Nahemow's theory of environmental press as a foundation, environmental gerontology has examined how older adults respond to incongruence between (1) their changing competencies, needs, or preferences and (2) their physical surroundings.[18] Early studies applied a range of objective criteria to assess how well residential conditions met the needs of frail older adults, particularly those living in long-term care facilities. Later work expanded the model of "person-environment fit" to better understand how community-dwelling individuals respond to changes in function or residential circumstances as they age.[19] More recent elaborations of this approach have proposed models of the sequence of events that occur when there is age-related incongruence between persons and places: the coping, adaptation, and interventions that result; and an eventual, perhaps provisional, resolution, at some new level of capacity or emotion.[20] As an example, the subjective assessment of living environments plays a central role in Stephen Golant's theoretical model of residential normalcy.[21] A lack of perceived congruence between one's needs or preferences and one's physical environment will give rise to negative feelings that the individual seeks to manage by either adjusting expectations or changing the environment.

These demographic and ecological approaches have built a body of knowledge about residential choice and preferences, and they have established a set of explanatory factors for residential decisions that encompass social factors, environmental features, and individual dispositions.[22] The environmental features that affect relocation might occur at any scale—the dwelling, the neighborhood, the community, the climate—and also include factors such as economic contexts and government policies.

People's own reports about why they move are more likely to credit their own agency than social structure and so cannot be the whole story about relocation. Yet people's reasons for relocation are worth attention because that is their own understanding of what they are doing when they move. When panel members of the HRS surveys are found to have moved in the preceding two years, they are asked their reasons for having done so. HRS staff can code up to two responses into one of more than forty categories, reflecting the abundance of reasons that people can have for relocation. These many categories can be classified into fewer. For example, Kelly Haverstick and Natalia Zhivan distilled five reasons (family, finances, better location/house, retirement, health, and other) among a relatively young cohort of retirees, then used these reasons to sort movers into two kinds: planners and reactors.[23]

Qualitative interviews allow people to give extended explanations for having moved. In the Elder and Family Study, Julie Sergeant and I drew on such conversations with thirty-eight movers (aged 60 to 87) in thirty households, along with the separate accounts of fourteen family members (mainly adult children) who had been participants in the events. In this study, the residential relocation decision was made by the householders; couples usually made the decision together. And, more often than not, decisions were made within an extended family context, with the elder receiving input somewhere between "support" and "pressure." The daughter of an 84-year-old woman put it quite succinctly: "Well, she moved because my sister and I decided she was going to move. But she wanted to move. It wouldn't have happened if we hadn't decided that she was gonna move. It was a little complicated."[24]

Multiple issues surfaced as reasons for moving, but these motives are not isolated from one another. They cumulate and interact to generate a move decision. In these narratives, a change of residence (in the previous year) might occur because of health events; inability to carry out daily activities; concerns about safety; desire for lifestyle changes; the proactive feeling that "it was time"; inability to perform home and yard upkeep; proximity to needed services and support; role change, such as widowhood or remarriage; friends as positive role models; finances; and the existence of available housing options. These are all accounts from households that did move. It is also likely that many more households might have had these same circumstances but did *not* move because they found ways to cope with the situation while staying put.[25]

Some elders cite a clear, single reason for a move that eclipses all others. For example, in the Midwest Study, a doctor encouraged a move to separate places for a mother and daughter who lived together. In another case, a man moved because of smoke and water damage from a fire in his apartment building. But, more often, reasons for moving came braided together as interviews proceeded, especially when wives and husbands both contributed their views. For Sheira Engel, the proximate cause of her move was a road-expansion project, for which the state took her condo building by eminent domain. She also allowed, however, that she had serious health concerns and needed to move anyway to be closer to her family. In another interview, we asked Carolyn Tingey for the top three reasons why she downsized to a smaller place. She replied: "Top three reasons. Tired of stairs. Tired of cleaning all them rooms. And tired of cutting grass, shoveling snow, washing windows. Which all sounds like home maintenance." Yet earlier in her interview, we learned that her mother, the home's owner, had recently passed away. There had been a reverse mortgage on the property and the daughter had had up to two years to exercise an option to buy the house or it would revert to the mortgage holder. So what was the real reason for her move? Again, mixed motives for moving were cited by Janis Flatt, a widow. Her husband had been hospitalized and in a nursing home before he died, and she found that hard: "Well, after he passed, then I said no, I'm not going to—I don't want to be here, like by myself." She added later, "I just couldn't keep up the grass and stuff." She hired the work out, but was not happy with the results:

> People that cut your grass don't cut it like you cut it and edge it like you edge it. My husband was always particular about his stuff. He always wanted things looking nice. And so I would have to get someone to cut it, and it just wasn't the same.

Moreover, she no longer felt safe in the neighborhood. And finally, she learned of a new senior apartment building not far away, which is where she moved. Loneliness and grief, property maintenance, the neighborhood, an attractive alternative—multiple reasons explain her transition.

THE REASON BEHIND THE REASONS

Standing back one can discern a dominant theme within most move stories. It emerges like a "hidden image" in a stereogram, when a viewer gazes steadily at a drawing of, say, trees in a forest, until the scene refocuses so that a horse appears. Behind many of the reasons for moving lies the prospect of declining health—stated outright, or when people say that they are looking for a more manageable home or proximity to kin support, or they say that "it's time," or certain destination options appeal to them. One woman whom we interviewed was happy to move to a smaller place and relieve herself of the obligation to be the family center for "Thanksgiving, Christmas Eve, Christmas Day, and Easter dinner." Reasons such as these are rolled up into the all-purpose explanation that one is "getting on in years," aging away from a younger, healthier, more capable self. But when older adults engage in "residential reasoning"—about where they could or should live—they also understand themselves as aging *toward* something.[26]

Catheryn Koss and I have argued that older adults continually evaluate their housing. "Residential reasoning" is an ongoing process wherein one thinks about the suitability of the current place but also about possible *next* places. We contend that such reflection entails a forward-looking flow of thought that is motivated by the rising specter of the fourth age.[27] "Fourth age" is a term commonly used in gerontology to describe the last stage of life, which follows the "third age" of active, healthy, self-directed retirement. The fourth age is "deep old age," marked by progressive dependence and decline, by frailty and infirmity, by "extraordinary needs and vulnerabilities."[28] In everyday talk, not many people would recognize the term fourth age, but they do say that "there comes a time" or that things "reach a point" when they might cross into a life stage of increased dependency, of limitations. This realization is borne in on older adults by the awareness of age-related change, especially in physical and cognitive function.[29] And it is borne in by the "social imaginary" of the fourth age that is part of an idealized life course. This social imaginary is a "collectively imagined terminal destination in life," the old age that is unwanted and often feared, marked by the loss of independence as well as by irreversibility. Its onset (unpinned to chronological age) is uncertain. As older adults reason about where to grow older—about whether, when, and where to move—such reflection occurs in the gravitational field of the fourth age.[30]

In qualitative interviews for the Ageing as Future project, we found that concern about the fourth age appears to influence and motivate many older adults as they think about housing, and well before they experience significant declines in physical or cognitive health. We asked our participants whether they had plans for where they would live in the future. Replies fell into two broad categories. In the first type of reply, participants foresaw themselves staying put and also expressed reasons for thinking that they could do so even in the face of declining health or function. Several reported having already moved to places that would accommodate them as they aged. Whereas some described having made anticipatory moves ("That's one of the reasons we bought this house"), others described anticipatory remodeling. When asked about her plans for housing, Teresa White, age 72, insisted that she would stay in her home. She continued by describing upgrades that she had already made and will make in case she needs a less challenging environment in the years ahead:

> In fact I've put stair railings in. Put a garage door opener. Put a fence for the dog over here. I'm going to put one of those high-rise toilets in. And the safe-step tub so I could—so I'm doing as much as I can think of. I have to haul the garden hoses around. So I may put in, even though I hate to do it, in the backyard some automatic sprinkler systems. But every year I do two or three more projects so I can make the house easier to live in.

Beyond this, Ms. White's intention to age in place was perpetual: "And can I be buried in my backyard? So my hostas will benefit from me?"

In the second type of reply, half of our thirty participants, when asked for future plans about where they might live, conceded that a move might become necessary—even if unwelcome—and in each case they had some idea of what or where that destination might be. These decisions were not yet necessary but would be in the event of health decline:

- "I realize that there will come a time perhaps when I won't be able to stay here." (Female, aged 96)
- "Well, you know, you look into the future and what could it be? And you think of where you will need the help to get through the day. I have friends in Bella Springs, and you look at that and you think, well, that's possible. And oddly enough, it's a very pleasant place." (Male, aged 85)

- "I've looked at a couple of the retirement centers over there. That's not where I belong now, but I certainly have looked them over and would know where I would want to go." (Female, aged 81)
- "Am I making preparations? I think about it. I look ahead. Also I look at senior housing around here." (Female, aged 67)

Mixing both types of reasoning, Sylvia Reynolds, a participant in the Midwest Study, explained her residential status. She and her husband moved from a "much, much bigger" house into a more modest three-bedroom house:

> That was one of the goals: to get a place and get it like we wanted it so that if anything happened to either one of us, the other person would be ok and not be forced to have to move and have to move alone. We said this is our last move unless we go to Oak Villa. And that is still where we want to end up eventually, but we're not ready for that yet.

Such residential deliberations, either as to how people would age in place or the options they might see for living elsewhere, lead us to suppose that residential reasoning is common, continual, forward-looking, and driven in large part by anticipation of the fourth age. Even though set for the time being, these elders were nonetheless imaginatively engaged in planning and strategizing in case they someday had need of more environmental support for declining health. They talked about options with peers (residential co-reasoning) and measured themselves against the situations of others who had already moved. These participants' very language referenced a fourth-age threshold as thinkable, possible. They spoke in the conditional: "If we had to do away with steps. . . . If we needed caregivers. . . . If I have to get a wheelchair. . . . If it gets to where I can't stay." They acknowledged the chances: "I realize that at some point. . . . It will come to the point, possibly, someday. . . . There will come a time perhaps. . . . That may not be our choice. . . . We have a [continuing care] contract that will take us all the way through."

Based on our interviews with family members of older movers, it also seems clear that the specter of the fourth age is apparent to family members, especially in their concern for the safety and security of elders.[31] Almost certainly a factor in this residential reasoning—by older people and by others on their behalf—is the fate of the material convoy. What's to be done with all the belongings? So, even absent a move, the ability to manage possessions and household property comes to the fore as the fourth age looms.

MOVING AND DOWNSIZING: THE ORDER OF EVENTS

Residential moves to smaller homes require possession divestment. As one man said: "When you go from a two-bed to a studio, you gotta shorten sail and reduce!" How moving and downsizing coincide can play out in three basic ways. In the first, de-accumulation spans months or even years in advance of a move. This is the process that life course theory might predict (figure 2.1 in chapter 2), people pruning from their convoys the objects that no longer have, or are likely to have, utility or emotional value for daily life. De-accumulation is also consistent with the prudential anticipation of the fourth age. The backstage areas of the home are emptied of unneeded items, gifts and donations are made to the appropriate parties, significant heirlooms and major items of furniture are earmarked for eventual disposition. An extended process gives householders time to optimize divestments, such as making gifts to just the right persons and managing to get the best prices for sale items. The purges could occur in periodic waves to take advantage of, for example, neighborhood yard sales or the fact that a younger relative needs to furnish a new apartment or house. The benefit of a leaner material convoy is flexibility in contemplating a move and the ability to promptly take advantage of residential options that might arise. The peace of mind that anticipatory downsizing might confer for elders (and their families) is exactly that advocated by the advice manuals directed to the problem of elders and possessions.

Such farsighted downsizing is not likely to be the general pattern, as our report on age and possession management suggests (figure 2.2 in chapter 2). Besides procrastination, there is sometimes a surprising obstacle to getting ready—one's family. Family members can resist not just the reception of objects but acts of distribution altogether, refusing to engage in conversation about who gets what as a way of denying the elder's mortality: "Oh, Mom, you're not going to die tomorrow."[32] In our interview with Kathryn Nurski, a widow aged 84 who had lived in her house for more than fifty years, we heard about her uncooperative sons. We asked her whether, anticipating a move, she had been packing or sorting things in advance, or whether she waited until she knew she was going to move. She replied:

> My daughter came—this was over a period of a couple of years—she would come and we would go through stuff that was in the attic. There was still stuff left, but we did get rid of a few things over a couple of years. The boys never helped at all! They didn't want me to [move]. . . . Well, one of them understood, but the other one really hated it because he'd lived all his life there.

Advance disbandments that are methodical and controlled are a particularly good idea because the timing of so many moves in later life is unexpected. Julie Sergeant and colleagues analyzed two waves of data in the HRS, comparing expectations about moving expressed in 2000 with actual outcomes by 2002. The researchers found that many older adults can indeed anticipate community-based moves up to two years in advance (not so with moves to nursing facilities). Among people with low expectations of moving within the next two years (the bottom third of a subjective probability scale), only 10.5 percent later made a community-based move, but among those with high expectations of moving, 43.5 percent did so.[33] This is a prospective reading of experience. However, when the data (authors' table 2) are read retrospectively, many moves appear as unforeseen. Among all the people who *did* make a community-based move, the majority, 57 percent, had earlier estimated a zero or low probability of moving, and only 22 percent of these actual movers had foreseen a high chance of moving two years earlier.

The unforeseen nature of so many housing transitions—prompted perhaps by health changes, by family events, by the vagaries of the real estate market—is all the more reason to lighten the household's load of belongings. A particular wild card comes up in later life relocation when people apply for admission to units in senior housing and retirement communities. Once approved, they are typically wait-listed and told that it could take some time, but sometimes a spot then suddenly opens up, and there is a quick decision to make and immediate downsizing to do.

The second relocation-divestment scenario is the usual one: downsizing proximate to a move. Activity commences once a move seems quite probable, the household sheds contents, and the divestment is more or less concluded once occupants are settled in the new place. The nature of real estate and rental contracts tends to put people on a six-week to three-month schedule for moving, and that has been the common interval among people we have interviewed. Waiting until the last few months makes sense because the dimensions and size of the new place, when known, can inform divestment decisions about what appliances, furniture, and other room contents to retain or release. Will there be space for tools, hobby materials, books, kitchen utensils? Will there be a garage, basement, garden, office area, or spare rooms? Knowledge about these matters will expedite the downsizing. "It's not a matter of what you can bring," said one of our participants, "but what you can't bring." A specific destination confers a "fit heuristic" on the divestment project, something discussed in the next chapter.

If people are selling a house, the requirements of this effort are daunting enough even without the need to deal with household belongings. In some of our interviews, "real estate talk" overshadowed the focus on possessions as people returned again and again to recall the house-selling project. This did not seem to them merely to have been a financial transaction because it was also the farewell to a place that had been a setting for personal and family experience, agency and independence, memory and belonging.[34]

As if selling a home, clearing it out, and the logistics of moving were not complicated enough, there is now the increasing practice of "staging" a home for sale. All sellers know to make their properties attractive and presentable, but staging, either as a do-it-yourself activity or when turned over to professionals, takes things to a new level. Before listing a home for sale, stagers will reduce all appearance of clutter, rearrange and redecorate at least in the main rooms, and perhaps even replace (temporarily) the homeowner's furniture and accessories with more appealing appointments. The staging practice has been rising for a generation and now has its own television programs. There are organizations of professional stagers with their own accreditation and training. The claims for staging are rosy, promising faster sales at higher prices. I heard one presenter at a professional meeting warn, "If you're not staging, you've lost 80 percent of your potential buyers." The 2019 *Profile of Home Staging* from the National Association of Realtors reports that the majority of surveyed realtors use staging at least in some instances. Just over a quarter use it on all houses.[35] Although moderate home prices are more important for successful sales than staging, about half of the realtors thought that staging could also increase the dollar value of offers on a home.

Staging maneuvers only add complexity to the downsizing task. Should one sort and divest possessions before listing the house, or store quantities of goods while the house is on the market? In the latter case they will be difficult to access so that possession sorting can go forward. Staging is essentially depersonalizing a home, erasing the owner's traces so that it will seem more appealing by some standard. This is exactly the kind of "divestment ritual" described by Grant McCracken, a ritual that eases the transfer of possession. The cleaning and redecorating of a home "may be seen as an effort to remove the meaning created by the previous owner. This divestment allows the new owner to avoid contact with the meaningful properties of the previous owner and to 'free up' the meaning properties of the possession and claim them for themselves."[36]

When Anita and Ross Duvall, both in their early seventies, decided to sell their four-bedroom house where they had lived for twenty-one years, the realtor sent a "staging person" to advise them. "They say they want everything to look spacious." Accordingly, the Duvalls removed items to a portable storage container—a "pod"—sorting as they went along, which imposed a sort of discipline on the downsizing. "They said: Don't have a lot of little things sitting around. Loading up that pod did help." The house had small closets, so they shifted clothes to the pod "so you could see how big the closet was." They rolled up area rugs to make rooms look lighter, took down pictures and all family photos, as well as some valuable prints that might make the home seem more expensive. In the end, said Ms. Duvall, "This one real estate agent we know said that it almost looked like we didn't live there." Mission accomplished!

In the third relocation-divestment scenario, one takes selected possessions and moves to the new place, leaving the still mainly furnished home behind to be emptied afterward and then in many cases sold. This way, the divestments again can be methodical and controlled without the pressure of a moving deadline. From the new place, people can second-guess and correct their retention choices. On-site sales of possessions will be easier to organize if the inhabitants have departed. However, this scenario presumes that the elder can bear the expenses of two homes (rents, mortgage, taxes, utilities) while the belongings left behind are processed. Unless one is well off, this is a self-limiting strategy. The move-divest sequence was exactly the procedure followed by Dale Swapp, 71 years old and a widower within the last year. In May he committed to buying a condo that was under renovation, and he moved in September. The selling of his old house lagged these events:

> I had listed the house on the market about the first of August. I didn't want to jam myself up and have someone come along—say, if I put it on the market in May or June and then have somebody come along and want to buy it and want me out in 30 days. I just didn't want to deal with that. And since the house is paid for, it wasn't a real issue of money. It was about a reasonable, controlled transition.

Upon moving, Mr. Swapp then scheduled an estate sale at his old house, where the estate seller had free rein to arrange and price things. When we spoke with him, four months after his September move, the house was still on the market.

Across the 79 households in the Midwest Study, 10 still had homes for sale at the time of our interviews (2008–2013), and 8 of these were in the Detroit area of our project. Our participants would have agreed that the Great Recession's slow housing market played a role in the failure of these homes to sell. In a more robust economy, some households in our Elder and Family Study also had unsold homes, so it is hard to say how common the move-divest sequence is. Prolonged postmove divestments can occur by choice or by chance, but they are costly. Joyce Leseur, age 85, moved to a senior living facility but still had not sold her house when we visited her. Asked how that felt, she said:

> Depressing, it's depressing. I have come down twice in the price. For instance, my electricity bill for last month or before, it was $345, and I had it turned down to 60. So pay for that. And the gas. Gas is only $14 a month, but the water and taxes, insurance.

Also costly is an option that bridges downsizing and departing, and that is storage in a commercial rental unit.

In practice, downsizing and moving will be temporally intertwined, one preceding the other, precipitating the other, awaiting the other, and interrupting the other. And downsizing often never actually seems to conclude because people still have, even months after moving, boxes and tubs and racks of things that they still need to go through, along with quantities of belongings nominally "stored" with family members. The work carries over. Elden Weale said that he and his wife "had a second culling once we moved here. There was too much to deal with the first time to make those kinds of decisions for everything." Three months after moving, Vera Sampson still had "boxes of stuff that I don't want." Chapter 2 presented HRS findings on the volume of possessions, on the percentage of people who claimed to have "more things than I need." Among persons aged

60 and older and who had not moved in the last two years, 61 percent said they had excess possessions. But even among those who had moved in that period and who almost certainly downsized, 44 percent still said they had more than they need. Moving may pause the encounter with one's material convoy but probably not end it.

THE DURATION OF DISBANDMENT

Disbandments are acute episodes of possession divestment but their time spans are sometimes a bit indeterminate. One could say that each episode begins when the move-related decision-making and sorting commence and ends when movers are in their new home. But downsizing activities might, as just noted, anticipate the transition and stretch on afterward. In our interviews for the Midwest Study, we made an effort to establish how much time there was "to get ready for the move," often repeating the answer back for confirmation. Of the 79 households, 27 (34 percent) disbanded in one month or less, and altogether 58 (73 percent) disbanded in three months or less. (In the Elder and Family Study, 83 percent of the 30 households had three months or less to get ready for a move.) Consistent with the time frames of real estate transactions, the most common duration was six weeks to two months.

The longest reported spell was six years in the case of a widow and widower, each with a home, who married but dragged their feet on merging one residence into another. Six households reported very short disbandment spells of two weeks or less. In one case, a woman had her house for sale and her realtor heard from a buyer who said, "I'll buy the house if she can be out of there in two weeks." "Two weeks!" the woman exclaimed. In three cases, people rushed to take advantage of sudden apartment availabilities at senior housing. And in two cases, our participants had health problems that set in motion immediate transitions to another setting. The moves and household emptying each took place over four-day weekends with prodigious help mobilized by family in one case and a charitable agency in the other.

Yet even for moves not as urgent as these, a month or two to disband still seemed fast. Iris Boettcher, an 88-year-old widow, decided to move from a two-bedroom to a one-bedroom apartment after she had a fall, and she had "one month" to get ready. "That was quick," the interviewer said. "It was too quick," Ms. Boettcher replied. "A lot of decisions. . . . Every cupboard door I opened had something I didn't know what to do with, right down to the spices." A two-month disbandment was a rush for James Dines, aged 74:

> Well, we started when we made the decision to sell our home, which we had owned for 40 years plus. And at that point, we realized that now, all of a sudden, we're not going to move into a home anymore, but into an apartment. Then we realized that we had so much stuff to dispose of. And we had no time to do it, because once we made the decision to sell the house, the house was sold, thank God, in two months. You do not get rid of 40 years of excess stuff in two months. So, it was a nightmare. It really was. So, we gave away, we threw away.

Divesting, however, can hang over into the new place. Two months was not actually the end of it for Mr. Dines. He reported that he and his wife really like the new place and all the activities that it offers, but "the only problem that we have, have even today, is still downsizing." In the second bedroom of their apartment he had a stack of boxes lining one wall, with a curtain around them, "for the time being. But some of those things, as soon as we can find somebody that we feel deserves them—we don't want to try selling them to anybody—we gladly give it to them, you know." Frances Lucas moved from one two-bedroom apartment to another, but said that she divested about 20 percent of her belongings to do so. And she still feels that more must be done. We asked how her belongings fit in the new apartment and her reply was, "I have too many things." She still needs to empty a storage unit. She tried to sell some "antique type things" on Craigslist, but there have been no buyers, "so they sit there in my daughter's garage." Asked about photos, she responded, "Still too many photos"; and as for seasonal decorations, "Um-hmm. Too much of those, too." For Mr. Dines and Ms. Lucas, the conclusion of the disbandment episode did not end their wrestling with the material convoy. In chapter 8, on the emotions of residential relocation, I will return to discuss the time pressures of disbandment.

CONCLUSION

Moving residence is a major occasion for possession divestment in later life, for pruning the material convoy. Older adults are not frequent movers. They generally do not want to move at all, but they can readily imagine the need to do so. And if they move, they will in all likelihood need to fit their households into a smaller space. Relocation and migration by older people have been much studied in the social sciences, and there is a solid set of explanatory models to account for this behavior. People express a great variety of reasons for moving; motives for a single transition can be complex and braided together. Yet one can detect a reason behind the many reasons: the prospect—proximate or remote—of declining health and function and the need to live in settings that would make life more manageable physically, financially, and socially. "There will come a time, perhaps . . ."

So the showdown with the material convoy occurs within a more significant and enveloping event, the decision to change residence, which in turn may be playing out in the larger context of concessions to age-related limitations. Of the two processes, downsizing and relocation, the move is the bigger story. Yet the two are temporally coincident, whether people divest in order to move or they commit to moving and so obligate themselves to the labor of divestment. Both dynamics are liminal—that is, symbolic of crossing a threshold to a more reduced life, leaving a place behind while releasing the things that furnished activities and identity there. As Donald Redfoot and Kurt Back observed about movers, dealing with one's things in "breaking up housekeeping" is likewise a confrontation with one's own mortality.[37]

The story being told in this book is one of people and possessions and their shifting relationship. Though not the main concern, what is also liable to change across the disbandment process is the meaning of the home itself. Place attachment and the meaning of home has been a great theme in environmental gerontology.[38] Memories and emotions of familiarity and comfort merge into feelings of being "at home," where one finds centering and belonging, refuge and retreat. Naturally, we heard participants' regrets about leaving. "We raised all our children in that house. You know, it's got a lot of memories, a lot of Christmases. We had such a good time during Christmas time, you know. Our children always did holidays, I should say. It just seems that it's hard to let go really." Yet "home" memories could be so poignant as to push people to move, and move on, after becoming widowed. And for several of our participants who were newly moved into subsidized senior housing, the old place was not replete with positive meaning. They were, to a person, tickled to be in a "better place," more secure with nicer amenities. One man moved from a "hellhole" apartment plagued by vermin and crime. We asked what it was like when he left the place. "When I left for over here? . . . I was smiling all the way, baby, all the way here." Later he added and laughed: "I was glad to get out of there. I told you what I did, I wanted to do that Toyota thing, the little thing with your feet [a joyful leap]." All of these diverse experiences departing places with "too many memories," leaving places where one is not invested, or an empty house not seeming the same—all in their way nevertheless confirm what environmental gerontologists say, that the extent of place-making—and that would include furnishing—is the extent to which people feel at home.

4

CONTOURS OF HOUSEHOLD
DISBANDMENT

Household disbandment is the "breaking up" of the household, its setting and contents. Compared to ongoing possession management and the occasional big purge, what differentiates disbandments in later life is that they are necessary, liminal to mortality, and comprehensive. The previous chapter addressed how these episodes are *necessary* when moving to smaller dwellings and they are *liminal* (threshold crossing) because moves in later life are often undertaken in the shadow of the fourth age. This chapter is about the *comprehensive* confrontation with the convoy that coincides with residential relocation. What will emerge in this and the following chapters is a picture of a challenging experience. The aim is to understand exactly why and what may ease the chore. The outlines of the disbandment process have emerged from our interviews in more than 120 households for the Elder and Family Study and the Midwest Study. This chapter's topics include the labor of divestment as a cognitive task; sorting for retention or disposal; the mental shortcuts that aid people's decision-making; the typical hierarchy of disposition strategies; how the meanings of things shift as the process proceeds; and important contexts for the effort, such as health and family support.

A COGNITIVE TASK

What sets disbandment apart is the thoroughness of the project, the clearing out of those "cupboards, closets, drawers, balconies, garages, attics and cellars which comprise the hidden spaces of the dwelling."[1] Our participants needed to imagine how they would establish housekeeping in a new, reduced space; imagine the disassembly of a material environment that they had arranged over a period of years; conceive strategies for decision-making about, and disposition of, their belongings; and anticipate who could be enlisted to help—and those were only the cognitive tasks. The work then had to get done. While this was underway, disbanders were also managing other details of the relocation, such as stopping and starting utilities, scheduling the actual move, and—not least—conducting a real estate transaction.

People dealt with the cognitive challenges by making lists. "I'm a list maker," they would say. "You just have to think it out, think it out. What are you going to do? How you going to do it? What you gonna do with this stuff, putting it in a small cubbyhole?" The "cubbyhole" was a one-bedroom apartment to which the speaker, Janis Flatt, a 78-year-old widow, was moving from a five-bedroom house. Colleen Andrews recalled that she and her husband, downsizing from their home of forty-three years, began with lists:

> We had a couple of trips planned during the summer. And I took a big pad of paper with us, and while we were driving to and from, I was making lists. I said, "Now just walk through the house in your mind. Walk through the living room and tell me what pieces of furniture, what pictures you see." And we listed everything that we had, furniture-wise, lamps—how many lamps in each room and that kind of thing. And then on the way back we got to thinking, "Okay, now I had the floor plans, but not all of this is going to fit. What items on here do we REALLY want to keep?"

Inventories made a big job manageable for Isabel Arnold and her husband:

> I'm a list maker. Once I can have it on paper, it isn't clogging my brain so much. I listed categories. I am not organized, I'm so right-brained it's pitiful because I'm a musician, but there are some things that I do see that way and that's probably from reading music, too, you know. I was pretty much able to get it down and the most difficult part was when it came to just the little bits and pieces. I just—it was too much! But for the most part I just organized by groups and set aside a week for certain things and, I don't know. Somehow we made it through.

People made lists for their children, asking them what items they might like to have, or suggesting what they might do. "For my kids, I make a list of things that had to be done as I thought of them and they would look over the list and see what they could do." Moving tasks were scheduled, and box contents were logged and labeled. For some people, lists were a daily coping strategy:

> I'm a great note writer, I make lists galore. . . . So, lists; I would sit down in the evening, and I'd make a list for the next day, what I need to do, what I'm going to do. (Belva Carter)

> During that last two months, in particular, I was trying to stay organized and I was having my physical problems. So every night I would make a list of what needed to be done the next day, and I was kind of doing it in priority terms. And I would get through most of them, that day, and it would turn out that that night I'd make another list and it would be just as long as the day before, only with different stuff in it. And that went on right up until the very last week. I closed on the house, and it was now a week afterwards, and finally the list began getting shorter. (Gerald Saltzman)

But when he was in the middle of things, Mr. Saltzman added: "There was a sense of that list never going down."

One cognitive strategy is magical thinking, just wishing it all away. For her ethnography of older movers, Tam Perry actually helped people sort and pack. After an entire afternoon of work together, one woman told her, "The decisions are agonizing. I'm almost to the point where [whispers] I could just throw it all away." A little later she said, "I'm beginning to envy people who have left, or more, lost all their stuff, or they just don't have it any more."[2] In our Midwest Study, two people had fantasies that "didn't happen." An 86-year-old widow said, "I remember I used to sit there and think, boy, I hope I die before my husband does because I don't want to get rid of all this stuff. But it didn't happen that way." Another widow, Frances Lucas, imagined a fire.

> I found myself wishing that I would have a fire [laughs] and it would just disappear. I know that sounds silly. The decision making was so hard that I just couldn't—I didn't have a way to deal with that. I thought if I just had a fire and it all disappeared, then I wouldn't have to worry about it anymore. But that didn't happen.

SORTING BEGINS

Getting down to it, people begin to partition household contents, conceptually and physically, into what will be retained and what will be dispersed by some means or another. Although it might seem logical to set aside all the objects to be kept and then move on to distribute and disperse the rest, given the short durations of disbandment, activity proceeds on all fronts all at once. And assignments to the "keep" and "rid" categories are provisional. (More complete treatments of the major disposition strategies—giving, selling, donating, trashing—will appear in the chapters that follow.)

As things shift about, so does their meaning and their status in the material convoy. It cannot be otherwise when people must divest themselves of 20 percent or 40 percent or 60 percent of their belongings. Nicky Gregson observes that the moving and handling of things brings them into heightened zone of scrutiny: "In being moved, touched, and handled, things are positioned to be looked at, felt, smelt, considered, and thought about." Once out, there is a "gap" in their accommodation that allows their holders to decide whether the belongings should stay or go.[3]

In talking about their retention decisions, our participants moved certain kinds of possessions to the foreground of their narratives. One category was the "major furniture" to be used in stocking the new place, starting with specific beds. Next would be dining room tables, whether they would be kept or not, followed by mentions of dressers, chairs, china cabinets, and sometimes large appliances. Other belongings at the fore for retention were clothing, kitchen things, family portraits, antiques, TVs, and computers ("I can't function anymore without the Internet and my computer"). Then there were idiosyncratic must-haves: guns, scrapbooking supplies, a drafting table, a sewing machine, "the piano, . . . my husband!"

A second category at the fore of decision-making comprised things that are especially beloved and carry a high symbolic value. "Cherished" or special possessions, which have been the focus of so much research (see chapter 2), are treasured for their personal meanings or because they are believed by kin to be irreplaceable and inseparable from the family. The cherished things become inalienable when, as keepsakes and heirlooms, they are passed from one generation to the next.[4] Cherished and inalienable possessions assume an outsized importance during disbandment not because there are so many of them, but because their meanings must be conserved, either by retaining them or else ensuring their "safe passage" to new caretakers.[5] Mentions of cherished possessions were spread across our interviews. For example, we asked one woman what were the most critical things she had to bring along. Her reply: "I have my husband's cremains. That's the most important thing." An instance of something on its way to being inalienable was a collection of crystal figurines that had belonged to Carolyn Tingey's mother. Ms. Tingey shared some pieces with family members but wanted to honor the set as a whole:

> I knew I wasn't going to get rid of all my mother's crystal. Because
> over the years [for] Mother's Day, birthdays, Christmas, all them, we

always gave her crystal. . . . My mother was a family person. She was the matriarch of the family. So she had plenty of crystal. So I gave crystal away to family members as well. But I knew I was not going to get rid of all that crystal, so I had to find a way to house that crystal, and I wanted it to be on exhibit. So, I was about the business of trying to find me some cabinets, so I went furniture shopping. Now, remember I'm low income, I'm working everyday, I'm trying to find me some inexpensive curio cabinets.

Ms. Tingey's plans suggest something else about heirlooms, that they can be an obligation and a burden. This was quite clear in our interviews when people talked about the quantities of old photographs that they felt bound to retain, even though the identities of some of the ancestors were unknown.

Continuing this theme about protected things, personal collections are a third category that tends to come in for extra consideration and care. The following text box lists the various kinds of collections reported by participants in our interviews. Collections are more than sets of similar things, such as china or cookbooks. There are several facets of collections that complicate their disposition. First, they are an achievement; they memorialize a long-standing habit of searching for, acquiring, and assembling a composition of objects. Theorists of this activity stress that collections encode not just agency, but passion.[6] Second, they are a part of one's public persona—one becomes known for curating such items. Third, being known as a collector of teddy bears, people then make gifts of teddy bears to the collector, creating ties to others. Fourth, the display of the collection is often important, so keeping obligates special space in the household. Fifth, the collection is meaningful as an ensemble, so it should best remain intact if ever transferred to others. Collections are, in these ways, singular and perplexing constituents of the material convoy. In Gregson's study of households and possessions, she found that collections were "rarely rid."[7]

Georgina and James Dines talked about their more difficult divestments: "And the other thing that was hard, over the years, he's been a collector of [model] cars. And in the basement we had this

The following collections were mentioned by participants in the Elder and Family Study and the Midwest Study. The list does not include mentions of books, china, jewelry, phonograph records, and videos as collections.

Ceramic and glass figurines of angels, bears, birds, buffalos, cats, chickens, Easter eggs, elephants, frogs, gnomes, rabbits, shoes, snowmen, unicorns, and people reading books
Souvenirs of the 1893 World's Fair
Antique clothes
Antique dishes
Antique telephones
Antique toys
Beer cans
Beer glasses
Bibles
Bottle brush Christmas trees
Brass
Buttons
Coins
Company credit cards
Costumes
Dolls: china, miniature
Drink coasters
Fenton art glass
Fish plates
Gallon jugs
Garfield note cards
Guns
Hunting decoys
Jars
Kabuki prints
Kewpie dolls
Lindbergh material
Longaberger flower pots
Madame Alexander dolls
Masks

Matchbooks
Miniature covered wagons
Model cars
Currencies
Music boxes
Navajo rugs
Objects with a Kansas City imprint
Old liquor
Paper napkins
Placemats
Playing cards
Postcards
Sailing pictures
Santa Clauses
Smoking pipes
Spoons
Stamps
Stuffed animals
Teacups
Teddy bears
Toilet paper from travels
University mugs
....

great big display, two displays, about as long as this wall with all kind of little—what do you call those?" He replied, "Was 1/18 [scale] diecast cars. Yeah, 1/18." Ms. Dines next started to say that he had had to get rid of them, but he interrupted to point out:

No, I still got my cars. But they're in storage. And they're in part of that pile I got against the wall [in that second bedroom, with the curtain around it]. Some of those, plus a friend of mine is letting me store some stuff in his storage space. . . . I love my cars. Think about it now. When you collect those, every car I got in there, it's by choice, you know. They're not just something to buy; no, it's all about choice. And I think I have about 100. About 100 of them.

What Mr. Dines actually divested were the cabinets that displayed the collection. Before the interview concluded, he vowed, "I'm going to get back to my cars." For some of our participants, one compromise solution to the space problem posed by collections was to divest the set but retain sample or token pieces for memory and display.

Attention to big furniture and special possessions hardly begins to handle the disbandment process. One thing about sorting that impressed our participants was the disorder that it created, which might interfere with efforts to show a house for sale. Maureen and Marty Sable, both in their late seventies, were selling a three-bedroom condo, and she recalled: "During that six or eight weeks we were showing the house so much, too, that slowed us down. You can't have a big mess when you're showing a house!" Later in the visit, Mr. Sable added:

> Well, the sorting is a bit of a problem. You have to sort out and find a place for the things you're going to give away and a place for the things you're going to throw away or things for charity, so you have to stack all that. So the charity things we did stack out in the garage. So it was just kind of take it as it came, and call the kids when we came to something we thought we should check with them. We don't want it, do they want it?

Nicole and Matthew Rink, both aged 80, also recalled the difficulty of living in the middle of a work site at their two-bedroom apartment:

> We tried to go through the drawers and get rid of the junk. In every household there is junk! It was kind of difficult too because we only had so much space and we had to keep living there. It seemed like the boxes filled up faster than we had room for! You're bringing all these memories back!

Putting things into a rented self-storage facility would seem to be an option halfway between retention and divestment, and it sometimes was a temporary solution while shifting quantities of belongings about. In the long term, however, keeping is keeping and off-site storage is retention, the same as a box in the home. On that point, Marilyn Howerton observed, "Once you put stuff in a box, nine times out of nine you don't go back and use that stuff."

DECISIONAL HEURISTICS

As noted, disbandment is a whole-house encounter with the material convoy. "That was the one thing about the move that made it the hardest move I've ever done: you hold everything in your hand that you own, everything, and make a decision about it." Fortunately, when it comes to these decisions, movers can use mental shortcuts—what cognitive scientists call "heuristics." In this instance, as on other occasions of complexity in daily life, people use cognitive or emotional rules of thumb in evaluating possessions for retention or divestment. Heuristics are the ways that minds deal with an uncertain world, "how real minds make decisions under constraints of limited time and knowledge."[8] In the face of large amounts of information and many possible consequences of action, heuristics simplify and economize search processes, recognition tasks, decision-making, and judgments. Other terms for these mental mechanisms might be scripts, schemas, or rules. Herbert Simon identified such shortcuts as the "approximate methods" that humans use to handle most tasks, practical ways to proceed when knowledge and time are limited.[9]

Elden and Margaret Weale had their own term for this expedited thinking. When we asked them how they made decisions, Mr. Weale said: "Yeah, you have protocols." We asked, "Like what?"

Elden: Well, you know, the food is an excellent example. If it's expired—

Margaret: [interrupting] If the clothes don't fit.

Elden: If it's something you're not going to eat in the next months, throw it away. And/or give it away.

Margaret: If it's something that is going to cost too much to fix.

Elden: We had lots of files and I think I developed a protocol there. If, you know, it was something that was an original work by [one] of the family, then I would probably save it. If it was a clipping from the newspaper or something, I would almost certainly pitch it.

Writers on clutter control promulgate similar rules of thumb, such as, "If you haven't used it in a year, you don't need it," or "You should discard one item of clothing for every new item that you acquire." The clutter guru Marie Kondo's dictum is that the only things worth keeping are those that "spark joy."[10]

Heuristics enable people to deal with things in batches rather than one at a time. Several of these expediting rules stand out from disbanders' recollection of their experience. I discuss three of them here—the *fit, household utility,* and *me/not-me* heuristics. Of note, Mary Kalymun also observed the importance of fit and utility for decisions about living-room items by older women. Later chapters cover another three heuristics that I call *offer-claim, gender-kin,* and *deadline.*[11]

Fit Heuristic

The "fit" of furniture was a ubiquitous topic with our participants. When asked about having made "choices about what to bring and what not to bring," most people recalled the early use of a floor plan or map of the new home in order to evaluate their furniture. They may have done the measuring themselves or obtained the plan from the building manager or move-in coordinator. The rooms' dimensions, walls, windows, and doorways created a discipline and set limits on what was spatially possible. "Takes a lot of measuring and a lot of saying: What can I bring and what can't I bring?" Until the new layout is known, people cannot be sure about their decisions; this uncertainty is probably why downsizing for many movers does not begin in earnest until the destination has been fixed. This is also the reason, along with utility, that movers' narratives foreground mentions of major furniture (beds, tables, sofas) as well as the furniture that accommodates other possessions, such as bookcases and cabinets.

The fit heuristic tends to be framed in the negative: what won't fit. When asked what were the easiest things to deal with, one woman said, "The furniture was easy—it wouldn't fit." Edward Sluman, who had to get rid of his double bed when moving to a small apartment, went on to say:

> Got rid of that and, uh, there were things like that. The analogy, or metaphor I used was: Suppose I was a sailor living on a submarine. You don't have much space but you're going to have to make do, make it do and organize it. So with that theory to start out with, that premise, that's how I progressed.

William Copple and his wife moved into a two-bedroom apartment that was, by square footage, one-third the size of their former home.

> Remembering the reality of the vast difference in space was sort of a reality check. "No, I don't have room for that." "No, I can't take that." Etcetera. The reality of that was upon us so there was no kidding about what we could take or not.

Martin Hawk, who had been a housebuilder, also moved from a large house to an apartment. He teed off on our question about choices with this:

> Making the choice? Well, A, if it doesn't fit, I can't bring it. Like I had a—well, they call it a blueprint machine, in the basement. I had a copier that was old, big and stood on the table on the floor. I had stuff that didn't fit, just no room. So, I had to get rid of it.

For all this foresight about fit, some participants moving into senior housing discovered further space constraints. In one building, things had to be placed at least twenty-four inches from the wall heaters. In another, the space in front of windows had to be clear, in case of fire.

The location of electrical outlets and TV jacks also limited where things could be placed, so the way that things fit needed rethinking.

Household Utility Heuristic

Equally pragmatic but positively framed was the judgment that possessions were useful and necessary to the new household. In chapter 1, I observed that utility is one of two generic motives for keeping any possession. Useful possessions are things for instrumental control of the environment, things that enable the capacity to enact everyday life.[12] Our participants retained things that were needed to provision functional homes, such as linens, lamps, kitchen utensils, and Christmas decorations. One couple evaluated the continued utility of furniture pieces based on the amount of storage space they contained. If people retained a car or still had a yard, there were tools and accessories to keep. If a necessary household item was misplaced in the move, people were annoyed at having to repurchase it. Married couples found themselves yielding to the spouse on those items that the other judged to be personally useful. So a home needs certain things, no question; but how many of these things to continue to accommodate or in what variety is, of course, a further problem.

Surprisingly absent from our transcripts was much mention of electronic products. A few people referred to their reliance on computers and laptops, but they were not, in most people's telling, a focus of decision-making. (To be fair, we did not directly ask about such items.) To be sure, people had computers, telephones, radios, and TVs (we saw them) but did not talk about them to any extent. It may be that such things have the status of appliances, serving their purpose and taken for granted as long as they work.

Me/Not-Me Heuristic

The other generic motive for keeping possessions is their value for symbolizing something, especially self and identity. Possessions as representations or artifacts of the self are a great theme in consumer studies—how they signal who I am or who I will be.[13] When downsizing, the choices can be streamlined by the individual's evolving self-story. One's identity can guide the downsizing, but the downsizing chore can likewise prompt examination of the life that one has had, has now, and will have in the future. Facing the material convoy is likewise facing oneself and is thus a developmental encounter.

"Me" possessions narrate one's life, and their retention is a given. These are the (idiosyncratic) cherished possessions and inalienable family things that rise to the top of people's recollections about moving. In some households these are things that have already survived previous postretirement moves, having been deemed worthy of the labor of possession. When we talked with Debra Stinson about keeping decorative pictures, she said:

> Most of them that I have back there are just regular pictures. I've got, you know, one of Jesus on the mountain and one of angels— one of little, baby angels that I just LOVE. My youngest granddaughter there, or my younger granddaughter, gave me that at Christmastime. And I just love that. Nobody's gonna have that until I'm gone.

"Not-me" choices are based in self-admissions that life is changing. Participants made blanket declarations about how their moving meant leaving former lives behind. "It was a great house for entertaining . . . but we couldn't do it anymore." "[Our garden] was very pretty, we spent a lot of time on it, but you know what? I'm done." "Toward the last couple of years, the lawn wasn't that much fun anymore. We weren't boating. It's like you've been there and done that." For William Copple and his wife, a conclusion about life change eased the shedding of books.

> In the past my wife and I had conducted some classes and seminars and that type of teaching. As a part of that we had quite a library, but we decided that we had not in recent years done that and we

would not do it in the future. Although [the books] had been very important to us at one time, that time had passed.

The humanities scholar Stanley Fish once reported a similar disengagement with books. He moved to a smaller apartment and so sold books to make room. "But the deeper reason is that it was time. What I saw on the shelves was work to which I would never return, the writings of fellow critics whom I will no longer engage, interpretive dilemmas someone else will have to address."[14]

A not-me rule was used to divest clothes: "We don't really dress up anymore." "Shoes," said Francesca Tanner, "I knew I couldn't wear high heels anymore. So I had to give all those high heels and stuff away." Anne Gunter, aged 88, talked about clothes with her daughter sitting nearby:

> When I was in a home, then I entertained or I went to various things, so a lot of my clothing—and things that I wear to church, things like that—you don't wear around the house or nearby. So when I moved, I knew that I wasn't going to need some of those things anymore. . . . I only have one dress left now, and I picked that out and I told her, "That goes on me when I die."

Betty Mahan's rules for divesting clothes were these: "Things that I did not wear, that I haven't worn for a long time, that, I would finally have to say—Well, I'll never be that size." Martha Farnsworth likewise cited sizes she will never be:

> I decided my size 10s I probably could get rid of. A size 12 is like midsize. I give my eye and tooth to be in a size 12 or a 14. So, no, I decided a size 12 and 14s could go. I've been that way for 30 years. . . . The sizes 10, 12, 14, forget it and give up. Give up, face facts.

Life change facilitated the divestment of material associated with hospitality. Both Frances Lucas and Josephine Merrill made donations of domestic goods—"the entertaining things, the dishes and serving things"—and had the same observation: "I knew that I wouldn't be using things like that" and "I knew I wouldn't be doing it here." Entertaining was something about which Patricia and Sam Phail did not hold the same view, and the point of contention was a dining room set, furnishings that were at once "me" and "not me." Ms. Phail was giving away her "beautiful" nine-piece set to the daughter of one of her friends after failing to sell it. "I had the tablecloths, I had the extension, I had the pads." However:

> My husband was very upset. He gets dramatic: "We'll never have any company, that's the end. If you are giving it away, that's the end. We won't be able to have company, we won't be able to have anybody over, we're done, that's it." . . . He was angry at me over that dining room set, I couldn't believe he was that attached to it. It wasn't anything from his side of the family or anything. I said I was not going to keep a dining room. I am getting to the point where I am beyond this. My daughter and daughter-in-laws put all the food on the stove and on the countertops and they all work and everything and just help themselves and people eat all over. And I am going to set up linen table cloths and have water goblets? I am done with this formal entertaining and he was very upset that we were going to be done formal entertaining, very upset. I could not believe he was that attached to that.

Thus, when spouses do not agree about the direction of their lives, decisions about shared objects will be difficult.

In a confluence of fit, utility, and "not me" decisions, several widowed women talked about reducing their place settings of dishes, as if calibrating the reduced size of their lives. All of them, entertainment careers over, settled on the practicality of service for four or for six:

- "I could have furnished a three-bedroom home with what I gave away, with dishes and all that. I didn't bring any; I have no need for them. I have just four cups and four plates, in case I ever wanted to cook a couple of eggs."

- "I only brought four of everything as far as my dishes: four glasses, four plates, I did that. I didn't want all of them things I had before, which is a lot of dishes, a lot of glasses, cups."
- "I brought six white plates, mostly for my use. And I brought another set of my favorite dishes. I had holiday dishes—for Christmas and for Easter—and some had been given to me, some came down through the family, some I bought, but I didn't bring any of that. They all went into the garage sale. I'm pretty much down to bare bones and I still have too much stuff for this little kitchen."
- "I had service for 12 in everything. That was because over the years at Christmas time and other holidays I would do all the family dinners. I made the decision—the way our family has evolved, we don't do that so much anymore—just to keep service for four or six."
- "I sold a lot of my dishes; I don't need service for 12 anymore. And so I brought service for four. And instead of six dining chairs, I brought four."

Emotions about the lifelong companionship with deceased husbands led two widows in opposite directions when it came to their husbands' belongings. Debra Stinson, a widow for seven years, had a chest by her bed and another in storage that held "all the memorabilia from my husband":

> But the stuff from my husband . . . there was a lot of stuff that I wanted to keep from him. And I have sent some stuff to my son that was in the army, that's in California. He wanted some of his dad's military things, so I sent him some. But there was still a lot of stuff, because Mark and I, we were married 50, 51 years? . . . And so we had a lot of stuff that I wanted to keep.

Ruth Ann Barber, on the other hand, was widowed for three years by the time of our visit. One week after her husband had died, she moved all of his clothes to her daughter's home for eventual sale or donation. "I think that was the wisest move I made. . . . Then I didn't have to, you know, continue to look at that." In the later disbandment, many household objects reminded her of her late husband. Packing up with her children:

It finally got to me that night. I finally broke down, and I just couldn't take it anymore, because, you know, just so much of the stuff was, that he had loved, and everything. But, I didn't need it anymore. So I just, I told myself just, "Ruth Ann, don't get upset, just go ahead, because if Ted was here he would want you to go ahead and do just that."

Not everything in a household is as emotionally charged as the belongings associated with a late spouse, yet how one deals with them, as with other possessions, is a material way to tell developmental truth about life course continuity and change.

POSSESSIONS AS POSSIBLE SELVES

People can use heuristic thinking to efficiently embrace things or dismiss them based on their relation to the self, who I am and who I no longer am. Another, more limited category of possessions can survive the downsizing because they represent a self that I may become. Research on the "social convoy" of family, friends, and acquaintances concludes that we maintain some members in the convoy for their potential supportiveness. Interaction with them is slight but someday ties may be activated for practical help or emotional support. Likewise, material goods can stand by— stored, shelved, closeted—ready for the moments when they are useful.

Some belongings, as noted in chapter 1, are kept because they have the ability to conjure a time to come, helping us to imagine a "possible self." According to the definitional work on this idea by Hazel Markus and Paula Nurius, "possible selves" are ways that individuals think about their potential and their future.[15] Possible selves are ideal selves that we would very much like to become, or selves we could become, or the selves that we are afraid of becoming. According to these authors, hoped-for selves might include the successful self, the creative self, the rich self, the thin self, the loved self. Dreaded selves could be the alone self, the incompetent self, the depressed self, the unemployed self. Whether longed for or dreaded, possible selves are of interest because they motivate action and behavior. Whatever the origin of these personal ideas about who one could become, people keep or release selected possessions motivated by possible selves. Those cookbooks: I would like to be the person who has tried those recipes. That piano: I would feel so accomplished having learned to play it.

Among the households in our studies, certain objects endured through the downsizing because they held the promise of a future self. A car parked out back symbolized optimism for a return to health from present eye problems. A toaster oven, purchased two years earlier, made it to the new place, although "I've never used it, but I have a book from the library on using a toaster oven." For several women, materials for hobbies and crafts, now idle, nevertheless held potential for interest and creativity. When we asked about hobbies, a 64-year-old woman identified her pursuit: "I'm a seamstress and I did bring my sewing machine and my serger, but I seriously doubt that I'll get it out. I had to have it with me for comfort but it will be interesting to see if I do anything with it." Hearing about a lot of yarn sold in a garage sale, we asked this 85-year-old woman whether she was a knitter, but we were corrected. "Crochet," she said. "I haven't done any since I've been here and I keep telling myself I got to get my hooks out and start doing something like that again." Chapter 1 cited a woman who painted and held on to all of her materials but had not resumed the hobby. Another woman, age 75, pointed out where in the room her brushes and paints were stored, and then continued:

> I used to paint but I'm not sure I'm going to again. I guess when it gets warm I could paint out on my porch. I don't know, I didn't need to bring—. I suppose there's always the hope that you're going to do something you haven't done in a long time so you bring the possibility with you.

Daryl and Gladys Staples moved mainly because she had been diagnosed with incipient dementia two years earlier. During the interview, Mr. Staples sometimes spoke on her behalf. In this exchange, he guides her to say something about her new interests, but her attention remains fixed on a particular object, a spinning wheel.

Daryl: Gladys, would you say that in downsizing, that you were initially very afraid of it because you were giving up all of your things that you have worked for all your life and that meant something to you? But coming here, and engaging in other activities, and your friends made the downsizing easier, because you were able to put aside your old interests and develop new ones?

Gladys: I don't think it's so much putting aside my old interests. I have changed my interests and brought them here. I still want to bring the spinning wheel.

Daryl: Where are you going to put it? [Aside to interviewer:] That's what I say about everything that she wants to bring.

Gladys: We can probably lock it up in the knitting room downstairs.

Daryl: You got to talk to them about that.

Gladys: I have a spinning wheel and one day, I want to learn how to spin. I've been saying that now for eight years. . . . As long as I have the wherewithal to learn, I want to be able to use it. I don't want to die yet. I don't want my brain to die quite yet. I am trying. That's why I keep on knitting. I think it's important for all the things up in here [points to her head] to keep on going as long as I can and to keep on reading music and doing all those things. So that's why I want to keep active and keep on doing it. And I don't think there is anything wrong with learning as long as I still have some ability to learn. So I do want to spin.

Whereas the spinning wheel seemed to be something of a bother to her husband, to her it was a beacon for a mind that she was resolved to maintain.

SEQUENCE OF STRATEGIES, DRIFT OF MEANING

Those household contents that will not be retained must be divested by some means. The exact strategy may be one appropriate to the object, but the relative availability of a recipient or outlet may also decide the matter. Given the volume of items and limited time, the process is fluid and improvisational. People try some tactic, and if it doesn't work, then they try something else. One of the most remarkable regularities in our participants' accounts of ridding themselves of things is the fairly consistent sequence of strategies that people attempt for divestment, a structured pathway for relegated goods.[16] People tend to think first of giving things away, then perhaps selling them, then donating them, and finally discarding them.

People referred to this sequence in interview after interview. For example, when we asked how she went about deciding what she was going to bring, Linda Shill said:

> Well, I tried to go through it and, you know, sort of pick out what I thought I could bring and then try to decide on, well, first of all, let the children take what they wanted and then decide what I was going to sell, what I was going to give away.

Talking about furniture, Anne Gunter recalled: "I wanted to give things to family if they needed it or wanted it rather than to worry about putting it out for some sale. So that's the way it worked and what we have left, we put in consignment [a shop that sells used goods]." Her daughter added, "And all what she didn't sell, went to the DAV [Disabled American Veterans] or Salvation Army—we kind of spread it around—or St. Vincent de Paul." Maureen and Marty Sable described their progression through the give-sell-donate sequence. First they asked their children, "Do you want any of it?" Then the couple had a garage sale: "There wasn't too much left after our kids took things, so it was mostly little stuff by then." For anything left after the sale, they "gave it to charity," which valued the remaining items at $300 for tax purposes.

The sequence might be applied to batches of possessions, as above, or even to single types of material or single things. Sylvia Reynolds divested herself of a piano. "I had a baby grand piano I had to get rid of—that was hard!" She had wanted to keep it, but there was no room in the new place. The piano had "a lot of memories." She wanted her daughter-in-law to take it in hopes that the grandchildren would take lessons, but the family said no. So Ms. Reynolds sold the piano on Craigslist. "If I didn't get the piano sold, I was going to donate it to our church, but it did sell."

As things are remaindered by passing through the sequence of divestment strategies, their meaning drifts. Perhaps something that I appreciate will likewise seem valuable or useful to my family. No? Then perhaps a buyer will be willing to pay for it? No? Then perhaps a charity will take it? Maybe not, as Frances Lucas found out:

> You have attachments to stuff, and it is stuff, but you have attachments to those things and until you go through that process, you don't realize what your attachments are. Then, some things are valuable to you, but not to someone else. When I wanted to give things to charities, I was astounded that they didn't want a lot of things. They were specific about what they would take and what they would not take. That was a shock to me. You think charities will take whatever you want to give them (laughs), especially if you think its good stuff. That is not the case.

As divesting proceeds, the drift in meaning also contributes to a way that people speak about belongings. The meaningful shifts toward the merely material. Initial talk about single items of furniture and special family things gives way to catchall terms for undifferentiated batches of belongings; by the time people are donating to charities, they denominate the goods as "bags" of things that were dropped off. The all-purpose word *stuff* was commonly invoked to encompass undifferentiated quantities of possessions. Ms. Lucas used it three times in the quote above. It frequently came embedded in the phrases *a lot of stuff* and *all that stuff*. Yet there is also a special way that people sometimes said it, drawing it out into two syllables: *sss-TUFF*. Uttered this way, it sounds categorically dismissive (though less so than the coarser term *crap*). Our transcription rules instructed the typist to capitalize words that were spoken emphatically, or place them in quotation marks. And so we can hear William Copple distancing himself and his wife from their possessions when he said: "Through the process our reference to the stuff was 'the stuff,' trying to remind ourselves that it was just 'stuff.'" Burt and Colleen Andrews talked over each other when remembering what was included in their estate sale. She grew more expressive as she concluded:

> Oh, we had everything. All kinds of stuff in the basement: tools, leftovers from my framing business, linens—table linens, mostly, big table linens. I didn't have a whole lot of linens. Knickknacks. . . . The washer and dryer, though, a lot of the yard stuff, lawnmower, snow blower, patio furniture. You know, all of that STUFF. You know, I said I didn't need any more STUFF! I got of rid the "STUFF" (makes quote signs in air), knickknacks and stuff.

Ms. Andrews said all this in the middle of the interview, and would say the word *stuff* fifty-four more times before it was over, three uses of which merited more capital letters. Carolyn Tingey, who moved after her mother and sister died, was also emphatic about the sheer materiality of it all:

> Thank God I had friends who would come over and help me, 'cause I couldn't go up and down those stairs. We had a lot of stuff. We had a lot of stuff, a LOT OF STUFF! Believe me. Sixty years in the house. My Momma is a pack rat. My sister and I had closed down our individual houses, and our stuff was there, too. We had a lot of stuff. It was unbelievable! I was like, I open a cabinet and I was like, "Oh God!" We had Tupperware up the yang-yang.

For Ms. Tingey, the household's contents had morphed into an infrastructure of "stuff" with an unintended material agency (see chapter 1), inducing bother and dismay.

One of the tenets of environmental gerontology is that place-making is essential to a feeling of being "at home," and this experience of familiarity and comfort draws on the memories made in a place and also the way its contents have been assembled and composed over time.[17] With disbandment, with the drift in the meaning of possessions from the singular to the material, it follows that the home itself could lose its hold as a place of belonging. Elden Weale confirmed this very point. He and his wife moved from a two-and-a-half story, hundred-year old house where they had lived for thirty-three years and that had been "a wonderful home for the children." When we asked what it had felt like to sell this property, Mr. Weale said:

> Um, it was a little, there's an emotional attachment to it. In the process of doing all this we—because the house was very full of stuff—we tried to get 80 percent of it out. So we lived in the house for about six months with very sparse furnishings. And after the "stuff" moved out the emotional attachment wasn't as great.

Disbandment sends the meaning of possessions into motion, and this can include the large possession that is the house itself.

CONTEXTS

Aside from individual differences in the way that people keep house or are attached to possessions, certain contexts color the disbandment project. These include marital status, health, prior experience with moving, special skills, and the involvement of family members and others. Another important context, whether the household is rich or poor, is a subject to be taken up in chapter 8, on emotion.

Marital status is a primary context. Earlier in this chapter, widowhood was seen to prompt a stance toward those possessions that should be protected and those that can be dismissed. Downsizing while still married has its own wrinkles. On the plus side, there are two people to share the cognitive, physical, social, and emotional labor of divestment. On the negative side, a two-person home likely has more material to deal with, and those two persons can differ in their readiness to move, in their possession habits, in their motivations, and their feelings of urgency.[18] We interviewed seventeen couples jointly for our Midwest Study, along with another eight married persons individually. They told us that they cooperated and that sometimes they squabbled. They called one another pack rats. They snuck things from the "keep" piles to the "giveaway" piles, and vice versa. Essentially, they brought long-accustomed marital styles to this new episode.[19]

Consistent with a spatial separation of homes into male and female domains, husbands and wives addressed belongings within different areas of the place.[20] Couples, asked how they worked both together and independently, often explained that the husband dealt with *his* areas of the house—generally the garage, basement, and other workshop-type spaces—while the wife would deal with *her* areas—usually the rest of the dwelling. In one example of separate spaces, Sylvia Reynolds completed the sorting and packing of the household herself while her husband performed maintenance work at their new residence. Gendered space served as a way to easily establish who does what. Although the distribution of work was unlikely to be equal—the garage versus the main rooms—couples rarely addressed the fairness of this arrangement.

In even more disparate situations, a few couples openly reported that the wife did all the sorting work for the household disbandment. When speaking with us, neither member of the couple objected to this entirely skewed division of labor, though they did in some instances openly make light of the husband's lack of effort. A passage from the interview with Joseph and Christine Black illustrates the situation. Mrs. Black described how taxing this period of disbandment was, as they rushed to vacate their previous residence:

Christine: We did not want to be paying two rents [for old and new residences,] and the new apartment was to be ready in three weeks. So, we really—it was the most stressful occasion of my entire life.

Joseph: For her. She did all the work! It didn't bother me a bit! [laughs]

Christine: [laughs] He didn't do anything!

Later in the interview, the Blacks revealed that when Mr. Black was called upon to assist in the decision-making, he failed to follow through. Reiterating his earlier contention, Mr. Black recalled, "She did it all." Mrs. Black further explained the problem: "I would say, 'Please go through this box of your family's letters.' He would start reading them and that was it!" In a different household, William Connell impeded the process in another way. He simply refused to sort through the items deemed "his" and instead brought them all. As his wife made decisions about household objects in preparation for their new, smaller living space, Mr. Connell avoided the process. Consequently, as his wife Patricia recalled, the trunk of the car, post-move, was still full of the tools and sporting goods that he had yet to sort. "I told him last week: You know honey, that trunk is getting kinda full with golf clubs."

The gendered nature of disbandment occurred in yet another way. Three widowers, now without the domestic know-how that their wives might have brought to the effort, ceded agency to their children. The men, ages 74, 82, and 87, cast themselves as passive and detached from the proceedings, aware of some divestments but clueless about others. Said one man to his daughter, "You gals set it up, I'll live in it."

Health is an important context. Downsizers who are fit can reach, bend, stoop, and lift; they have stamina for repeated days of physical labor. People with health problems will have a more limited role in the proceedings. Their condition may have prompted the move in the first place, made it more urgent and hurried, with more control ceded to others. Advancing age raises the risk that health will complicate the move—hence the piece of advice from so many of our participants that people should not wait to downsize until it is "too late." Said one woman, "You need a lot of help at our age, at this age—86 and 88 was our age when we moved. That's crucial. If we had been 10 years younger, it would have been easier." Specific impairments could affect the work. Carolyn Tingey, as noted earlier, could not use stairs. Gladys Staples, with her incipient dementia, would make repeated and different decisions about the same items, to the point that her husband put the items in black garbage bags to conceal them.

One's stage of postretirement life can also color the experience, particularly if the household has already relocated once or twice in later life. Our participants reported that the character of these subsequent moves was different, but not necessarily easier. If one had already transitioned from long tenure in a house to a condo or apartment, there would be less to move this time. Veteran movers can generalize from the prior episode, the effort it took, the logistics of breaking house, and especially the talking about it afterward, comparing one experience with the other. The prior move will also feed into residential reasoning about a next move, appreciating what the job entails. These are all advantages. At the same time, the material convoy now has a higher concentration of items that are more central to the self, and the paring down may not be emotionally easier. And this second move may not have the benefit of being a spousal undertaking. And one is older. Maureen and Marty Sable, ages 77 and 81, were asked if they'd moved a lot in their lives.

Marty: Oh she has more than I.

Maureen: Yes, we both have. It's not a new thing. I've moved 19 times in my adult life, but none of them were as traumatic as this last one because of all the downsizing.

Marty: This one was too late in life!

Maureen: Well yeah, that's another thing, our age. Before, we were younger, had more energy to do things.

Some people have special skills. One of our participants had worked for a shipping company and claimed to know all about packing, stacking, and organizing material. People in four households had worked in real estate as brokers or property managers or had experience in home construction. Details around selling, renting, and building condition held no mysteries to them. And one woman had been—of all things for our research—an estate seller by profession and so could readily appraise the value of every item in her house, an activity that other participants frequently wondered or guessed about.

Reliance on nonfamily agents enabled some households to delegate various chores. For one couple, this agent was a handyman they knew who had a truck. The all-purpose answer to our questions about who did what and what went where was simply, "Jim." For another woman, "estate sale lady" was the answer to those same questions. Twelve households availed themselves of the services of "senior move managers," service providers with businesses that specialize in assisting the residential transitions of older adults. Move managers might simply consult for a few hours or they might take over major phases of the sorting and divestment. There is a growing membership organization, the National Association of Senior Move Managers, that lists services for more than nine hundred companies in the United States and abroad. Among our households, nine used move managers or home organizers that were recommended by the retirement communities to which they were moving. A limited consultation was actually one of the amenities offered by two communities; people moving in were then free to hire more time. Todd and Cathleen Koenig, ages 87 and 75 and moving between a four-bedroom house and a two-bedroom apartment, were very pleased with the move manager that they hired:

> [The retirement community was] very helpful in offering a lot of advice or information, and then part of it was recommending this [move manager], a company which is owned by a husband and a wife, and they are very, very nice. It is not cheap, but it is a tremendous amount of help. And so they helped us prepare for the moving. And then they were here when the movers arrived to help us unpack and settle. And then somebody from their company, golly, for two or

three more months, they said whenever we had [used] boxes, let them know.

Later in the interview, Ms. Koenig endorsed the company again: "It was worth it, it was expensive but worth it." Frances Lucas, however, questioned her expense for a different company:

> I hired an organizer for an outrageous amount—$50 an hour. I would never do that again. In my opinion it comes down to, you're the one that has to do it. You have to make the decisions, someone can come in and help you put things in certain places, but I had to make the decisions and the decision process is very stressful.

What Ms. Lucas said is something that applies to all agents and helpers, family and nonfamily alike: that decision-making about possessions is ultimately personal. Said another woman, "People can't go through things like you do."

The family context for disbandment was a focus of our initial Elder and Family Study. In our report from those interviews, Julie Sergeant and I described the many ways that kin, principally adult children, "attend" the events of downsizing and moving, observations confirmed in our larger Midwest Study.[21] The next chapter will explore how family members are an outlet for divestments; here the focus is the decision-making and sorting. Based on the reports of family members and elders alike, it is fair to say that the next generation is generally less invested in their elders' possessions and their disposition. Family members have not (or not recently) lived among the things at issue, and family members' presence at the household dismantling is typically intermittent. As an example, one uninterested son teased his parents that "if anything happens to you and we have to come and take care of [your things]," he would rent a dumpster. At the same time, because certain objects might be regarded as shared between the material convoys of elder and child alike, adult children can object to divestments. Of her children, Sylvia Reynolds said, "They were the worst to get rid of stuff because they just wanted to keep everything." Marjorie Curtis had a set of china that her husband had bought for her in France after World War II:

> And my daughter-in-law said she'd like to have that. And my daughter said, "Yeah, because I don't entertain. Jane does. Jane has the biggest family." And all the reasons why my daughter-in-law should have it. But when it came down to the day, my daughter said I couldn't give it away, I had to keep it. She said, "That set of dishes is a part of every memory."

Some family members affected the proceedings because they were not on board with the entire project, having discouraged the move in the first place. Kathryn Nurski's sons were of little help because they were hesitant about her leaving the family home of fifty-two years. When Dale Swapp moved within several months of his wife's death, his daughter objected: "Dad, you are moving too fast." Grieving her mother, she wanted him to wait a full year. Mr. Swapp invited her to participate in making decisions, but she declined.

When involved, the family role can be characterized along a continuum that locates agency for the numerous tasks of divestment. At one end, elders have complete agency in the disbandment, as in those cases we studied in which family members had no sustained involvement. In the middle of the continuum are cases in which family members supply assistance but cede autonomy to the elder in a pattern of collaborative decision-making. At the far end is family paternalism in the disbandment, executing the activities of relocation to protect and secure the elder's eventual well-being. The three stances can be labeled "absent," "assist," and "assert." About the first, *absent*, involvement is so common on the part of children and relatives, local and distant, that an interviewer waits for talk of it. So it is surprising when relatives are absent from the story, or nearly so. In some cases there are children nearby, but the elders say that they do not want to bother them ("They have such busy lives") or hint at strained relations. People who moved all by themselves tended to be couples, and younger ones.

Our interviews were full of reports about the supportive *assist* style of help. Family members who had adopted the hands-off helper role explained their stance in response to our question about the advice that they would give to others. In reply, they said to be respectful and let parents decide. Besides, "there is no way you can do that for someone else. You can't tell your parents what to keep." As an example from the Midwest Study, Anne Gunter, moving at age 88, gave a lot of responsibility to her daughter but said this about the arrangement: "She always brought everything to me—now do you want this? What do you want me to do with this? She always asked before she got rid of anything." Her daughter had sat in on our interview, and later agreed:

> I think working together was a good tactic, because she had the final say on everything. All I could do was offer suggestions and show why she would or would not need certain things. But she made the final decision on what she was keeping and getting rid of and where it was going and what she wanted done with it.

Cooperative relations might be a longstanding family style, but in a few cases the elders told us that cooperation had been strategic behavior on their part. Georgene Mullins, a widow aged 65, moved from a distant city, from a four-bedroom house to a small bungalow. We asked whether there had been any disagreement with her daughter and son about what to do with things, what to keep and get rid of. She said, "No, I didn't argue about anything, 'cause whatever they did I would accept that because I needed the assistance and support. . . . To accomplish the mission, I needed their support." Josephine Merrill, aged 91, also had a daughter present when we visited. Asked about any disagreements between them during the downsizing, Ms. Merrill said:

> You know, I only have just one daughter and I don't think I would say [she is] spoiled but I always wanted to get along. We fight or argue, but I like for her to be happy and I don't want to give her too hard of a time, especially now, with my husband gone, I only have

her and my granddaughters. I don't want to alienate affection, I don't want to be a burden. . . . Let's face it, I am dependent.

These sentiments—"I go along to get along"—are exactly what the exchange theory of aging would predict about intergenerational interaction.[22] People are, by nature, self-interested actors. If older people have fewer resources and less power than younger people, it is less trouble for elders simply to comply.

Another variation on the collaborative family story came about for five women, all heads of their households, who lived with other relatives. Three women each lived with a single daughter, one lived with a daughter and two grandsons, and one lived with a sister. The disbandments in these cases, already a parting with others, were really more a division of property and selection of belongings. There nevertheless were divestments of the elders' personal things and also the relegation of possessions to storage at the relatives' homes.

Family members were likely to *assert* themselves into the sorting and packing when elders were more frail. In the Elder and Family Study, children's assertion of control, even if it ruffled elders' feelings, was felt to be justified on the grounds of necessity. Children rationalized their actions as a means to relocate elders to a more protected and secure environment. One daughter allowed that her father regretted losing his lawn and garden tools, "But that's OK—he shouldn't be doing much anyway." Getting rid of things behind the elder's back was the far extent of arrogation. Some of this paternalism has to be evaluated in light of family's larger interest in accomplishing the move, which they in turn might regard as part of a longer caregiving career.[23] And feelings were ruffled. Laverne Cherwinski, age 86, was a participant in our Midwest Study. She had traveled with her husband to a distant city for his medical care. They took up temporary residence in a retirement community, but then her husband died in the nursing home there. It was decided that she would remain in the new city where two of her children also lived. Together her four children took over disbanding the home place where she and her husband had lived for forty years. She traveled back for some of this activity but mainly directed events from afar. It all felt abrupt and rushed to her, and her family did not accommodate her wish to be at the old house more often.

> I made the decisions what to bring, for the most part. But isolated things, if I had been there, would've been done a different way. Part of it, too, looking back, I realize I resented that, and it was partly because gas was so high at that time—way over $4. . . . I felt, looking back, I needed to go back and help look at these things and see where they were going, because it was my grieving. It was the end of my life with my husband. Those things represented more than just the physical thing. So I think, I think the move was grieving. I resented my son and my son-in-law for treating me that way, because they're wonderful people otherwise. But I knew—I'm beyond that part now.

Family paternalism might be grudgingly accepted. There were cases where one child stepped forward as a motivator. Betty Mahan, aged 65 and divorced, said that "having my son nag me was good." She credited him with organizing the other children and offering the frequent refrain, "Yeah, just throw it out." For Vernon and Margaret Woods, both in their 80s, it was a daughter who flew in several times from out of state to crack the whip on weeklong visits.

> *Margaret:* She's, uh, she's very with-the-program, and she STAYS with the program. And every time she was planning to come she was also planning what she would do during that week.

> *Vernon:* It was pretty, pretty tough. I did pretty good with keeping my mouth shut. She did all the "Dad, that stuff goes to the trash. That goes to Goodwill. That goes to anybody that wants it. Do you want to move this?"

> *Margaret:* "Surely, you don't want this."

> *Vernon:* "Oh, you don't want this. Give it to Goodwill."

Margaret: And even if you did want it, you didn't get to keep it long. But it was necessary.

Later the interviewer asked what the hardest possessions were to deal with. And Margaret's reply was:

> I would say that [our daughter] was probably one of the harder things to deal with! I expect a lot of people would share that, too. And I don't know, I actually think that the easiest part of the move, and the most indispensable part of the move, was the help our children gave us. I don't see how someone could make a move—THAT move—without somebody helping, like family helping.

Yet later, the interviewer said: "So your daughter was mainly in charge?" And Margaret said: "She TRIED to be."

Stronger family interventions were mainly in the direction of challenging decisions and discouraging retention. Donna Crandall had relatives and friends to help her sort and pack.

> So, I got people over to help me to move. They put stuff in the box, I take stuff out the box after they left. They come back the next day and say: Why is this out when we packed this? I say, well, because I'm going to keep it.

Her helpers' tactic, then, was to seal the boxes up and take the boxes with them. "That's a good way, too, because once you seal it and tape it, and someone takes it out for you, that'll make you not go back in that box and be sadder." Boxes were also a point of contention for Janis Flatt, moving from her five-bedroom family home of forty-five years. "I told you my kids took my stuff and put it in boxes. They taped them up and dared me to go in 'em. [Mimicking children:] 'Mom you've had this so many years.'" She returned to the point later:

> The kids helped me but still, I still had to pick through it because the kids were like "Why do you keep touching stuff after we put it over

there. Why do you have to go through and touch it?" . . . But they put
a lot of it in boxes and taped them up and it was just stacked up stuff.

A lot of these boxes went to the Salvation Army donation center. "I
was mad at first but after that stuff left, I was glad. That made it a
little easier."

The family role was a prominent theme in most of our interviews,
but many other kinds of people appear as supportive in these stories, too: neighbors, friends, church members, tradesmen, cleaning
women. It is the social convoy activated to confront the material
convoy. The social dimension of relocation was exemplified by our
interview with Gerald Saltzman. When we visited his new apartment, he was waiting for his "surrogate daughter" and her boy-
friend to come and hang pictures. Mr. Saltzman was 78 years old
and moved from a large house in a nearby city. He had been widowed
two years before. It was a second marriage for them both, and between them he and his wife had eight children, but none lived in the
area. So he forged a kinship of assistance, which was crucial because
he was hobbled by an injury during part of the disbandment. His
mainstay was a young man with a truck "who stuck by me right to
the very end." For friends, there was the surrogate daughter; an in-
terior designer who advised him about what to bring; two women
who scouted for his new apartment; two men who organized his garage sale along with two couples who helped with that and later
with sorting and packing; and two women who took all his books
for donation. Mr. Saltzman's advice to others was this:

> Well, if you're older or are limited in any way, you're going to need
> help, and you're just going to have to somehow find help. I was fortu-
> nate in doing it. The two guys that did the garage sale, that was great.
> I mean they did all the work, and it really didn't cost me anything,
> and I ended up getting something from what was sold. But beyond
> that I still needed help. And it can be friends, it can be family, but you
> might have to pay somebody. And don't be shy about seeking help
> and getting it, even if you have to pay for it. It's a very hard thing to
> do all by yourself. Really it is.

CONCLUSION

All of the households faced some version of the challenge that one man enunciated as "how to squeeze an eight-room house with a basement into a three-room apartment." As this occurs, one is also appraising the self, making the disbandment a developmental event. People undertaking this effort will, on a daily basis, need to think through endless details. They will reassign large portions of their material convoys, pondering the continued value of keeping even the important things. They will live for a time in the middle of a mess. Mental shortcuts—heuristics—will help them economize decisions based on what fits, what will be useful, and what kind of person they are, will be, or hope to be. They will see the meaning of things change as they revalue some possessions and devalue others as less relevant to their lives. It will matter for the project whether they are married, single, or widowed; how healthy they are; what competencies they have or are able to hire; and especially how the social convoy of family and friends mobilizes to support them. It will matter whether they are women (wives, daughters), who are more likely than men in the household to shoulder the various downsizing tasks. Just as the possessions are "there" in their materiality, so the labor of moving and divesting them is irreducible. Specific strategies for doing so are explored in the chapters ahead, starting with the attempt to give things away.

5

GIFTS TO OTHERS

On the face of it, what could be more simple? Confronting the need to divest a good part of one's material convoy, one could try to just put the things into the convoys of others. The previous chapter outlined a rough sequence of strategies that people attempt, and they tend to think first of giving things away. Family members are most often the intended recipients in these efforts, but neighbors, friends, and household workers can also find themselves offered belongings. In our interviews, giveaways occupied a larger amount of narrative space relative to other methods (selling, donating), and not necessarily because more goods were dispersed in this way. Perhaps people take more time with gift stories because the anecdotal point is actually the speaker's connection with the lives of others in their social convoys, or because the afterlife or whereabouts of things makes a good tale. Whereas gifts are a potential solution to a practical divestment problem, the act of giving is likewise a way to discharge one's responsibility to the things, to oneself, and to the welfare of the recipients.

Gift exchanges are a topic that has been well visited in anthropology, economics, and other fields.[1] Gifts function both to create and ratify bonds of affection, obligation, and solidarity among groups, individuals, and generations. In later life, one focus of study has been pre- and postmortem transfers of financial assets from older to younger persons.[2] Who makes transfers and what motivates them—altruism, need, intergenerational reciprocity? Such research is feasible because the object that is the gift—money—can be measured by survey methods. Aside from wealth, older adults, while alive, also distribute personal possessions along the way. The most thorough analysis of gifts of cherished possessions was conducted by Linda Price, Eric Arnould, and Carolyn Curasi, who broke down the who, when, and how of divestment decisions. These authors saw the long-term protection of cherished things as a primary motive for such transfers but also saw intentions to send a "meaning bundle" along with objects.[3]

This chapter observes gift giving within the accelerated schedule of downsizing for relocation. Variations of this strategy include intentional placing of things with others, and how decision-making for placements follows gender and kinship lines. Alternatively, elders make offers of things ("Come take what you want") even as others in the social convoy may, unbidden, try to claim things. Such tactics, however, are not assured of success and may result in ambiguous transfers or outright failure. The interesting feature of gift giving is the way that it mixes material with emotional exchange.

PLACING THINGS

Facing a moving deadline, older adults will not have the luxury of careful deliberative processes such as Price and colleagues have described for gifts of cherished possessions. Getting the right thing to the right person on the right occasion—such solutions will be uncommon in a household downsizing. Nevertheless, even in the accelerated context of a move, gifts to family members and friends can be expedited by prior calculation and planning. Some placements are already decided, perhaps having been talked about for years in the case of heirlooms, collections, and major furniture. This is the "sticker method," whereby objects are marked or listed as assigned to specific individuals; with the move imminent, all that remains is to put plans into action. Here is an example. Taking advantage of a visit by their two sons and their wives, Burt and Colleen Andrews gave each couple a card with colored stickers, telling them, "Now . . . we're going to go down in the basement. You take these cards and go around the house, and just pretend that we have to move into an apartment next week. What would you like out of this house? . . . If there's two stickers on any one item, we'll decide which one gets it." In this way, the Andrewses' antique furniture was predivided.

Whether scheduled or improvised, the matching of objects with recipients aims for some sort of congruity of interests between the giver and the acquirer, the hope being that things will continue to be valued, appreciated, and properly cared for. There may also be the hope of a kindled tie with the object's new holder.[4] Careful transfers ensure continuity in the cherishing and use of things, thereby fulfilling a responsibility toward objects with which there has been a relationship—giving them a "good home."

Along with these gift motives—the protection of the object, the benefit to recipients, emotional bonds—the research on cherished possessions and their disposition speculates about another reason to bestow certain gifts: making a legacy. Gifts can be deployed in an attempt to transcend mortality, perpetuating memories and stories and transmitting values and indeed oneself into the future.[5] Whether such outcomes occur is a gamble; in prospect, such legacy-of-self sequellae are all imaginative.

In the Midwest Study, my colleagues and I identified a strong form of intentional placement, calling it a "safe passage."[6] Safe passage was what travelers in the Middle Ages received when escorted through perilous territory. Catherine Roster brought the term into consumption studies in order to describe ways that people at sales would steer their things toward congenial buyers.[7] The term can also be applied to gifts, and complete safe passage accounts would have up to three features. First, the owner has shown some initiative in bringing the placement about. Second, safe passage accounts describe an "afterward," an assurance about either the physical protection or the appreciation of the item by its new owner. Third, the placement is thought to project the values, personality, or identity of the giver—that is, it has created a legacy.

Gift stories with an aspiration to legacy were few in our interviews. Here are two such anecdotes. In the first, about a fishing reel, Jane Ferguson tells of selecting just the right recipient, how the gift was received, and how it deposits a memory of her late husband and herself as a neighborly couple:

> There was a whole bunch of fishing stuff.... And one of the things that my husband had been given was a reel that was rather expensive—it was still in the box. We moved from Columbus and went to Wisconsin. He was going to do a lot of fishing in Wisconsin but that didn't work out. He didn't become quite the fisherman he thought he'd be. So this was still in the box. There were young girls on our street who, as little girls, we'd take them to lunch once in a while. And one, when she was over one time she talked about what she wanted to be when she got older and she said she'd like a big house and to go fishing. So we thought about that, and had special feelings for these girls. So after he died, I asked Amber, "Would you like this reel?" So we found it and I had no idea what it cost—I'm thinking it was rather expensive. So she has the reel now. And she was quite thrilled with it at the time.

For Marjorie Curtis, plans were in place for gifts of books to grandchildren with an eye to their readiness for the books and with an explicit intention about legacy:

> I have some [books] that are very, very old. Some I have already designated to go to grandchildren because they are books I read when I was a child, so see that's a long time ago. They won't appreciate it right now, but my good intentions are to write a note for each book to each grandchild ... and tell them what I did with the book and why I had it. I would like them to keep it. So that's something I'll do.

Safe passage stories that lacked the legacy intention were more common and included the specific placement of gifts and the recipients' pleasure at having them (and thus the giver's pleasure at the protection of objects). Jane Crawford's husband had a big, antique workbench that he gave to a local arboretum. "He has some friends who work out there and stuff, his golfing friends." The friends came and got the workbench, "so that was a good thing for us, too. That's something they will enjoy for a long time." Marilyn Howerton could not bring her birdbath to her new place, so it went to the home of a grandson and his wife, "and they love it, so that made me happy." Cara Deaton's daughter in Nashville "had my whole living room furniture shipped out to her. And she called me the other day and said, 'Guess what, Mother! The green that was in the sofa and love seat matches the tile in my fireplace exactly. I'm so excited!' To me, that really feels good, that really feels good."

A small wicker rocker belonged to Cathleen Koenig as a child, and it had already been in the family for an additional generation. With no toddler among her grandchildren, she gave it to the handyman who was helping with the move, and he in turn placed it at his parents' house. The handyman told her a week later that he had been at the house, and "there was his dad sitting in a rocker and his little nephew, four years old, was sitting in this little [wicker] rocker, rocking in his chair next to his grandfather. So you know how I felt—it was going to a good place."

Initiative and object protection featured in Ruth Ann Barber's gift of her houseplants. She shrewdly engineered their transfer to someone who would really want them:

Interviewer: Did you have houseplants, or—?

Ruth Ann: Oh, yes. LOTS of houseplants.

Interviewer: Did you sell those?

Ruth Ann: I gave them away. Yeah. Up at the Warburg Bank there was a, oh, the president of the bank up there. She had done a lot of helping with a lot of different things. And so I was up there one day and I said "You've been down to my house and you've seen all of my plants," and she said [gasps, mimicking,] "Oh, can I come down?" And I said yes. So, I come down and I let her take whatever she wanted. So—.

As expressed on the sound recording, the concluding "So" was an expression of satisfaction at things having gone as planned.

Sometimes gifts are unplanned, occurring on the spur of the moment. Moving truck drivers might find themselves gifted with furniture that won't actually fit into the new place ("Don't take it off the truck"). Once a downsizer is in gear, any available recipient will do. Martha Farnsworth told us:

> My friends—the people I know, sometimes people come for dinner. One of their daughters just loved a painting I had, and I just took it off the wall and handed it to her. It gave me a lot of pleasure. I gave a lot of things I knew some of my friends liked. I just handed it to them because I figured I'm not going to get much money selling this stuff. It's really going to be pennies. It means nothing and it would really mean something to this other person, either before they said they like it or I knew they would love it. So I gave a lot of stuff away to friends and family and things like that.

At the same time, for all the memories of gratifying transfers, we also heard gift stories that were matter-of-fact, lacking happy notes about the giver and receiver's delight in the exchange. In the telling, the objects were less bestowed than off-loaded. For example, Gerald Saltzman, a widower, simply recited the destinations: a piano to a daughter; several boxes of tools and a table saw to a son and grandson; his late wife's desk to the daughter; a sewing machine to another daughter; heirloom china and silver split between the daughters. "So there was that kind of peeling away of things."

THE GENDER-KIN HEURISTIC

Mr. Saltzman's distributions demonstrate an important heuristic that economizes gift decisions. As he gave tools to a son and grandson and china to daughters, he was reproducing the objects' circumstances of possession by passing items to the appropriate gender and within family lines. Gender and kinship are primary axes for divestment decisions that are intertwined with considerations about the cherishing and conservation that items might enjoy.[8] Chapter 4 noted that there are gendered zones of a home—his areas and her areas—that a couple might address in downsizing. Likewise, separate objects will also encode gender.[9] Many consumer goods are designed specifically for the enactment of male and female identities. The taken-for-grantedness of things as male and female—by design or ownership—simplifies the list of potential recipients when it comes time to distribute possessions during a household downsizing. The preference for retaining family ownership by first-degree relatives of appropriate gender also narrows the range of recipients. So-called family things should preferably "go down" a female or male line. Our interviews did contain accounts of gender-crossing and family-slipping dispositions, but the practice of reproducing gender and family circumstances of possession is so pervasive that Aislinn Addington and I thought it worth naming. We would call this practice *homoctesis*, from Greek roots meaning "sameness of possession." In the case of residential downsizing by older adults, homoctesis, as facsimiled ownership, is a cognitive pragmatic for the "to whom" of dispositions.[10]

Besides speeding gift decisions, the homoctesis heuristic has another, latent effect: the replication of social structures. The gendered passing of items (and the values that those items hold) is at once the passing along of expectations for gender identity. The items potentially instruct or assist a person in how to be a man or a woman—whatever that may mean for the family or social group involved. Likewise, the inclination to bestow things within family bounds is part convenience, but it also reproduces ideas about family and kinship.[11] The gifts signal who "counts" as family members and what counts as family wealth. Gifts thus can "materialize" gender and kin roles even without the givers' explicit intention.

Our participants commonly spoke of objects in a gendered way, passing jewelry to "the girls" (meaning daughters and granddaughters) and tools and hobby materials to men. Vera Sampson, when asked about her seasonal decorations, said, "I gave a lot to my daughter"; in comparison, she said, "I gave my son his dad's golf stuff." She distributed these gifts in expectation of her children's interests: *she* would use holiday decorations, and *he* would use golf equipment. Ruth Ann Barber thought first of her son when allocating things from her late husband:

> I gave that [man's diamond ring] to my son, and then any of [my husband's] personal things. I had Jimmy come because I felt like he and his dad were so close and he should come before the girls. So he came and took anything he wanted of his [father's] . . . then each of the girls came and, you know, picked out stuff of their dad's.

Gifts were deemed appropriate because they might kindle sentiment but also ongoing gender role enactment. Thomas Stinson's father had been a hunting enthusiast who began a gun and decoy collection. Mr. Stinson inherited the collection and enlarged it and, when downsizing, gave it to his son and grandson, thus conveying traditional masculinity to the fourth generation. Ms. Sampson's four-year old grandson got his late grandfather's bow ties because the boy played at being a grown man by dressing up in suits. Lorna and Jim Stoner matched things man-to-boy: his pool table to a grandson with whom he played and his woodworking tools to another grandson who had that interest. "So that's how we did it, anything we knew they would use and enjoy and it would mean something because it was grand-dad's." Sheira Engel's fine dining items, symbols of her domesticity, were routed to a daughter ("my good dishes"), a granddaughter ("my good silver"), and another granddaughter ("my crystal").

Many of these gendered dispositions were obviously layered by degrees of kinship. Assuming that there are gender-appropriate kin at hand, there is a strong preference for possessions passing to first-degree relatives, especially to sons and daughters. Lacking those recipients, people will still tend to attempt same-sex transfers, but to second-degree relatives or to in-laws. Belva Carter raised not only biological children but also nieces. Whereas there were a few family items that she felt those nieces would feel closer to than her biological children—things they had grown up with—Ms. Carter nonetheless offered these items first to her biological daughters. Degree of relation was also apparent in the convention of letting daughters have first choice over daughters-in-law. Betty Mitchell could not take a dining table to her new, smaller residence. Her daughter-in-law had shown an interest in this particular piece of furniture, but before relinquishing it to a relative by marriage, Mrs. Mitchell first checked with her daughters to see whether they wanted it.

When we asked Roberta Davis about family heirlooms, she told us about a ring and her intention that it move "down" in the family.

> I have my mother's diamond. When she died she had told daddy to take it off of her and she wanted it to go down with the girls. I was the oldest and my daddy had it, so I said to him, "When Dick's getting ready to marry me, you should offer it to him." So he did, and Dick bought it and [showing her hand] had it set up like this for me. This is years and years old, probably 90 years old. This will go to one of my grandchildren or my children. We haven't decided yet. One of the girls—the boys aren't interested. Kathleen would like to wear it right away. But it will probably go to one of those twins if she gets married first. But I would like them to be sure that it stays in this family and moves down. That's the only thing that's antique-y that I have.

When her own children weren't interested, Nicole Rink placed a legacy set of china with female cousins:

> One thing that was outstanding to me was a set of dishes. They had been a wedding present to my mother when she married my stepfather and they had been his mother's . . . so they went back to 1900 or a little before. They were Bavarian china. None of my family wanted them; I didn't want to sell them, didn't feel right about that. I talked to a cousin and she didn't want them but had a daughter that did, so that's where they ended up. I felt good about that.

In all, the gender-kin heuristic expedites distribution decisions but also creates extra benefit in the transmission of family tradition.

OFFERS AND CLAIMS

Alongside intentional placements, quantities of items can be passed to others by means of offers and claims. This is a batch method of giving and perhaps more suited to the accelerated schedule of household disbandment. The mover invites a taking of possessions, and others—typically family members and friends—cooperate by volunteering to accept them. This could be a whole-house invitation or one confined to certain categories, such as Christmas decorations or jewelry. In our studies, nearly all households tried these low-initiative giveaways, and the technique has certain advantages. It's a practical way to dispatch a lot of things that shortcuts decisions about who, when, and how. Multiple claimants for the same thing can sort out any fairness issues among themselves. And even if the take-up is disappointing, there is less emotional risk from refusal than there would be in direct gift attempts.

Along with gender and kinship, offers are another kind of disbandment heuristic. Jean-Sébastien Marcoux observed how older movers invited children and family members and any other potential recipients, together or separately, to choose among things.[13] Our participants recalled initiating offers with their children: "The kids had first crack at it, and then it went in the sale." "I let my children pick first." Donald Enloe told his kids, "You know you guys have got to get over here and start thinking about what you want and what you are going to take. If you don't want any of it, it's going to be donated."

Offers also adhered to gender and kin lines. Brenda Valkos told it this way:

> Basically it was family. There were certain things, I asked the grandkids what they would like to have. As I said, my grandson wanted that bed with the bookcase headboard. I had a chest of quilts that had been in my family for a long time, so I spread them all out up in the bedroom and I had my daughter and the daughters-in-law and the grandkids come in and pick out the quilts they wanted. I had enough to go around to all of them. So they did that before I actually moved. I made sure all the grandkids had an opportunity to get—. My

daughter didn't want me to leave out the boys even though you don't think of boys and dishes and that kind of thing. So she talked to the boys and picked out things. I really let the grandkids and the daughters and daughters-in-law pick out things.

The voluntary quality of such transfers was conveyed by William Copple's use of the word "selections": "Our son, who lives here, came and made some selections, and our daughter who lives in Tucson, as I said, she came and made selections." Roberta Davis offered anything that she was not taking to the new place, and with modest results:

I knew exactly what I wanted to bring here. Called the kids over, the five of them, and said, "Take what you want. Here's what I'm taking: my front room, my kitchen, my bedroom. Whatever else, you take!" And they did, they picked around. But they have all their own homes, so they don't need lots.

A variation of the offer was used in congregate housing, where things were "set out" for any other resident to glean. "Down in the lobby, that little stuff could go. I put a lot of little stuff out on the table so people could just pick it up as they go." This was a distribution recited without much emotion, but there were likewise family offers that lacked any kind of story. As people told it, things were taken, picked out, spoken for, or wound up with someone.

Offers sometimes came with nudges. Movers could add a somewhat stronger obligation to take objects because they were family things: "Would you like this, it was your grandma's?" Such a situation could be awkward, according to one woman's adult son: "You almost felt you had to take things. She would ask: 'Do you want this? It belonged to your father.' You didn't want some things because it was junk, but on the other hand it belonged to your dad and you didn't want to hurt Mom's feelings."

Claims—unbidden, someone asks to take a possession—are quasi gifts to others because the owner agrees to the transfer and can take satisfaction in the object's "afterward." The move and its household disbandment are a turning point that signals to others (and they may have seen this coming) that things may be available to them, that they can have "dibs." Claims have an element of surprise; otherwise, if the desire had been known, the elder might have given or offered items outright. In retrospect, claims make it possible for downsizers to conclude that some possession has ended up with just the right person. Surprising claims are all the initiative of the recipient. Jill Crosby was prepared to toss out a quantity of vacation slides, but they were rescued by a grandson-in-law:

> We had traveled a lot and took a lot of slides of our travels. And we used to give slide shows when we came back. We had boxes and boxes and boxes of slides! I thought, "Oh, I just hate to throw those away, but I'm not going to take them with me." Well, the husband of one of my granddaughters just thought that they were the most wonderful things in the world. And he was delighted! He took them all and he took the slide carousel. So that worked out well.

Marjorie Curtis's son took her cedar chest for his daughter: "I think that was the most surprising part of the move. Things that I never would have thought my children wanted were what they wanted." Another son "wanted my sewing machine—which was a shock. I planned to either give it or sell it, or whatever. And he said 'No, I want that.' And it was an antique; we bought it in 1946." Later in the interview, she was asked about any collections, and she said that she had had a collection of spoons:

> Because, well, we travelled considerably. So I did, I had two of those spoon cases. My oldest granddaughter asked for those. [Interviewer: Oh nice.] Yes, I was very pleased. And very surprised. I didn't think that she was interested, but she said, "Oh no, I want those!"

All of the things mentioned above—clothes, slides, furniture, spoons—had found good homes. Yet these happy outcomes had occurred not by the elder's initiative but rather by accident.

Some people lightened the giveaway chores with a sense of humor. Jill Crosby laughed as she recalled telling her children and grandchildren: "You can't leave till you take books! You can't leave till you take records!" Linda Shill had a barbecue grill and a turkey fryer to give away: "I gave those to one of my best friends and I told her—she came over to my house a lot like when I would deep fry a turkey or chicken—I said, 'Okay you've got to return the favor now.'" Alice Frawley's granddaughter, who was moving at just about the same time, was an outlet for many things, such as pots and pans.

> I had it set to the side for her. When you go through stuff you don't realize how much you had. I also had a bunch of chemicals, I guess you'd say, under my sink—all the spray cleaners and stuff. I let her just come over and go through that box. I just said don't take everything but take at least half of it.

One theme in studies of inheritance—whether postmortem bequests of money or objects or transfers among the living—is fairness. Jill Crosby solved this in part by having made "a book of various items for when I passed on, who they should go to. And I had taken pictures of things and put them in this book and had someone's name underneath it. So I had an idea of where I wanted things to go." In creating this postmortem book, she took a lesson from an earlier episode in her life that left a simmering grievance.

> One of the reasons I [made the book] was that, when I was growing up, I grew up in my grandmother's house. She had one thing that I dearly loved. It was an Irish tea set, a pot about that tall and four cups and saucers, hand-painted. For some reason I really took to that and she said, "Oh you can have that someday." Well, when the someday came, one of my aunts was living in her house and she just took it! And every once in a while I would see it in her house. Then after a while she didn't even have it out anymore. And then she passed away, and I didn't say anything. But my cousin said to her

kids, "If you find a tea set packed away in the storage room, it really belongs to Jill." [Laughs] So, ah, the next day I wasn't there but one of the daughters told my cousin, "We found it, but Aunt Jane was here and she recognized it from the house and she took it!" Well Aunt Jane didn't have any place to put it, so Aunt Jane gave it to her son who has a big house and a breakfront in the dining room. There it sits in Herm's breakfront. So the last time I was over there and it happened to be my Aunt Jane's 100th birthday and she was sitting next to me, and she pointed to the tea set, and said, "Do you recognize that, that's from our mother's house?" So that's why I made a book!

To check this idea about equity in distributions, we directly asked our participants whether there had been any disagreements about who got what. And we did not hear much in reply—there were very few heated stories about family conflict, at least over things. Before concluding that our sample households were models of family harmony, it is likely that any wrangling over special objects had taken place outside of the disbandment or was blunted by the tactics of offering and claiming. Grace Brown had such a reply about conflict-free claiming. "Well, basically, people just said, 'Well, I'd like to have such and such.' And it was just mutually agreed. I don't think we have any hard feelings, you know. That was better than I thought it was going to be, actually." According to Bill Ahlstrom, "Whoever wanted it. We offered it. There was no really—I don't think the kids really got into any arguments over it." At least as far as we heard, there was not much within-family conflict about who got what.

Whether by intentional placements or invitations to take, people can recall themselves as having been careful with things, as having seen them through. (I will say more about this in chapter 8.) There can also be contentment in reflecting that family transfers have demonstrated, across generations, how to protect the special things ("safe passage") but also how to manage responsibly the mundane things. Gifts well concluded are thus a transmission of values.

AMBIGUOUS PLACEMENT

In the comprehensive possession management that downsizing entails, there are a few gray areas along the otherwise bright line between mine and not mine. Some possessions are not mine at all to give away, and some possessions are given and kept all at once. In the former category are objects that reside mutually in more than one material convoy, a possibility already mentioned in chapters 1 and 4. One person holds things, but their ownership and treasuring are communal. Scholars dub such material as "inalienable"— inseparable from the group.[13] More colloquially, these are the "family things" whose exclusion from the kinship circle is hard to conceive. The items carry tradition and legacy and command special responsibility for their care. Family members pay particular attention to the possession circumstances of these pieces, and a single person is rarely at liberty to dispose of them.[14]

In our Elder and Family Study, the daughter of one of our movers explained how furniture from grandmothers was reassigned within the family during her mother's downsizing:

> And really, the piece of furniture that will always be in our family is, like, this china cabinet. My dad brought these dishes from Maine on a plane and I don't know what you call them, but there is a name for them. They were his mother's. So my grandmother on my dad's side collected those dishes. . . . And this buffet was my grandmother's on my mom's side. When I got this house, I knew that wall [pointing] was made for the buffet. So I got these two pieces of furniture. My one sister got granny's desk, an old rolltop desk. So it took a while to decide who was going to get what and divide things as evenly as they could.

Inalienable things do not need to be heirlooms to be jointly cherished. For example, the possessions of recent decedents can so hold a loved one's presence that survivors have a mutual stake in the items' disposition. One son described how the adult children had objected to their mother's disposal of their late father's things. The mother had started donating her husband's clothing during his final illness:

So she started before he died. Then, after, she really began sorting through stuff and disposing of it. And of course it was hard on the family because my mom was trying to be very practical about it, and I think my siblings and I were acting very strongly like it was getting rid of dad. We know, rationally, it was a very important step, but it affected us all emotionally.

Collections of photographs, if not retained by the movers, are an example of possessions that are not so much given as relocated to new hands. Other studies have shown that elders consistently list photos among their most cherished possessions. In almost every case during our Elder and Family Study interviews, family members said that the trove of family photographs remained intact through the move, as this granddaughter relates when we asked about photos:

> We have them. They are in a giant trunk in Ohio. I think when we actually took the thing home, we went through the storage and there were like ten boxes of photos. Like, everybody. I don't know—my parents don't know half of the people. And oho [grandmother] didn't know everybody. But we've got really old photos lying around.

Photos were commonly entrusted to be kept by women in the family, a variation on their traditional role as kin keepers. A daughter asked her father for custody of the family photographs because he "has a really bad memory. I feel I'm most responsible for them, the keeper of that sort of thing. He gave them to me on loan and I have never given them back." Ruth Ann Barber reported giving all the family albums to her daughter and granddaughter. It had been Ms. Barber's responsibility to maintain these things, and now she passed the role on to the next generation. Vera Sampson described her daughter as the "clearing house" in the family, keeping whatever objects needed a home.

In the category of objects at once kept and given, things such as records or artworks might be stored with family members even as the elder had not yet ceded their possession. One family had half a basement devoted to storing their mother's excess things against the possibility that she might move to a larger unit at her retirement community. Some storage was described as provisional to eventual ownership, as with this piece of furniture:

> Probably [my mother] didn't care about anything that she left behind except a kind of curio cabinet that her brother made. There was just not room for that, and that's at my house. But the reason I say it's there, I'm not really storing it for her because there is no way she will be able to have it back. But yet it's still hers.

Another type of gift that is half-given and half-retained is an exchange akin to "archiving."[15] The giver places things with designated people, with the understanding that the items will be visited in the future and could be reclaimed. One man had his collection of beer cans, four hundred in all, at his son's house. Another man told us:

> We had the cash register from my father's hardware store, almost 100 years old. Everyone loved that cash register; worked just fine. They played with it. That's at my friend's house. We love having it there. We don't have any room for a cash register.

"We love having it there"—it would be interesting to learn whether the friend was equally delighted with the arrangement. One reason that adult children may refuse gifts from downsizing parents, a topic I turn to next, may be that they are unwilling to undertake duties as curators and exhibitors of treasured items.

GIFT REFUSALS AND FAILURE TO PLACE

Gifts test the meaning of things and of personal ties, the hazard being that potential recipients do not want what is offered. Early in each interview we asked a broad question: Did you give things to your family or friends? More than a few replies described a disappointing take-up, typically expressed with the words "not want" or "not need." Here is a sample:

- "Our kids really didn't want much." (Cheryl Palmer)
- "Like I said, everyone had their own things and didn't need much." (Yvette Timian)
- "You find out that nobody really wants your stuff that much." (Martha Farnsworth)
- "Actually I had one son-in-law that I gave stuff to because all the rest of them didn't want anything. They had plenty of their own stuff." (James Kanaga)
- "Uh, nobody needed too much. I mean we tried to give things to the kids, especially the one in town here, uh . . . and, she took some things. She's got a small house that she's moving into, so that was handy. But her house is tiny so it didn't take much to fill." (Elden Weale)
- "My kids, none of them are living here. And all my stuff was 58 years old, so there wasn't everything that they wanted. You know, everybody today has a different lifestyle, different decor." (Kathryn Nurski)
- "[My daughter's] style is completely different from mine, so she didn't want anything." (Frances Lucas)
- "We asked them to come and take things. . . . And we found the fact is that they are operating pretty well themselves. There isn't a heck of a lot of things that they wanted." (Bill Ahlstrom) "I think that that is a fallacy that you pass everything on. They don't want it." (Christine Ahlstrom)
- "What surprises me, and I thought about this as Harold got rid of his things, the things that we thought were so important in our early marriages—like china, crystal, and silver—is not really desirable this time—now. My kids won't, don't care for it because it's work and it's not very serviceable and it's upkeep, and they, none of them (my two), have room. It's storage, and they are kinda against that." (Barbara Jones) "Unless they're a sharp heirloom and still of functional use, our kids' generation don't really want much of what we have." (Harold Jones)

From our interviews, we can't know what reductions people were trying to accomplish with gifts and offers. With some frequency, we did hear that family members' takings fell short of expectations, but those expectations may have been too optimistic.

In the reports just listed, family members' indifference to give-aways was recalled with a shrug, but sometimes emotions were stronger. Other studies have described hurt feelings upon the refusal of intentional placements.[16] Some of our participants were frustrated in placing things that they had thought would be well received. For example, three people had wanted to give pianos to specific children who had turned out not to be interested, and the pianos went elsewhere. When one woman tried to give either of two oil paintings owned by her late husband to one of his sons, he said, "I don't want either one—I hate both of them." A daughter called a halt to taking things from her mother:

> Well, [mother] was kind of disappointed, but I didn't want any more stuff. I'm not a big stuff person and so I have been minimizing my stuff for a long time. And my brother didn't want anything, even though he came and I asked him if he wanted anything. [Interviewer: Do you think that was hard for her?] Yes, I think the fact that nei-ther of us wanted anything or took anything bothered her.

Gift refusals by adult children are a staple of popular media sto-ries about elders and downsizing. The portrayals are potentially un-flattering to both generations, featuring three themes that none-theless would find some support among our participants. First, older people have possessions that are out of style. Roberta Davis had a mink coat—a long-ago reward to herself for raising a large family ("I deserve a mink coat!")—that she now could not give away. "The girls say, 'Mom, you don't wear mink coats anymore.'" Passages cited in this chapter had admissions that "all my stuff was 58 years old" and "china and crystal are not really desirable." Second, older people have possessions that are worn out. An older son said, "You didn't want some things because it was junk." Third, adult children are thoughtless and self-centered ("I didn't want any more stuff. I'm not a big stuff person.").

Jonathan Marx and colleagues argue that diverging or even clashing appraisals of an object are predictable when two cohorts at different stages of life in changing resale economies look at the same thing.[17] But there are yet two more mundane reasons for gift indifference. As noted in chapter 4, family members are less invested in elders' things because the family members have not lived among the things and may be unfamiliar with what they mean. Hence, a son half-threatened to rent a dumpster in the event that the downsizing responsibility falls to him. Another mundane reason for indifference to gifts is the unfortunate, joint life course timing of giveaways. Anyone moving in their seventies or eighties likely has adult children who are already middle-aged with fully stocked households of their own. Said our participants: "Everyone had their own things." "They had plenty of their own stuff." If the material convoys of the middle-aged are not lacking for contents, there is perhaps an outlet among the grandchild generation if their need to acquire aligns with elders' need to dispose. For some of our households, grandchildren reportedly absorbed a lot of material. For example, Donald Enloe said:

> Let's see. My granddaughter got a leather couch, a beautiful leather couch, leather chair. She got that end piece in the dinette, she thought she wanted that. So she gets to take that, and I can't remember what else she got. That one grandson is up at college, in his second year, he was moving from the dorm into a house. So they needed a house full of kitchenware. So he got more than enough pots, pans, casserole and all—everything you needed to furnish the kitchen. So he got all that.

Among his four grandchildren, he also gave "two or three TVs to different ones."

The fate of the material convoy is intertwined, in part, with that of the social convoy and sometimes sadly so when "heirs" for cherished possessions are unavailable. Marcoux's ethnography of downsizing in Montreal called this event "the death of the thing." He recounted the case of "a childless single woman who invited her brothers and sisters, her nephew and her nephew's children to choose among her belongings at the eve of her move to residential care. She expected that her belongings would interest someone." She had a quantity of things that were still useful and that mattered to her. "But nobody came to choose them. No one responded to her invitation." She tried other family recipients to no avail, and the things went to a charity organization. She felt hurt and pain.[18]

One of the elders in our studies was, like the woman in Montreal, a single woman, never married, and even more isolated from family. She was among our respondents who had no substantial family help with disbandment. Friends had helped her move, as had a brother and two nieces who drove from some distance to assist her over two separate weekends. She said that she had not had the energy to keep up with her helpers owing to health problems and her depression. When asked about gifts to family, she said that they didn't want anything. She tried to interest her nieces in "sentimental family stuff" but did not get far. She had three old-fashioned photo albums that contained pictures of her grandparents, and she wondered whether perhaps the county museum back home would want these artifacts: "These pictures should go back to where [my grandparents] were born, married, and raised kids."

CONCLUSION

Gift giving figures prominently in the recollection of downsizing because people can reflect with satisfaction on having "taken care" in three respects. Care has been taken of oneself by attempting a continuity—a safe passage—in the cherishing or use of things and perhaps by creating a memory of oneself and one's values in the mind of the recipient. Care has been taken of the objects by conveying them safely to a new setting where they will be appreciated. Care has been taken of relationships, demonstrating affection with recipients, sharing material resources with them, and affirming ties. Gender and kinship relations are a heuristic that economizes decision-making for dispositions, and those dispositions in turn can express and uphold the social order. In their giving, downsizers can seek intentional placements, make open-ended offers of things (another heuristic), or allow others to claim this or that. Gifts are sometimes more than mere transfers. "Family things" are not so much given away as reassigned to other kin for their dutiful keeping. Other items are half-given, half-retained by storage and archiving. Gifts test the meaning of things and ties to others, so gift indifference or refusal is always possible. This may arise from mutual, generational misprizing of the value of objects, but also from life course timing. The middle-aged children of movers already have full material convoys; everyone has enough and does not need more. Finally and regrettably, the chain of possession breaks when special things find no heirs.

Gifts presume the moral cooperation of others. Into the future, givers hope that recipients will care for the objects. Based on intergenerational interviews, Carolyn Curasi and colleagues have reported that the new guardians of family heirlooms do tend to take their role seriously.[19] And, in the immediate present of downsizing, it is the role of others to take things. Jean Sébastien Marcoux writes about a "duty of reception," how the act of receiving is also an act of generosity: "It is the recipient who is doing the favor."[20] This is the nature of gifts, that the transmission is a social affair, and thus the material and social convoys intertwine.

6

SELLING POSSESSIONS

In the common sequence of divestment strategies, people tend to think first of giving things to others, then of selling to others: "Whatever you kids don't want, it's going in the sale." The previous chapter described several features of gift giving that can also be true of selling but with certain twists. The strategy is apparently convenient but can later prove frustrating. One's social convoy gets involved because sales schemes often require the collaboration of family and friends. As with gifts, there are attempts at protection, placing objects with suitable buyers whose congruity of values, it is hoped, will give the items safe passage to good homes. Sales test the meaning of things ("People will want this") but now in a way that can be quantified and sadly so when an item commands little or no money. Thinking back, particular sales can make good stories, but sales (like open-ended gift offers) edge toward a batch method of divestment and are thus more suited to the compressed schedule of household disbandment. And when things go in batches, there is a drift in meaning away from sentiment.

This chapter is about older movers' capacity for selling possessions, with a focus on three topics.[1] One is people's experience with sales procedures, their practical ability to exchange things for money. Another topic is the emotional processes that help sellers detach possessions from the material convoy. Finally, is making money the bottom-line motivation for selling things?

ONCE COMMODITIES, COMMODITIES AGAIN

A lifetime of consumer experience with the retail rituals of buying and selling should give older people some aptitude for commerce on behalf of their own belongings. For elders who are divesting, selling is commonly encouraged; a review of advice manuals about elders and downsizing shows that all authors suggest the strategy.[2] The rise of online auction sites and also the spread of reality television programs about antiques, pawnshops, and storage unit scavengers may likewise encourage people to imagine the material convoy as salable items—commodities.[3]

This book takes the view of possessions as a convoy of material that adheres to a person or household across time. Objects serve the human life course. Anthropologists have offered an alternative view that things themselves follow their own life trajectories and have their own biographies; possession by me or you is just a phase in their material existence.[4] This perspective is helpful in thinking about sales and the way that they put items' meaning into motion. At any age and circumstance, whoever resolves to sell a possession will put that item on a journey or, more properly, a further journey. Most possessions originate as commodities—objects with an exchange value. In the course of being kept, the object withdraws from the sphere of exchange and takes on other values in a process that has been called decommoditization, singularization, or appropriation.[5] To later sell a possession—heretofore regarded as "mine"— is to reinsert it into the sphere of exchange. In this intervening time, the object has aged in ways that make it perhaps more or perhaps less valuable; even if in mint condition, the market for it has probably shifted. Not only does the thing for sale need a price, it somehow needs a presentation to likely buyers. Cleaning, refurbishing, and repair may be necessary. The successful recommoditization of the object thus takes knowledge, skills, and effort. One would need to know the retail value of similar things, the sites where they could be sold, and how to interact with strangers or how to direct intermediaries who could manage the selling.[6]

For older adults who are downsizing, additional considerations about this stage of life may affect their abilities as sellers as well as the emotional process of divestment. Aging can make sales more difficult. Some objects in the household, by virtue of their owner's age, have been out of the commercial context for a long time, and so their present worth may be difficult to estimate. Physical limitations may interfere with the labor needed to retrieve, clean, organize, and present items, and limit the energy available to negotiate and bargain with buyers and agents. The moves are constrained by time, with household disbandments typically occurring in a modal period of about two months (chapter 3), and this constraint precludes exploratory sallies into various sales methods—trying this and that. Yet, the exigency of disbandment may make sales easier. The time constraints on a residential move will focus efforts to more efficiency. Moves in later life occur in the context of reduced role involvements that will discount the practical utility and social value of some goods (e.g., tools for home projects, housewares for entertaining, sporting equipment), making them easier to divest. Finally, moves by elders often mobilize family members to help (chapter 4), and this possibility could extend to assistance with sales.

WHO TRIES IT?

Of the combined 109 households in our Elder and Family Study and Midwest Study, one quarter (27) claimed to have sold nothing in conjunction with the move. This is a good share of movers foregoing a major strategy for divestment. Yet older Americans in general do not regularly sell possessions, a conclusion drawn from our questions in the 2010 wave of the national Health and Retirement Study (chapter 2). Among persons aged 60 and older who had not moved in the last two years, fully 81 percent reported selling no belongings in the last year via a yard, garage, estate, or community sale; on consignment; or online.

Our participants forwent sales for various reasons. Situationally, it was perhaps impossible to stage sales in an apartment or condo building, or the time of year was wrong. The move might have been hurried with no time for selling. The neighborhood was unsafe:

> You have to understand the logistics of my old neighborhood. . . . If I had set up my furniture in the back yard to sell it, I wouldn't have sold anything. People would probably be trying to walk off with stuff, you know, trying to sneak out the backyard with something in their pocket. A yard sale would not have been successful. So no, I did not sell anything. (Juan King)

Other nonsellers had personal reasons—for example, "I don't believe in selling stuff if somebody needs it." Sheira Engle cited the difficulty of sales: "I helped a friend many years ago with a garage sale and found that it is not as easy as you might think that it is. You know, you have to spend time being there. You have to wait for people that you don't know to come in your home." When we asked Marie Udall whether any things were sold ("No, not really"), she said she lacked computer know-how: "If I had known more how to do that probably I would have done it. Like on the computer—I don't know how to do that. I wish I did." Some of these various difficulties with selling were likewise cited by participants who nonetheless went ahead with sales of one kind or another.

Another one-quarter of our participants had low engagement in selling for their moves, having sold only a small number of things, typically to friends or neighbors, or to the buyers of their houses. These objects tended to be kitchen appliances and pieces of furniture, and the deals mainly came about opportunistically. Because these were off-market transfers to people whom the movers knew, several spoke of nominal sales prices in exchanges that were nearly gift-like:

I was just going to give [the cabinet] to her, but she didn't want to take it like that. So she gave me some money for it. You could say that I sold that because she gave me just about the price for it. (Sandra Graves)

The modest proceeds of these casual sales led several interviewees to say: "I really gave it away." Gretchen Herrmann has also reported such token or giveaway prices at American garage sales.[7] Lorraine Morse was a low-level seller whose interest was not profit but moving things along. She sold some furniture to a family, and we asked whether the money she made was important to her. "Nah, I would have given it to them. So what I [sold] it to them for was like nothing." She gave things to her caregiver knowing that the woman would turn around and sell the goods: "I told [her] she could keep the money because she took it out, packed it up, took it out. That's all I wanted to do was get rid of it." One other kind of low-engagement selling was a proxy strategy of contributing items to a community, church, or charity sale and thereby passing belongings to (unknown) buyers without profit to oneself.

The remaining half of the movers had greater engagement based on more extensive lists of things sold, multiple modes of selling, and having mounted multi-item sales either on their property or through an agent (estate sellers, auction houses, dealers, consignment shops) or on Internet sites. For example, Sam and Patricia Phail were multimethod sellers: they used Craigslist, a newspaper ad, a sign on the bulletin board at the hardware store, and word of mouth, and they told friends. In these efforts, people offered every sort of indoor and outdoor belonging, along with automobiles. The experience of the high-engagement sellers informs the sections that follow about sales competence and possession detachment.

The extent to which people turn to sales should depend on their knowledge and skills but also on the value and quality of their stock of possessions. As a rough indicator of human and household capital, we found that households with higher educational levels were more likely to sell things; 62 percent of households with a college graduate had high engagement in sales, as compared to 41 percent in households with no college graduate. Again, compared to college graduates, those with no degree were twice as likely to have sold nothing.[8] Selling possessions, thus, is a more conceivable strategy when households are better off.

COMFORT WITH SALES PROCEDURE

Private, person-to-person sales seemed the least fraught of all options. These transactions could develop by word of mouth. Jim Kanaga initiated sales to his neighbors:

> I sold a lot of stuff and I didn't even have a garage sale. I just went next door and asked Aaron if he wanted to look at some stuff, to see if he wanted to buy it. The guy was cutting the grass next door, and I said I may have something you may be interested in. So I went back and forth across the street.

Hearing of a downsize and move, people also came forward offering to buy things. Dionne Peasley and her sister were set to move out of the family home after the death of their parents. "And I'm like, what are we going to do with all this stuff? . . . So she's like 'Let's ask so-and-so, let's start talking to people, start trying to sell a few things.'" We asked whether they put ads in the paper.

> Actually, word of mouth. A lot of word of mouth. Different people at my job knew that I was relocating, coming back, and [my sister] started spreading it among her job that we had things that we were going to sell. People started coming by and hauling stuff. . . . We had enough with just the people that were in the community.

Informal sales, in the main, held positive memories in our interviews. There were stories of "safe passage," as when Patricia Phail sold bedroom furniture: "That was nice. People were enthusiastic, they were happy, they were going to use it. It was kind of nice to see your possessions were going to somebody who really appreciated it."

Anita Duvall sold the patio furniture that had once belonged to her parents "to a neighbor, a young couple that were putting in a pool. Her mother had the same lawn furniture, so she was thrilled. We were glad that it was going to be around her pool." Some anecdotes came with a tinge of wonderment at what got sold. Two households sold wheelchair ramps. "Would you believe," said Carolyn Tingey, "the ramp off the back of the house." Really?

> Yeah, that's what I said. You want the ramp? He said, "Yeah, I want the ramp." Said, OK, if you come over here and take it off, go for it. They went over and took it off. Yeah, you'd be surprised at the things people wanted.

The Ahlstroms simply left a considerable quantity of things behind when moving, which surprised the new owner, but he made it good. He sent a check and, for Ms. Ahlstrom, two dozen long-stemmed red roses. We asked if the check was a fair amount. "More than fair," said the husband. "Yeah, faith in people again," said his wife.

Twelve households in the Midwest Study developed buyers online using Craigslist, a classified ad service, or the auction site eBay, and in half the cases the business was handled by children or friends so there was little firsthand comment on procedure. This method was tried only for selected items—a car, a set of dolls, a piano—and with inconsistent success. In two cases, the sellers thought that they were being scammed.

The other major do-it-yourself method was the garage, driveway, stoop, or yard sale, a method intended to dispatch lots of belongings in a short period of time. The verdict was neutral on the success of such efforts. The method seems to have worked well enough that a number of households held more than one prior to moving—one household claimed to have held five such events. People marveled at what would sell. Gerald Saltzman's sale "had a lot of dinky things, you know, a lot of dishes, extra stuff like that, some of which sold." He continued, "It was weird what sold, because I had all kinds of strange stuff, like plastic tubing for a drip system in the garden. And some guy bought 50 feet of plastic tubing." At Anne Gunter's sale, a dispute broke out between two men ("two guys were literally fighting") over a collection of *Mechanics Illustrated* magazines from the 1940s. Also at her sale, one browser spotted a pair of deer antlers bolted to a beam in the basement "and this one guy wanted them so bad, he said give me a wrench—I will take them down myself." Belva Carter put some family rosaries in her garage sale "and I thought: Does this ever sell, I wonder? And this gal came along, and she's got an 'Our Lady' bathroom." Sensing a lack of respect for the rosary, "I took it from her cart."

The main drawback to garage sales was how laborious they are: promoting the sale with signs or an ad, selecting items, lining up helpers, setting up, pricing, the time involved, the handling of cash, the haggling, the disposition of what goes unsold. "It's not as easy as you might think it is." "Those are so much work!" Lori Kovar, who did not sell things, explained, "My neighbor asked me why I didn't have a garage sale, but I didn't want to deal with it, itemizing and pricing everything, so I just donated it." Roberta Davis, who had difficulty walking and would downsize from four bedrooms to one, recalled:

> Then I had a garage sale. Well, I hate those—that didn't do too much good. Then I had another garage sale. . . . Yes, two garage sales. And I don't like garage sales! The kids came over, friends came, neighbors came and helped me mark things and get it set up. . . . A lot of work to get it all ready and marked.

Other troubles beset sales: bad weather, theft, low traffic. Elden Weale wondered whether buyers are getting more picky: "Yard sales don't work so good. They used to work real well, but I think yard sale people have a lot of stuff, too. They're pretty selective now [laughs]. If you just want to dump things, a yard sale is not a great idea."

Turning to mediated sales, movers sold things through, or guided by, agents such as appraisers, antique dealers, resale or consignment shops, and jewelry merchants. This route, however, is open only to households with merchandise that looks to be profitable. Agents relieve some of the sale-related labor, but there is nevertheless effort (monitoring them, paying fees) in engaging these go-betweens. Such professionals were appreciated for realizing more profitable sales. For example, the agent for Luke Ries and his wife sold break-front bookcases for $1,000 apiece when the couple had thought they were worth only $150 to $200. Said Mr. Ries:

> This lady is good at what she does. And she knows quite a number of people in the business of collectibles primarily that the average person would not have access to at all, or if they did, it would take a lot of gumshoe work. You would have to sort through a lot of things and make a lot of calls. The owner doesn't have to do it. . . . It would have been a terrible traumatic strain to have to do all of the labor, bickering and bargaining and planning the whole thing. We were relieved of all the what I call mental anguish.

Although agents were generally prized for unlocking more value, they could also devalue things by assigning lower-than-expected prices.

The agents for truly batch sales were the businesses that conduct estate (or tag) sales and auctions. If necessary, such businesses could try to sell the entire material convoy. Estate sales received mixed reviews. Fourteen of our 109 households in the two interview studies participated in such arrangements, which sometimes occurred after the move but before the house sold. These sales are conducted in the home or, alternatively, things are mingled with other sale items at another property. By arrangement, the estate seller displays the goods, affixes prices (tags) on items, conducts transactions and discounting at the actual event, and manages leftover unsold items. Several of our interviewees endorsed the estate seller's work and expressed admiration for the time spent on arranging and pricing things, the way workers came equipped with canopies and tables, and the thorough clean-up afterward. Burt and Colleen Andrews, who moved from a large house, chose this solution for a simple reason: "Somebody else doing it!" And they were very pleased:

Colleen: They had that two weeks to come in, go through the house, arrange it the way they wanted, you know, to get it priced and whatnot for the sale, and then they cleaned up afterwards, so there was nothing. We didn't have to do a thing!

Burt: That's the way to do it. It would be difficult to have your own sale, because I just think it would be a lot harder to set up. They had, you know, a lot of extra tables.

Colleen: And the staff. And they knew how to do it.

Another woman said, "I could not have done it. I COULD NOT HAVE DONE IT! Trying to sell my furniture on my own." These estate sale enthusiasts acknowledged the expertise that they did not have, and they deferred to it.

At the same time, estate sale procedure was also a source of complaint, some of it arising in retrospect from admitted unfamiliarity with the ground rules:

> The estate sale was a dismal, stressful trial because the man that I chose ripped me off, in essence. I just really felt like he did not do an effective job of advertising. He had it on a weekday when people that would want tools and stuff like that couldn't come. I wasn't savvy enough to realize that at the time. (Frances Lucas)

Another woman had not realized that her seller would not display anything that might sell for less than twenty dollars, leaving the woman to stage a later yard sale for the cheaper items. Jane Ferguson admitted to being "a rookie" about estate sales. She would be charged 25 percent or a $1,500 minimum for the sale. She was displeased that her seller pressed to add someone else's tools and furniture to her sale, because "your house is kind of bare. And I said, 'Yes, I'm downsizing—I didn't die, I'm downsizing.' And she said, 'Well, we get more people if we get more stuff.' And I said, 'That's beside the point. We had an agreement.'" Ms. Ferguson thought that the sale was held on the wrong days of the week. Because she was required to stay away from the sale, "I have no idea what anything sold for. . . . The numbers could have come out of the air." From our interviews, we could not tell whether modest proceeds were the true basis of these complaints.

Because sales schemes are physically and cognitively challenging, they almost require the help of others—the social convoy mobilized to assist the divestment of the material convoy. Word-of-mouth news about a move produced cooperative buyers and purchase bids from among neighbors and acquaintances. From movers' social networks came advice about estate sellers and consignment shops. Adult children had cooperated in the divestment first by agreeing to take things, and then by helping with sales. They routinely appear in yard and garage sale recollections as supporting players, even sometimes taking over. Debra Stinson (age 90) told how her daughter organized a two-day sale that involved "four people from her bridge club, and another four people from her book club and some from her church." The absence of help was likewise a reason for not selling. Marjorie Curtis (age 87) moved from a trilevel house to a two-bedroom apartment. In addition to selling to friends and neighbors, we asked whether she had had an organized sale. And she said, "No, no. I couldn't quite handle that by myself. And with my children all working, and they have children, I couldn't ask them to come up and spend the week with me."

PRICING KNOWLEDGE

In yard sales and mediated sales (e.g., estate sales, sales through antique dealers), the eventual prices of things tended to surprise our participants. As Gretchen Herrmann observed about garage sales: "Sales contain an enormous range of items and few sellers have a command over the retail value of the items they are selling."[9] Our participants may have been in the seventh or later decades of life, but they were babes in the woods about the economic value of their belongings. One exception was Ruth Ann Barber, who held an estate sale and had herself been in that business. Her pricing acumen was apparent in an anecdote about a furniture item that her granddaughter wanted. Ms. Barber estimated the estate sale price at $1,500, and the granddaughter offered to buy it from her ahead of the sale. But Ms. Barber said no, wait for the sale because it may go cheaper. And it did—the granddaughter got it for $1,200.

There were very few anecdotes about undiscovered "treasures," items revealed to be far more valuable than imagined. Rather, we heard disappointment about the exchange value of things as they returned to being commodities, disappointment about how low prices had to be set to move the merchandise. Part of this could be a cognitive bias called the endowment effect—a general human tendency to overvalue the things that we own.[10] One man thought that he could sell clothing: "But heck, that didn't work." Joyce Leseur told us that her estate seller had underpriced the china, silverware, and glass bowls. One couple accepted an auctioneer's estimate of what their goods would bring, but "it was really lowball." Marguerite Heinen, whose illness limited her active involvement in some aspects of the move, had an estate seller handle some china, "but I went over there and she had $5 apiece on each item, broke my heart."

To other participants, the downward price-bargaining seemed tiresome—buyers were already getting bargains, but they wanted more. When we asked Gladys and Daryl Staples how their yard sale went, Mr. Staples said, "Splendidly, everybody made out but us!" His particular example was a crystal set that had been purchased for $13.50 a glass nearly fifty years ago. At the sale, "I was asking $3.00 and [the buyers] dickered and got it down to $2.50." The discounting also demoralized Frances Lucas:

> In the estate sale, someone would say, "Can I give you a dollar for this?" and I knew they were [worth] hundreds of dollars. I would say that if you have an estate sale, don't be there. I was curled up in a little fetal position by the time I heard all that stuff.

Finally, Grace Brown felt that her whole collection of belongings was discounted by the estate seller's decision to mingle outside items into her sale. "The lady came in and she says, 'You don't have anything fancy.' And I thought, well thanks a lot. It's fancy to us, thank you very much."

Disappointed about prices, some objects were retained instead of sold. We asked Edward Sluman if some things were harder to deal with than others, and he talked about testing the market for his art books:

> When you go to a used bookstore—you probably know—you get nothing, you get zilch for it. You're practically giving those away and that hurts. And the art books, which are valuable, I finally drew the line and said, "I'm keeping those." . . . So that part hurt a little bit. Yeah, that's about it. The books hurt the most.

Vera Sampson had "a very large Tiffany-style lamp, a very old one." She took it to a local antique shop and "was very disappointed." A friend of hers, she said, may try to sell it at auction. The Great Recession was cited by some movers as a reason for not getting a fair price. Patricia Phail had some success on Craigslist, but not with a nine-piece dining room set: "In this economy, who is buying a dining room set? It was down to $950, it was down to like $200." She eventually gave it to a friend. An appraiser told Cathleen and Todd Koenig that "nobody is buying, the estate sales are just about dead—this was like the end of October and she said you get about ten cents on the dollar." Another object, the appraiser said, "would be worth about $200 but nobody's going to buy it right now." Ms. Koenig also had a set of hundred-year old books with a gold binding that was in pristine condition. Her daughter had looked up their value on the Internet "before the big crash this fall." A bookseller came to appraise them and "he was giving me the story that nobody is buying anything. Oh, maybe he'd give me—I forget whether it was $150 or something. I thought, eh, I don't think so." Her daughter encouraged her to bring them to the new place and [pointing] "there they are."

DETACHMENT: LETTING GO

When consumption studies focus on divestment and disposal, the issue of emotional detachment—dispossession—arises.[11] If people's possessions are an extension of the self, what happens to such sentiment when the parting comes? Questions about self and meaning are usually analyzed when thinking of single objects—so-called cherished or special possessions. But in the context of an all-convoy sorting out, one that occurs over mere weeks or a few months, detachment will tend toward the wholesale. Chapter 3 pointed out that the decision to move and the decision to downsize are intertwined. This circumstance sets in motion a commitment to dislodge the contents of the material convoy from the places where they had been accommodated; this "gap in accommodation" opens things up to scrutiny and reappraisal.[12] The decision to move guarantees ipso facto the likelihood of emotional detachment. In the previous chapter on gifts, detachment could be a feeling of having fulfilled one's responsibility. Movers could cull belongings from their material convoys, comfortable with the blanket thought of having taken "care" with things, seen them through.

For anything put on sale, the sentiment has already been draining away. Some goods have been through a sequence of relegation, having been offered but not taken up as gifts. The fit heuristic surpluses other goods on the basis of their redundancy or the sheer materiality of their being "stuff." The same life change that prompts the move also obviates the use or need of numerous things (the not-me heuristic). As the selling proceeds, the monetary value of sale items may prove insufficient to extinguish existing possession motives (and so the art books and the Tiffany lamp are withdrawn), but the main point is that sellers are at least willing to let that calculative meaning supersede other meanings.

Yet even within selling schemes, there are "divestment rituals" that can further ease the parting of person and thing.[13] One such tactic is storytelling to pass along personal meanings with the sale item and kindle the acquirer's appreciation. Abbey Sala was a habitué at the auction house where her own things were being sold ("They called me by my first name"):

> And I would talk to the people after they bought [something]. I would give them a little background story about where it came from, who had it. And it's like getting a puppy. . . . I probably could have donated it someplace, but didn't know how it would end up. And at least I could go watch it at auction and talk to the people who bought it and things like that.

Her analogy to puppy adoption was most apt. Another tactic: manipulate prices to steer objects toward or away from certain buyers.

If storytelling fosters memories about the qualities of an item, other practices foster forgetting.[14] Things for sale will be cleaned or fixed to erase associations with the seller and ease passage to a new owner. One of the objections to on-property sales is that they expose the householder to opinions about one's taste and the quality of one's possessions. Said LeNora Russel, "To have a big estate sale where all your things are actually laid out on your furniture, and your furniture has tags on it, I think that would be difficult. I think that would have felt like an invasion of privacy or something." Auction sales have the specific advantage of removing the owner's traces: at auctions "the owner recedes from the selling context."[15] Several households in our study sent things to auction houses, where prices are set by bidders. Auctions anonymize things because the goods are taken to another place, severing the connection to the individual or household (a connection that Ms. Sala tried to restore). Belva Carter downsized a large home and was glad that she could auction things out of town:

> There's a place near Springfield that does this, they have auctions once a week. They come and they pick up all the stuff that you want on the auction, and then you get so much percentage. They get a certain percent and you get a certain percent. So I didn't have to have one in my hometown, which I DID NOT want. It was too small of a

place. I didn't want to have a sale of any sort, so I discovered this place. It was out of town and it was great.

The goods perhaps got a better price in Springfield, a larger town, but they were also distanced there from any link to Ms. Carter.

Weakening of sentiment is also helped by sellers' absence from sales of their own things.[16] This may happen by choice or as the ground rule of a mediated sale. Although we heard complaints about the stay-away rule ("I have no idea what anything sold for"), it does ensure that objects relegated to a sale will stay relegated and not be pulled out. Staying away forestalls the reemergence of sentiment. Carolyn Tingey was barred from her own sidewalk sale by her friends: "To keep me from being, from—how can I put it?—to keep me from not allowing stuff to go, they sent me to get food and stuff to keep me, to get me away." Disheartened by sale prices, Frances Lucas advised, "Don't be there." Nicole and Matthew Rink packed up forty-five boxes of belongings for an auction. "[The auctioneer] came and picked up everything for the auction and then took a certain percentage, which we thought was very fair. We did not go to the auction because I didn't want to, neither one of us wanted to see." We asked Harold Jones whether he and his wife went to their estate sale. "No, we elected not to stay for the sale and that was our election. We could have gone up. There are people from here that went up. I had given everything that I thought of value out of my shop. I was a handyman all my life." Having said that, Mr. Jones went on to talk proudly about all the tools that he did put in the sale. These objects had been part of his identity, but he had chosen to absent himself from witnessing their new status as commodities.

THE BOTTOM LINE

Once things are gone—and the advantage of sales is that buyers take things away—the lot of them can be reduced in the telling to some sum of money. The obvious criterion for evaluating sales as a downsizing strategy is making money. So, if people sold things, we asked them directly: "Was any money made? Was that important to you?" Profits, of course, would depend among other things on how many and what kind of goods the owner was selling. From our participants' replies, the proceeds from these activities seemed to them modest. Two yard sales netted $300 per weekend; five garage sales brought in $1,000 altogether; and there was another $900 from Craigslist. A few sales totals reached to the low four figures, but one household realized $7,000 from an estate sale and another made nearly $20,000, principally on the sale of extensive collections. The former estate seller, Ruth Ann Barber, claimed to have made $28,000. But more commonly, people said they "didn't make much," "it wasn't a lot," or they received "a little return"; money was made but "it wasn't that important." We asked Maureen Sable whether her garage sale was successful: "Oh no. It wasn't very much and we were selling it pretty cheap." People were happy to have the money and some applied it to moving expenses or the first month's rent in the new place. Deborah Richards got less than she wanted for the sale of a TV, "but it took care of the packing bit"—the $300 she paid to a couple who helped her move. Deborah Mohatt said that "any money you make is important, sure, to use it to pay the bills."

In at least a dozen cases, the response about money was paired with a higher benefit of sales: getting rid of things. "We got a little money from [the auction], and we got rid of it!" "I didn't get much money for [the furniture pieces] but at least they were out of the apartment. Even more than money it was 'do something' with it!" Gladys Staples, who had seen her crystal glasses go for $2.50, said, "We needed the money, but the main thing was to get rid of that stuff because I know I'd have to end up paying to get rid of it." After Gerald Saltzman's estate sale, there were unsold things that the movers packed up and brought to the new place:

And when I got here, there was no place to put this stuff. And it was all kinds of weird stuff. Like a chafing dish. I mean, I haven't used a chafing dish in 15 years, maybe longer. So those I now have those in an antique mall in Melrose. . . . It's just not here. That was the important part.

"It's just not here." Selling had been the means to an end—downsizing for a relocation. Money might be made, emotions might be managed, but ultimately getting rid of things was the goal. "Why did you decide to sell some of the items?" we asked one woman, who answered, "Just to get rid of them, so I could move here." In these accounts, with the use of the word *rid*, the objects had now drifted quite a way from any privileged place in the material convoy. Things that "went in the sale" indeed went away.

CONCLUSION

In our sample of older movers, three-quarters of the households downsized by selling some of their belongings. Amid this transition, sellers cannot optimize the market value of possessions as they might have without the time pressure of the move, their limited skills at recommodifying things, and perhaps their physical limitations. Do-it-yourself (DIY) sales could be laborious, but even those who used agents (estate sellers, consignment shops) nonetheless paid for the necessary labor of selling by accepting the agents' terms and agreeing to commissions. Fortunate households, overall, could better afford to hire help with selling, had more marketable goods, and lived in neighborhoods that were safer for DIY sales. The social relations of possession divestment have been observed in other settings.[17] Such relations and networks eased our movers' selling efforts, as helpers and buyers came forward. As belongings left the household's material convoy, emotional detachment from things was already underway as they were deemed salable and therefore alienable. Parting with things was also helped by divestment maneuvers that managed both the transfer and erasure of meaning.

We asked our movers to evaluate their experience by citing the money that was made by sales. Although money in these narratives might eclipse other measures of value, it did not always dissolve them. Viviana Zelizer maintains that there is no bright line between calculative, neutral money and nonpecuniary values, between the rational and the sentimental.[18] In Daniel Miller's terms, the price of things can bridge values that are irreducible to money.[19] So informal sales might close with token, giveaway prices, but the satisfactory emotional etiquette of an exchange may be the real conclusion. People could be gratified or bitter about item prices because they are judgments about the practical or symbolic qualities of their things. And modest proceeds overall ("I wouldn't say I made a lot") could seem a reasonable trade-off for the desired outcome: being rid of things. The bottom line on sales may be that their worth is nonmonetary.

Household downsizing presents a different view of older people and possessions from the one usually conveyed in the research literature. Unlike studies of special possessions, the positioning of the self in relation to keeping and disposing was not much in evidence. Sales seemed more about the management of things in quantity and the achievement of divestment goals.

This chapter has discussed selling without reference to an important context: many of our participants were also selling their houses. The disposition of this one possession would likewise have involved all the tasks of item sales: finding a buyer, removing identity from the place, and seeing the meaning of a dwelling of long tenure distilled to the home's monetary value as property. The concurrent commodification of the big possession and the many possessions within it requires a more comprehensive treatment than is possible here. Another limitation is that our interviews were conducted during a period (2008 through 2013) of recent economic distress in many communities. Some households reported to us that they were dissuaded from trying sales methods because "the economy's not so good for that" or "nobody is buying—estate sales are dead." In better times, the reports from our households about the success of sales might have been sunnier.

7

DONATIONS AND DISCARDS

C ompared to the numerous stories participants told about their
giving and their selling, fewer specific stories were told about
making charitable donations or sending material out into the waste
stream. Some possessions had been relegated toward these destinations from earlier attempts at gifts or sales, but other things had
never qualified for those routes—donation or discard was always
going to be their fate. This pair of off-ramps from the material convoy tends toward batch dispositions, though there are efforts at intentional placement. Batch disposal is a further step along the continuum from things as meaningful to things as material. Whereas
some giveaways and sale items go unremarked (it "wound up" with
someone, it "went" in the sale), the talk here turns to quantities of
"bags" and "carloads." There are fewer person-to-person transfers
and more asocial dropping off of items. Both strategies have ethical
aspects to observe and each requires some labor of disposition.

One commonly hears the claim that older adults, having been
raised in leaner economic times (our participants were children during the 1920s, 1930s, and 1940s), are frugal and throw nothing away.
This generational trait may be true or not—it would be difficult to
prove in any event (chapter 2). Yet the reluctance to cast things out
appears to be a tendency among adults at all stages of life. Contra-
dicting the glib charge that contemporary consumer culture is a

"throwaway society," research has instead shown that adults have a disinclination to waste things if they can be reused by others, even if those others are not quite in view.[1] Thus, there is a care of things that also colors people's practices for donation and discard.

This chapter considers features of donation and disposal behavior—as downsizers get on with it—that are like and unlike other divestment strategies. The chapter reviews the flows toward and sites for charitable donations, along with the advantages of this technique. Similar to giveaways, donation has intentional and dispassionate forms. As with donations, trash is also an apparent convenience. The household's surplus reaches its last resort, and what merits attention now is the exhaustion of possession motives. Finally, the chapter explores three disposal topics: the problem of paper, ambivalence about the finality of disposal, and possession abandonment.

FLOWS TOWARD DONATION

Possessions flow from the material convoy to donation sites by two means: sorting and relegation. All popular advice about decluttering and downsizing directs the making of piles, and one of these required set-asides should be the cache for donation. Compared to the trash pile (also required), the goods for donation need to meet some minimum condition to be acceptable by the charity. For one woman's donation of canned food, "I checked the [sell-by date] labels to make sure it was still good." Another woman could not contribute her books because "I usually mark books when I read them. So it's hard to get rid of them when you do that—nobody wants them except your friends maybe. So, no, I haven't donated a lot." Indeed, a recurring library book sale with which I am familiar cannot accept damaged books (i.e., "moldy, dirty, water damaged, missing covers, missing pages, excessive marking") or obsolete media ("LP records, VHS tapes, cassettes"). Some sorted goods may be headed for batch drop-off whereas some others, in attempts at safe passage, are directed to intentional placements at community sites. Placements will entail some social interaction with the organization, and the possibility of refusal. Even drop-offs, however, risk a certain degree of social exposure. Iris Boettcher enlisted friends in "taking the stuff to St. Vincent de Paul" (a thrift store) while remaining incognito.

> Took three carloads of stuff to take it down there. And I didn't want to do it with the same person, because I thought after a while they would say: What are you doing bringing all your stuff here? So my friends from Glendale took one load, my grandson took one, and my son-in-law took some. That was handy.

Donations also come about as residual to possessions' earlier allocation to the gift and sell piles. In particular, donation is often the downstream destination for what's unsold at the end of a garage or estate sale: "Everything that's left over goes to Goodwill." "You can call the Vietnam Veterans or something, and they will come and take the stuff." June Crawford arranged a pickup for things that did not sell in her estate sale: furniture, china and crystal ("I guess people aren't buying those too much"), and bedding ("so much bedding left over"). The material filled "half a truck—a BIG truck!" After Sylvia Reynolds's estate sale, the Disabled American Veterans hauled off "everything that was left. There was a ton of stuff!"

In our interviews, there was little talk of having searched out sites for donations, probably because people were already familiar with local options. Results from our national survey of older adults in the Health and Retirement Study showed that donation was more prevalent than selling things or giving things to family and friends (chapter 2). Respondents were asked: "In the last year, how many of your belongings have you donated to a charity, a church, or a community group?" Grouping together replies for "a few things" and "many things," 75 percent of Americans aged 60 through 79 had donated something in the preceding year. Compare this with some activity toward selling by only 21 percent in the same age group, and some level of gifting by 67 percent. The proportion reporting that that they donated "many things" was 25 percent, whereas the proportion who gave "many things" to family or friends was only 14 percent.

Donation sites were many and varied: thrift stores, community agencies, churches, veterans groups, health facilities, arts organizations, museums, libraries, historical societies, and the humane society (one dog). Operators with national networks of thrift stores came in for the most mention, chains such as Goodwill, Salvation Army, and "Jimmy Carter's thing, what is that? [Interviewer: Habitat for Humanity.] Habitat, they took a lot of stuff." During our interviews, as we led people through a list of possession categories, donation reports were commonly prompted by our asking about clothing, kitchen items, dishes, furniture, toys, food, and medical supplies. Books were most often routed to public libraries for periodic book sales and sometimes to the reading rooms of residential facilities to which the downsizers had moved.

This habitual donation to many places testifies to a robust circulation of secondhand goods.[2] For example, charities' resale of donated clothing has created an international trade in used apparel that floods the global South with hand-me-downs and crowds out domestic textile industries.[3] The actual (rather than imagined) fate of donated items was typically not a matter of concern for our participants. Yet at least some them knew that their donated property was not going out on display at the thrift shop or passing directly to deserving persons. One woman actually checked up after a drop-off and reported that "we did not see any of that stuff on the floor of Goodwill." Donna Crandall favored a women's shelter for her donations. The big agencies, she said, "sell that stuff and if I want to sell it, I would put up a yard sale. I want to give my stuff to people who are gonna benefit from it. . . . But you give stuff away to these organizations, they sell your stuff."

WHY DONATE?

Donation is an attractive divestment option for several reasons: convenience, the thought that possessions will be reused, the philanthropic cause of this or that charity, and tax breaks. As to convenience, there is a wide choice of donation sites, at least in urban

areas. The main thrift stores are open during business hours and often on weekends and can offer guidance about their requirements
by telephone or online. For people on a tight schedule for moving,
this availability is no small advantage. Even more handy are the donation drop boxes that charities set out for used goods. There is no
need for human interaction, no presentation of oneself at these collection bins; the task of unloading into a drop box is an errand that
can be delegated to helpers.

Another convenient option, if the timing is right, is the donation
of goods to periodic, public sales events mounted by churches, nonprofits, and community agencies and run by volunteers. These events
could be rummage (miscellaneous) sales or sales of one kind of thing,
such as clothing or books. With these events, one's possessions are
not distributed outright to deserving persons, but buyers presumably find a use for their purchases, and sale proceeds will support
the organization's programs.

The apparent convenience of donations was disputed by some
participants. Frances Lucas, already cited in chapter 4, expressed
surprise that charities don't accept everything: "I was astounded
that they didn't want a lot of things. They were specific about what
they would take and what they would not take. That was a shock
to me." The policy on home pickups was another complaint. On
schedule for a move, some households found that there was a wait
for the truck. One woman called a social service agency but "they
couldn't come; they needed more notice than we gave them." Lorraine Morse's interaction with a charity's representatives "drove
me crazy":

> Getting places to come pick up your stuff is very difficult. Some won't
> go to the basement. The [organization] came once and because every-
> thing that I had in the garage wasn't on the list, they wouldn't take
> it. They would only take what was on the list and they had to come
> back the next day, which was a pain in the neck. And talking to them,
> that probably was the most frustrating. . . . Or they say they're com-
> ing and they wouldn't show up. And here you are you wanted to get
> rid of this stuff and nobody wants to take it.

Ms. Morse's comments then immediately turned in a different direction: a suspicion that her possessions had been judged.

> A lot of people think what you have is junk, too. Well, I didn't have any junk. And some people do. But I just didn't have any. Everything I have, or had, was usable, not stuff that should be thrown out. And I think convincing people that's what you really had [was difficult]. You have all that and it's not junk, you know?

It is worth noting that Ms. Morse was moving from one handsome residence to another. That was not the case with Francesca Tanner. She repeatedly called one agency for a pickup, but they never returned her calls. She tried another agency and was told that they did not serve her part of the city: "Isn't that something? . . . I couldn't believe it. . . . I can't understand that." Did the neighborhood—and by extension the presumed quality of her possessions—have something to do with the snub? In the end, Ms. Tanner did get another agency to collect her things.

Another prominent motive for possession donations was the idea that "somebody could use them." "I think I donated those things that people really needed, maybe not so much knick-knacks." In this light, charitable donation is a responsible, virtuous act that also protects possessions and eases detachment. Compared to gift giving, donations have an altruistic quality because the ultimate receivers are unknown (buyers at a thrift shop, museum patrons) and will never reciprocate the gift. In parting with things, we heard evident satisfaction in the imagined reuse, even valuing and gratitude, by (unknown) others. We asked Francesca Tanner whether she lost a bit of herself when she gave up her things. And she said:

> No, because it could help somebody else. Somebody else can use it. I was happy about that. I could give things away that could help somebody else because they weren't tore up or too raggedy to give away. Somebody else could benefit from it.

Marjorie Curtis complimented a local charity for homeless people as having been "most gracious."

> They came and they took, whether it was damaged, whether it needed paint, didn't matter. They said, "We will find people who can use all of this." So, um, it was emotional—seeing it go out the door. But, on the other hand, it was time that those things were being used.

And this from Andrea Cruz, a woman who had been married for fifty-four years:

> I will tell you one thing that was sentimental: I got rid of my wedding gown. I don't know why I saved it all these years, but I took it to what they call the Share House, down in the poor part of [the city]. And the lady said, "Oh, some bride will really be looking for this."

Besides reuse, another ethical motive for donation was sympathy with the philanthropic cause of an organization, for example, a hospice or a theological school in Africa. Abbey Sala reported that Habitat for Humanity was "happy to get everything. See, they have a resale store. They use the money to buy material to build houses with. And then, too, they furnish some of the houses that they build." Furnishing women's shelters was another donation project. Martha Farnsworth had an armoire, "it cost me $2,000 and I donated it to this woman who was starting a shelter for battered women." Donna Crandall may have been helping the same place. She imagined the shelter's clients and their needs:

> I was taking stuff to the shelter for battered women, because they're leavin' home without nothing. And when they get ready to set up again, they'll have—I gave away TVs that I didn't want to give away. I gave away a new microwave. I gave away a new baking oven, stuff I had nowhere to sit. You cannot continue to let stuff sit in a box and don't be used. Number one, it's a sin. When someone can use something and you're holding on to it, that's not right. That's not your

Christian heart. Your Christian heart is to give it away to someone that can use it. And those ladies is comin' back out into the world eventually, and I took stuff. . . . If you give it to the shelter, those women gonna wear that stuff today or tomorrow.

Finally, donations can bring a benefit at tax time. All advice manuals on clutter-busting and downsizing tout the tax deductibility of property given to a qualified charitable organization. The Internal Revenue Service publication that covers this matter (no. 526) directs that clothing and household items must be in good used condition. The "fair market value" of these items—what they would sell for at a consignment or thrift shop—can then be bundled with other itemized deductions when filing taxes for the year. This dollar amount—determined by the donor or the charity, the calculation can be tricky (IRS Publication no. 561)—affirms in a token way the dollar value of the goods, the same as an actual sale would. However, few households in our studies mentioned the tax break (and we did not directly ask about it). Maureen and Marty Sable, for example, were delighted to learn that their donations were valued at $300—they had assumed $100. Martin Hawk was in the middle of an argument with his accountant about the sum that he was claiming. Perhaps the relative silence on this donation incentive resulted because, having modest incomes, few of our participants used itemized deductions when filing their tax returns.

INTENTIONAL PLACEMENTS, DISPASSIONATE DROP-OFFS

Participants took effort in making intentional placements that had the hallmarks of "safe passage" (chapter 5). Some of these gifts to organizations were meant for specific use: a twenty-foot ladder to Habitat for Humanity, sewing supplies to the home economics department of the high school, religious books for a church reading room, costumes to the university theater program, a collection of Christmas crèches to a church with an annual festival of such displays. And then there were donations meant for public consumption—donations intended to protect the heirloom status of objects ("It belongs in a museum") and perpetuate the legacy of generations or times gone by. We heard of legislative records deposited in a university archive and documents and photographs given to historical societies, as well as antique clothing "for programs, for display"—clothing that had been "in the family for over 100 years" and that "could have been sold." Labor history materials that Patricia Phail inherited from her father were given to museums: "I gave all of this stuff that my father had put his effort in and saved. I was able to pass this on and it was going not to a person but to an organization that was going to treasure it and keep it forever." LeNora Russel placed wedding dresses:

> I gave my mother's wedding dress and my wedding dress to a charity and I'm blanking on the name right now. They collect wedding dresses and they have a re-sale thing but they also have a museum-type thing for historical wedding dresses. Mine made it into the historical one as well as my mother's [laughs]. But they refurbish them and clean them, which is a delicate job. So that was pleasing because what are you going to do? You can't just put your mother's wedding dress in the trash! You can't! But yet, you never look at it. None of my kids want this stuff. So again, finding homes for things.

Abbey Sala had books on genealogy that she no longer needed, so she donated them to the public library where her genealogy groups had met. "And when I was there, they took me [to the] back, where people usually don't go, and showed me all my books." Her donation had filled some gaps in the collection "and they were delighted to have them." For these intentional placements, the givers achieved safe passage into organizations that would "treasure it and keep it forever," provide "homes for things," and "delight" in having them.

Compared to the almost curatorial care taken with some donations, other material departed the material convoy en masse and undifferentiated. "Well, they took some things to the Salvation Army but that's—they were just minor things, I mean. I can't even remember what they were to tell you the truth." The word "stuff" was indispensable for recalling drop-offs. People described their dispositions using the following terms:

- Quantities: "quite a bit of stuff," "tons of clothes," "an awful lot of stuff," "you just wouldn't believe all the stuff"
- Trips: "so many trips to the Goodwill and Salvation Army," "the DAV [Disabled American Veterans] and Goodwill got tired of seeing us coming and we got tired of seeing them"
- Bags: "there must have been 35 garbage bags full of clothes," "18 bags went the first time to Goodwill," "dozens and dozens—literally—of bags of stuff"
- Carloads: "two carloads jampacked," "three carloads of stuff," "St. Vincent, we gave carloads of stuff there—carloads," "We had an UNBELIEVABLE amount of Christmas decorations. . . . We filled the car, absolutely FILLED the car, the back and the inside and everything, and took it to Goodwill"
- Truckloads: "two truckloads," they sent "a LARGE truck," a good friend with a truck "just hauled out stuff," "a pickup truck full of Christmas stuff"

Batch donation was nearly a master strategy for Marjorie Curtis, a personal heuristic. What her family did not take all went to one charity—no sales, not much thrown away: "I gave everything away. . . . [The charity] took most everything."

COMPLEXITIES OF TRASH

Turning to trash (garbage, rubbish, junk, waste, refuse), its manner of disposal (by discarding, pitching, throwing out, getting rid of, dumping) appears as the least effortful of the major divestment strategies. Yet not all trash can be mixed and disposed of in the same way, and so it, too, involves some sorting. My municipal waste collection limits households to a certain quantity per week and excludes yard trimmings and leaves, recyclables, hazardous materials (liq-uids, chemicals), large bulky items, electronics, animal waste, sharp items, car batteries, and tires (and don't even think about adding as-bestos, explosives, or prescription drugs). The excluded materials all have their own separate procedures for disposal, some sponsored by the city and some by arrangement with private companies. There can be waits involved. In all the communities where our participants lived, local regulations are similar.

The contemporary rubbish regime for the household reflects a growing global emphasis on sustainability and environmental pro-tection. This movement has prompted policies to reduce the amount of waste sent to municipal landfills and likewise encourage the re-cycling and recovery of materials for reuse.[4] Studies of consumers and consumption have been fascinated with disposal, by the ways that material waste returns and goes back into circulation and by the social practices around this reclamation of value. The neat lin-ear story about extraction, production, use, and degradation is too simple, as is the binary distinction between useful goods and trash.[5] Stuff never really goes away.

Moving, meanwhile, generates scrutiny of the material convoy, and some of it comes to be judged as fit for naught but the trash. To forestall this throwing away, the U.S. Environmental Protection Agency produced a 2004 booklet, *Moving Out, Moving In: Making En-vironmental Choices When You Move.*[6] It begins by advising citizens of their responsibilities when moving:

> Whether you are downsizing from a large home you've lived in your whole life to a smaller condominium, or moving to a different city, moving can be stressful, time consuming, and expensive—and can have a great impact on the environment. Throwing away old items and buying new ones can generate a lot of trash and waste natural resources and energy.

The booklet goes on to list many environmentally friendly ways to get rid of things short of tossing them away. All of these alternatives involve some extra effort to carry out. And so potential downsizers are enlisted to the cause of ethical consumption and its green mantra: "Reduce, reuse, recycle."

Somewhat to our surprise, the households that we studied had few complaints about trash restrictions. For example, when one couple reached their weekly, curbside limit of garbage bags, neighbors would simply add the extras to the trash they set out. As we asked about discarding things, people mentioned recycling (into curb bins or drop-off bins) as a matter of course. The Koenigs had a helper who "took two or three loads of things you can't—we had to take to a special place over on Pike Avenue—your inflammables, your paint, your fluorescent lights, all that stuff that you can't put in the garbage." Martin Hawk lodged the only real complaint about trash—how the city bungled his effort to recycle the leftovers from a yard sale.

Martin: We had stuff sorted out into metal, paper, plastic, and we called for a pickup and they didn't send the recycle truck. They sent—

Interviewer: A garbage truck.

Martin: A garbage truck. And they threw it all in together and it went [he makes noise].

Interviewer: It breaks your heart, huh?

Martin: Yeah, because at least they could've been recycled.

Whereas researchers have focused on the career of material waste— how waste recirculates and the cultural practices that bring that recirculation about—our participants largely saw trash as something that disappears. If we did not hear more about the rigmarole of rubbish, perhaps it was because household trash management (kitchen waste, paper, packaging, glass, plastic, metal) is already a routine, daily chore and thus unremarkable. Perhaps the matter of trash was left to helpers. Perhaps, in the time press of a move, people simply ignored the rules; for example, more than one participant recalled how contents of the medicine cabinet went in the trash.

MEANING AND MATERIAL: THE END OF THE LINE

Discarded items had been, heretofore, things somehow worth keeping. Until recently, they had been undisturbed members of the material convoy, but then the disbandment process redefined and residualized them. "Trash," observed Susan Strasser, "is created by sorting. . . . Nothing is inherently trash."[7] Disbandment disclosed that these leftovers were not useful to anyone, not salable, too personal to entrust to others, or simply of limited interest, even to family members.

We asked our participants directly whether they threw a lot of things away. In reply, talk about quantities of trash ranged from "lots" to "not much," but it's hard to know what these answers mean. The "quite a bit" reply at times came with specifics: one dumpster, three dumpsters, a pile in the yard that cost $325 to haul off, weekly piles at the curb, overloaded trash barrels. When people reported having had minimal trash, that indeed may have been the situation, or else the discarding had been handled by others and the mover just didn't know. The "not much" claim may also been a way to stress that one had acted responsibly in disposing of things. For example, one woman deflected our question about throwing a lot of things away by answering: "I don't think so. We tried to find a place for everything." This seems less an answer about quantity than about her care of things that she tried to keep from the curb.

Trash quantities, of course, would depend on how squared away the household had been prior to downsizing. Spouses were not shy in identifying who was responsible for the domestic landfill. This from Patricia Connell:

> My husband is a packrat, he doesn't throw anything away. He even had pieces of scrap wood that he had picked up because he had a workshop in the basement. "Oh, I may need this," you know. I said, "If you put anything else down there, we're going to have termites," and I said, "The meanest thing you could ever do to me is die and leave me with that basement to get rid of." I made him feel ashamed,

so he got down and straightened up a little, but he still had five truck-loads. He borrowed our neighbor's pickup truck—five truckloads of NOTHING but TRASH. I mean, we couldn't even give it to Salvation Army, it wasn't that good.

People had blanket dismissals for discarded belongings, expressions that excused them from further obligation to things when all possession motives—utility, exchange value, symbolism—had been exhausted. The discards were: "anything that wasn't in good condition"; "stuff that didn't amount to anything"; "it wasn't anything that meant anything to me"; "stuff we knew wouldn't sell"; "small, little bits of junk"; and things that were "worn out," "past the point," "knick-knack things, old stuff, not usable." Said Kathryn Nurski, "I think mostly it was, well, JUNK really. It would certainly be junk for anybody else. And certainly not what I was using anymore." Such a statement—"not what I was using"—holds an echo of the "not me" decisional heuristic (chapter 4); the surrender of a possible self can be heard in Virgil Frazier saying, "I threw a lot of things away, things I was going to do things with."

Another way to excuse oneself was to cast discards as items of little consequence that have receded from memory. Were things thrown away? "I couldn't tell you what." "Don't ask me what they were." "I can't think what right now." "I don't remember what." Again, ignorance may have been exactly that because family members had handled the tossing: "I don't even want to know what they threw away."

Trash motives nevertheless were stated for certain things, such as food from the freezer, half-used cosmetics (too personal to give to others), obsolete slides ("I hadn't looked at them in 20 years"). The downsizing uncovered other things that were simply ruined: moldy and water-damaged objects; dry-rotted furniture and clothing; scratched-up LP records; vermin-infested furniture; and an upright freezer, water tank, and mattress that "we had in the barn and the opossums were making a nest in it."

THE COMB THROUGH PAPER

The material convoy encompasses amounts of paper that have been saved or filed as administrative records of the home, one's affairs, and one's life. We heard specifically about documents such as medical records, bank and loan statements, investments, tax records, military papers, insurance papers, wills, advance directives, certificates of birth and marriage, old bills and receipts, news clippings, maps and trip brochures, old letters and greeting cards, personal and family memorabilia, obituaries, genealogies, instruction manuals, warranties, records from a business, documents from employment, materials from service on a community board, sheet music, and college term papers. Paper is relatively easy to store, and stored it remains until ousted during a downsizing.

Similar to other possessions, document keeping may have been an act of prudence ("we might need it") or inattention. Compared to, say, clothing, paper lies concealed, and so is unlikely to receive regular culling. Brought to the surface during preparations for a move, it presents a sorting task. And unlike bulkier objects, hours of work on paper and documents may not clear much space. A single sheet of paper can bog down progress—a letter or a discovery that action is overdue. Family members and third parties can help (as long as privacy is not an issue), but decisions ultimately devolve to the mover to separate the important from the unimportant. Despite the task, Bill Wagner found the exercise worthwhile. He told us that "a truckload" of papers went "in the dump." The interviewer followed up and asked whether that involved going through files one folder at a time ("Yes, it did"); was that time-consuming? "It was a good thing. You give some of them up; some combined, some of them brought back memories. By and large, we've had a pretty good life—good memories."

The standard divestment options are the same for documents: retain, entrust to family members or friends, perhaps sell or donate, or discard. If the documents are records of one's relationships and past accomplishments—much like trophies—can a mover continue to house them? "Postcards, Christmas cards, family letters—very difficult to get rid of. Gotta let go." How long to retain tax and business records might require consultation with others.[8] Unless there is a decision to retain it all, the task is irreducible.

Document culling generates batch disposal, and if the contents are not personal, the paper can be recycled. However, if privacy or the fear of identity theft is a worry, then the traces of the owner need removal. And so we heard repeated reports about paper shredding and some burning. Although bulk shredding events are sometimes sponsored by local organizations (e.g., banks), home shredding was the norm and it could be tedious. Alice Frawley recalled doing it.

> Well, the old tax papers I had [already] shredded. In the front room there was a desk in the wall, you know. I had to go through there and I had to do a lot of shredding! I had bank statements from 1988. I had papers from when I put siding on the house in 1986. But I had a lot of things to shred—bank statements, prescription receipts. When I was sitting around watching TV, I would just sit and shred. [Interviewer: So you have a shredder?] Yes I do. I just had it sitting right beside me and had a trash bag here.

We had asked Anne Gunter if, during her downsizing, she had worked steadily or on and off, and she said that her daughter (present at the interview) had done "all the work."

> *Daughter:* But mom you shredded for days, remember? We would bring piles of paperwork and that and I would say, "These are things you need to go through and determine if it's something you want to keep or get rid of," and she literally sat and shredded.

> *Ms. Gunter:* I forgot about that.

> *Daughter:* We had a big garbage bag inside of these cardboard boxes, and I just said we would keep dumping it in there, bag it, and take it out. She shredded for days on end. There was a lot to get rid of.

Ms. Gunter: I'm surprised the shredder was still working.

Daughter: Well, we almost burnt it out.

One woman went so far as to cut her name off all personal documents, and then shred the clippings. Another woman, "out of concern for identity theft . . . went through the tax returns and cut out the Social Security numbers from each page." A third woman, having no shredder, actually soaked the identifiers off documents. She had to throw away

> a lot of papers that I kept from working, old gas bills, old light bills, phone bills. So I had to throw away all of that stuff but, since I don't have a shredder, I had to take each piece of paper, old hospital bills, and run it through hot water, take my name, address and important information. And it took me some time because I had stored up a lot of old papers. I thought I would never get through with all of those papers. I had garbage bags and garbage bags full and asked why did I keep this?

A TWO-STAGE DISPOSAL PRACTICE

Researchers who focus on possession disposal have observed a two-stage maneuver that helps people manage their parting with things. Possessions that are candidates for disposal are placed in provisional exile at the margins of the household—for example, the garage, the attic, the basement. Only later, once feelings are resolved, are the belongings sent on their way.[9] Kevin Hetherington writes that this practice is akin to the first and second burial found in the funeral rites of many cultures. After an initial burial that lasts some time and during which the soul is assumed to leave the body, "a second and more final burial will take place." Analogously:

> If the intrinsic worth of a person is assumed to be their soul, the intrinsic worth of an artifact is its value—use value and sentimental

value as much as exchange value. Only when all forms of value have been exhausted will the [stored] object be permitted to undergo its second burial.[10]

According to Catherine Roster, by this two-stage process people are not merely letting go of the object, but "more importantly, those aspects of self embodied in possessions."[11] In another analogy by other authors, the garage "may serve as a hospice when it becomes the temporary resting area for items on their way to final disposition."[12]

In our studies we had hoped to hear about instances of this intriguing divestment rite but there were few, possibly because we concentrated on limited periods of time prior to a move, periods too short to let the burials play out. Perhaps, too, some of the doomed items had already been teed up for the trash in marginal spaces of the home by the time downsizing occurred. Marie Udall recalled using the technique during a prior move: "What I did there was I got boxes and put stuff in my garage that I didn't think I wanted. I labeled the boxes so if there were things I decided I did want, I could get them and bring them back in." One anecdote did stand out in our Midwest Study. Belva Carter and her daughter were clearing out her house and came upon a broken chair, a former heirloom, that had already been marginalized to a second-floor sleeping porch, and they gave it a joyous, final sendoff.

> So, um, there was so much there that I remember Sandra and I picked up one of these chairs that was broken and was out on the sleeping porch. And I said, "You know, I saved that chair. That's grandma and grandpa's." And I said, "You know what? What do you think about just opening this window and tossing it out in the yard?" So we did! (Laughs) And we had such a ball doing it!

LEFT BEHIND

We had not anticipated one more discarding practice: the abandonment of possessions upon exiting the old place. Prompted by our question about throwing things away, at least seven households in the Midwest Study reported having left things behind, and these were all low-income households. These movers had been unable to manage a complete clean-out. For some, belongings would not fit at the new place, or they ran out of room on the truck. For others, the new place was partially furnished and did not need more tables, chairs, or lamps.

People also ran out of time and energy. The buyer of Janis Flatt's house told her to leave things behind if she did not want to take them. "That was bothering me, too, what to do with all that stuff because it was nice stuff—nice beautiful lamps, tables, the kitchen set . . . and a nice bedroom set with dressers and mirrors." The interviewer picked up the topic: "Let's talk for a second about leaving that—some of the stuff in that house. How would you feel if that owner, the new owner, sold some of that stuff and made some profit. How would that make you feel?" Ms. Flatt replied: "I would not care because I left it there. If I cared, I would've tried to take it with me. But I didn't. I was just—like I said, I was tired, and it just made me sick trying to gather all that stuff." Looking on the bright side, some who left possessions behind contented themselves with the thought that the things would be useful to the new occupants. Juan King put it this way:

> There were a few things thrown away, but not many compared to what I left. I kept trying to justify in my mind that whoever they sold the house to would get good use out of the furniture, that it would be something to help somebody else. So I had a little workshop in the basement full of tools. I left the washer and dryer.

CONCLUSION

By sorting or as the leftovers from other divestment efforts, donations can flow to many receptive sites. The advantages of charitable donation are apparent convenience, moral contentment about reuse, philanthropic satisfaction, and perhaps a tax break. Even amid the carloads and filled garbage bags that flow to donation, there are yet attempts to give selected things good homes. As to discarding, our households handled the complexities of the modern trash regime without much comment; with blanket dismissals, they excused themselves from further obligation to things. One kind of belonging, stored paper, posed an irreducible downsizing and disposal chore. Also of note, we had expected to hear more about a certain two-stage process for managing ambivalence about disposal, but we had not expected to hear about the extent to which low-income movers abandoned belongings.

Despite the batch nature of donations and discards, it would be wrong to view these solutions as heedless or disrespectful of things. Movers made attempts at reclamation and reuse of the "stuff." Scholars of consumption who focus on cast-off things maintain that disposal is a way of ordering the world—into here and there, into then and now.[13] This is exactly the outcome of downsizing: a reordered, smaller material convoy that is, one would hope, more suited to a new life context in new environs.

The spatial redistribution of possessions by various strategies has been the main focus of the preceding few chapters. The next chapter takes up the emotional management of the transition.

8

EMOTION AND EVALUATION

Ready or not, there comes a moving day when the reduced material convoy is conveyed elsewhere. Move-in narratives could
be pleasant memories of a smooth transition, some people fortunate enough to arrive at new quarters with furniture already placed
and pictures hung. Other move-in stories were fraught, intense, and
vividly remembered for the trouble they entailed. Because the focus of this book is on possession downsizing, the immediate events
around moving day will await telling elsewhere.

Chapter 1 noted that downsizing for a move is at once a cognitive, physical, emotional, and social undertaking. This chapter considers emotional dimensions of the episode, though there have been
considerable references to emotions already. These have included
expressions of comfort in possessions, wonderment or embarrassment at their extent, and sadness about parting with a thing and
what it represents. People have recalled the need to practice patience
and forbearance with others as well as feelings of fatigue, stress, and
the pressure to get it all done. About some outcomes, there was anger and bitterness, but there was satisfaction in others. People
found humor in their predicaments. There was joy in having a new
place. Ohad Green and Liat Ayalon have likewise reported a wide
range of emotional reactions to the surrender of possessions among
movers to a continuing care retirement community.[1]

By the time we interviewed people some months after their move, emotions may have been softened or blunted by the passage of time or likely shaped by the retelling of how one came to live here. From a research point of view, there is no substitute for being there in real time, among people who are doing the household downsizing. Tam Perry conducted such a study, and she characterized the process as emotionally tough: "The anxieties associated with the decisions about the numerous objects provoked a lot of worry, including anxiety about getting good prices for items, checking whether adult children were interested in certain items, getting items to children if they were interested, and tax deductions for donations."[2]

Even when possessions divestment is voluntary—not associated with a residential move—and the possessions are cherished ones, disposition "arouses both extreme positive and negative feelings," according to Linda Price and colleagues. The same person could embody ambivalence: an older woman "happy" about leaving possessions as a legacy to children and grandchildren, but "scared" that interest in the objects may someday wane; an older man "happy" that his coin collection would go to heirs but "sad because I am old."[3] Whatever people feel about the loss of possessions, it is helpful to remember that such emotions are likely intertwined with other losses—of a spouse, one's function or mobility, one's home, one's neighborhood.

This chapter relates some features of the way that people looked back on their downsizing. Did they miss things? What made the experience stressful? What difference did affluence make? Some months now after the transition, how did they evaluate their efforts?

HAVING DIVESTED, DO PEOPLE MISS THINGS?

Even after possessions have left one's convoy, they may not be wholly gone, instead exerting an "absent presence."[4] An image that comes to mind is that of an empty bird's nest that still holds the shape of something that has departed. I also think of the sculptures of

Rachel Whiteread, who renders the absent present by casting the vacant space around objects. Elders who have downsized can continue to imagine the possible afterlife of things that they have given away, sold, or donated. Even with their garbage, they can perhaps take pleasure in thinking that recycling efforts have rescued items of trash for further use.

As noted in the previous chapter, stuff never goes away—certainly in a material sense—and sometimes it cannot help but persist in memory: "The erasure of an object is never complete. There is always a trace effect that is passed on by its absence."[5] We asked Marilyn Howerton whether there was anything important that she could not bring to her new place. "You're going to laugh . . . the birdbath that I have." With her "little binoculars" and a bird book, she had enjoyed her garden and the traffic around the birdbath. But health regulations forbade her bringing the birdbath along, and so she gave it to her grandson and his wife, "and they love it, so that made me happy." But she also said, "I didn't give them my book and binoculars," which for her still held the absent presence of her birdbath as she resumed her pastime. For Donna Crandall, it was her old house that was present to her. During her interview, she did a little memory walk—how she would come up the stairs from the basement and where she would set the laundry basket in the hallway near a coat closet.

> Now, once you [move] out, it makes a difference because you look back and see all the things you did, the love, the joy you had in that house. . . . Would I have stayed, if I could? Yes, I would have stayed if I could. But I won't go back. I've got to go on. I can't go back. I miss it still today—deeply. . . . I'll think about it forever.

At the same time, the exigence of a downsizing devalues the utility and symbolic properties of whole swaths of the material convoy, easing a psychological dispossession and parting. Decisional heuristics (chapter 4)—utility, me/not-me, fit—efficiently settle the status and sentiment of things. The fit rule, in particular, creates a barrier to further thoughts of accommodation. Reflecting on their choices about what they did and did not keep, people would say that they miss things, but yet there was no room in the new place. Georgina Dines said that "the only thing I think about is a lot of clothing that I gave away, some of the things that I do miss [that] I wish I had kept. . . . But we really don't have space for it." Donna Crandall mused, "Givin' away stuff, givin' away, givin' away stuff. Then you think: Should I have given that away? Should I have kept that? But where are you gonna put it? That's it—where are you gonna put it?" Absent presence is more difficult to conjure when the new place has little space within which former convoy contents can seem absent.

A wistfulness about certain possessions emerged when we asked people about things that were harder to deal with. The objects were singular and idiosyncratic, but the common thread uniting them was a longing for some role or some idea of oneself that the things had afforded or symbolized. They might have been business records. They might have been books:

> I've always been a reader and I don't know how many books I had, maybe close to one thousand. I had a beautiful custom built-in of-fice in my old house that was just lined with bookshelves floor to ceil-ing. I allowed myself to bring 50 books here. It was just so hard! I actually did have a little cry. (LeNora Russel)

It might have been a piano. Sylvia Reynolds recalled: "That piano was hard. Even though I didn't play much anymore, when I felt like I wanted to, I could sit down and play. Yeah." It might have been the dining room table, a loss remarked upon by several women. The table was the first thing that Claudia Radford gave away. "The big dining room table and the six chairs. We'd had that 60 years! And that sorta made a twinge when you realize what you're . . . [she stops and is au-dibly emotional]." It might have been features of the old place—a porch, a certain room, a fireplace—that meant contentment. For one couple, hard losses were "so many Christmas things" (for her) and "getting rid of my shop" (for him) and thus the enactment of do-mestic routines.

Through missing now-absent possessions, people missed marital and family relationships. The loss of one's spouse was felt anew in dealing with the spouse's clothing, letters, jewelry, or even furniture. "It bothered me to think that, knowing that we had collected all that stuff through the years, and then, you know, having to dispose of it. That's the only thing that was overwhelming." In clearing out her basement, Alice Frawley lingered over things and "thought about when the children were young, you know. It brought back emotions from that. When I saw the little trophies and things, I could remember them on the stage, receiving them at church and things." The downsizing diminished Sylvia Reynolds's capacity to accommodate grandchildren. "It was hard for us to get rid of the grandkids' stuff. That whole upstairs was toys and games and stuff like that. . . . It's definitely made a difference in how much they come over." In her ethnography of older movers, Tam Perry recounted the story of a baby crib. The Lewises were talking to a daughter-in-law about furniture from the early years of their marriage, including the baby crib that "we just got rid of." They had put the crib on the curb for the garbage. When Ms. Lewis heard the truck arriving, she watched at the dining room window, crying. "The arm of the garbage truck came down and just crushed it. And I said, oh, my babies teethed on that crib. . . . There were, there were Jack's teeth marks on there."[6]

Absent presences such as these confirm Russell Belk's observation that possessions are part of an extended self.[7] When certain things are disposed of, so is a part of the self, and that indeed is what people miss.

WHAT WAS HARD; DEADLINE STRESS

Turning from the emotions that attended the parting with things to those of the downsizing business itself, some people cited the hard work and drudgery of it all. "It was just work!" said Nicole Rink. "You'd put in a hard day and not really see that much was accomplished." Gerald Saltzman, widowed for two years, moved from a large three-bedroom house to a two-bedroom apartment in a new city, all the while coping with health problems:

> There were times when I would cry, but it was a release more so than a period of sadness. . . . Yeah, you know, basically I was disabled during a critical time in the move. I mean, that was frustrating. I was getting up early in the morning and it was like 9 o'clock at night before I'd eat dinner, and then I'd crash and do it again. And it was day after day like that. And I wasn't getting, personally, I wasn't getting as much done as needed to be done. So personally it was daunting.

Others reported being "exhausted" during the process: "It is just traumatic. It just stresses your body to no end." "It made me tired. It made me—I don't know. It just made me sick. I got headaches and lost weight, not that I was that big, you know." Sandra Graves had all of two weeks to move in order to take advantage of an opening in subsidized housing. She said, "I got tired because I was already tired. I was beat down from other things" (being a caregiver for her mother). Her conclusion: "Moving is a job, a big, big job." For their part, family members in our Elder and Family Study likewise recalled the physical work that they undertook as draining and time-consuming.[8]

Other unhappy memories were based on a loss of control over events when others asserted themselves in the proceedings. Georgene Mullins felt that she let others dictate her path to her new home and she just followed along: "I didn't take more initiative to do things. . . . Most of the time, you know what you want. Then you have influence from these other people, which are your support people [and they] can make it difficult." Siblings motivated the relocation of Grace Brown and her father away from a distant city, all in three weeks' time. Both had health issues. "We [the siblings] just got together and they started plowing through things." She described the sorting as "helter-skelter," with minor conflicts about what to bring. She added that "I wish it could have been slowed down." Some participants had bad luck that left them with sour memories: an instance of car transport fraud, a ceramic shoe col-lection stolen during the move, and a swirl of helplessness and pow-erlessness as a couple's house was about to be forfeited to the bank, emotions that were then channeled into anger at their son.

The most common stressor to which people pointed was the tick-ing clock, which brings up the consideration of another heuristic that expedites downsizing activities: a "deadline heuristic" that economizes and simplifies decision-making, but at some emotional cost. In general, deadlines have their advantages and disadvantages. On the upside, they focus attention and motivation.[9] In the reloca-tion context, they limit time for sorting and deliberation and may facilitate more expedient, if hurried, dispositions. On the downside, moving deadlines—both intermediate and final—ramp up anxiety and worry. Of the households that we studied, about 80 percent dis-banded and moved in three months or less; one third had only a month or less (chapter 3).

Except in cases in which the sequence was to move first and then finish up later at the old place, people thinned their material con-voys in a bounded temporal space. People frequently talked about this when we asked if things had ever seemed overwhelming, citing cognitive and physical strain with disrupted sleep as a hallmark of deadline stress. A few people reported that things got easier as they went along: "You become more heartless." "You become hardened, a little bit hardened. You start making decisions then because you know you have to." In remarkably similar ways but from completely separate households, people recounted how deadlines loomed:

- "Yeah, I started with books and we're talking starting in January, Feb-ruary, and the move was consummated in July, early July. So I started packing books and things like that, sorting knick-knacks and things, thinking, "Do you really need this?" . . . So I had this long range plan of six months. And come the end of June I'm still workin' at it, fighting the deadline, and pretty well exhausted! There's where I, uh, overestimated my abilities as an 86-year old to handle all of it. . . . By the time June came around, I was pretty much shot." (Edward Sluman)

- "[There was] the worry about getting things ready to move. I lost sleep at night. I couldn't think straight sometimes. Just too many things on my mind." (Kathryn Nurski)
- "Well, looking back over it, things went well, but going through it was stressful as the devil! I'd wake up at 3 o'clock in the morning thinking: We gotta do this, or that. You just worry about getting everything done." (Matthew Rink)
- "There was a time, I guess, we kind of wondered if our body was going to take it. I mean really, you know. I mean you're working, not going to bed at night and you're still going and going—can't go to bed because we know that deadline is there." (James Dines)
- "When it was, like, 2 o'clock in the morning and I could see the big stack of things I had to do and I was so tired, but had to go to bed, you know. That's when it became overwhelming." (Wendy Zaharis)
- "The worst push of all was at the end. We had to be out and we still had the garage to do. That was horrible!" (Sylvia Reynolds)
- "That last week was terrible. I kept thinking, you know, that old saying: Whatever doesn't kill you makes you stronger. I felt like that." (LeNora Russel)
- "If I had had more time, I might have done some things differently. I might even have advertised something for sale just for my own satisfaction, but I didn't have that kind of time, so it was overwhelming and what else can I say? I had a month and I did it in a month." (Iris Boettcher)

In addition to one's own energy and organization, movers depended on other people to come through on time. Cheryl Palmer recalled how "it got tense at the end. We had a hard time with the auctioneer. We were a week before we were to be out of there before we finally got the auctioneer to come out to get stuff. It was coming down to the last minute and we needed to have stuff moved out of there." Her husband added that "it was three days before we were to sign the papers when [a charity] came and got the rest of the stuff. We were beginning to wonder whether we'd get it all done in time."

In all the material that I have reviewed for this book, this one anecdote, from Audra Huddleston, stays with me as a snapshot of relocation strain:

One day I had the car loaded—Pier Street—I looked in the mirror—the cop stopped me. And I thought, oh dear. I was feeling especially helpless that day. He said, "Do you know what you did?" And I said, yes, something about speeding. He said, "That wasn't it at all." He said, "You didn't stop back there for the stop sign. You just went right through." And I burst into tears. I've got the car loaded with Salvation Army stuff, the movers—. I'm so upset. I've driven down this street a thousand times a week, but today wasn't the day. He just gave me a pat on the back. Up to that point in time, I had gotten control of my crying.

The deadline heuristic, however, could also become a motif for emotion-focused coping, the kind of stress self-management by which people regulate their response to the situation.[10] "I guess, all I said was: I've got to get this out of here in one month." People also invoked the fit heuristic to remind themselves that there was limited room at the new place: "You can't put 59 years of accumulation into a little apartment." They resorted to prayer: "I just asked the Lord to give me strength." "Please God, help me." They made themselves resolute by saying, for example, "You gotta accept change"; "Get over it"; "You have to do it—you just have to get in and do it—SO DO IT!" Wendy Zaharis told herself, "You got to be tough. You can't be emotional. You gotta get this done. Just have to look at reality. There it is." In another variant of emotion-focused coping, the pull of a new life was a comforting thought. Cara Deaton repeated "over and over" that "I made the right choice. I'm in the right place at the right time. I am forever grateful." Dionne Peasley's mantra was: "I need to get started on my new beginnings, the next part of my life." "What motivated me," said Sandra Graves, "was me getting over here." Finally, a few people were other-focused. "This isn't about you," Isabel Arnold reminded herself. "Really, I was doing this first of all for my kids so they wouldn't have to make the decision. Second of all, I really wanted to get my husband into a safe and comfortable place where he could get the best care." Josephine Maxwell's thought was, "This is what my family wants for me."

DOWNSIZING RICH AND POOR

The extent of ease or strain across a downsizing episode arises from many sources, such as individual differences in planfulness and coping abilities in the moment, but also one's lifelong habits of possession management that assembled the material convoy that is now at issue (chapter 2). The transition may be deliberate or rushed (chapter 3); it plays out in contexts that color the project, such as marital status, health, family involvement, and prior experience with moving (chapter 4). And then there is social class. Throughout this book, there have been many suggestions that more economic resources ease downsizing in practical ways. Positions in the social hierarchy can also become embodied as emotions, in this case, as feelings of insecurity or being in control.[11]

In the course of conducting our studies, others have suggested to us that possession downsizing is a more significant problem for affluent households. The labor and stress of possession divestment should be a greater burden for those whom consumer society has advantaged. Such observations may arise from the same inclination that voices the cultural critique of clutter among America's overprovisioned homes (chapter 2). Yet, across all levels of social strata, people do move in later life, and they tend to move to smaller places, so possession divestment will be common to most transitions. The question is whether it is a greater challenge among the middle class. One could hypothesize that middle-class elders, having higher incomes and living in larger dwellings, have accumulated larger material convoys to manage, multiplying the cognitive, physical, emotional, and social dimensions of the process. People who have fewer goods should have an easier time of it.

To answer this question so as to compare across socioeconomic groups, what would come in handy is a way to assess the size of a household's material convoy. Alas, we still await such a measurement technique and for this purpose would have needed to ask questions retrospectively, because our households had already moved. Potential proxy measures for convoy size come to mind, such as net wealth, former occupation, owning versus renting, dwelling size prior to moving, and neighborhood characteristics that might approximate a contrast between big-convoy and small-convoy downsizers. Few of these indicators, however, were part of our studies. There is one way to approach the question with our qualitative data, and that is to compare the experiences of people moving in to two types of destinations: expensive, gated retirement communities and low-income, rent-subsidized senior housing where people typically took one-bedroom apartments. Both types of places were known to us by reputation or by participants' own comments in the areas of our fieldwork. From the Midwest Study, this comparison was conducted between twelve affluent households and seventeen low-income households.

Reviewing these cases, it would be fair to infer that the retirement community movers had more objects and property to deal with. But on other characteristics, the households were diverse within the two categories. True, the low-income movers were less likely to be married and were more likely to be renters prior to the move. But some of the low-income movers were vacating multistory, multibedroom houses where family members had formerly or currently lived. As sites for the accumulation of other people's things, these places were filled with furnishings throughout, down into basements and out onto porches. Both categories of movers might have adult children in the area and so available for help, along with social networks of friends and neighbors to offer information and advice and receive giveaways. Movers in both categories testified to stress and pressure during downsizing.

What tips the affluent households toward the easier time of it was their ability to control the timing and circumstances of the move and their ability to afford to hire various kinds of assistance. They were better able to control the sequence of the transition. With the means to support expenses at two properties, they had the option to move first then later clear the old place. Their destination communities, within limits, accommodated these movers' wishes about the day and hour of moving in. They could hire the services of home organizers, decorators, and cleaners and line up businesses for packing, cartage, storage, and disposal. These movers could engage agents such as estate sellers and antique dealers to optimize prices for their salable items.

The folks moving into low-income buildings did not enjoy such advantages. In the first place, if renting at either end, the schedule for moving and downsizing tended to accelerate. Offered a unit in a senior building, one soon needs to start paying monthly rent in order to hold it. Who knows when there will be another opening? When giving notice to vacate at the current residence, departure usually must occur within thirty days. The luxury of taking an extra month or two for the transition would mean managing rent and utilities in two places. Alice Frawley had a brief overlap, but it was a stretch. In the process of vacating and closing the sale of her house—within two weeks—she had to borrow two hundred dollars plus "some odd-dollar security deposit" in order to begin renting her new place. Second, the urgency of the downsizing affords less time to line up sales of possessions. Consequently, giveaways figure more prominently in these movers' stories. These were not unhappy recollections, because their things found willing recipients among family and neighbors. Ms. Frawley put it this way: "Most of the stuff I mainly gave away because the people I knew who needed it really didn't have the finances to pay for it. I just felt like I would be better off giving it than trying to sell it."

Third, these movers had limited funds with which to pay helpers. They could not afford to be indifferent to the value of things or labor and so they were prone to recite the expenses of the episode. Carolyn Tingey said: "Every time I had to have somebody come to move stuff it cost me at least $50 to $75." After moving in, Darlene Hastings gave her boxes to another tenant. "This lady came down the hallway and she saw me and said, 'Can I have those boxes?' and I said sure. Her daughter was moving and so she took the boxes. So she made out, she got lucky. Those boxes cost me a fortune." Asked to reflect on the entire experience, Sandra Graves said this:

> I wish that I had had more help, you know, somebody to help me. If you don't have a lot of family and you're from a small family, it's hard to get people to help you. People have things to do, and like I said,

unless you pay them—you've got to pay them, you can't expect them to do it for nothing. So I wasn't in that position to pay nobody, you know, to help me with other things.

Toward the end of the downsizing, Ms. Graves also kept her food purchases to a minimum, "just buying enough to eat for maybe that day. Or what I had in there, I would eat that, so it would be all gone. So when I got ready to clean the refrigerator, I wouldn't have to throw food away. Food is too high to be throwing away."

In all, as if speaking to the potential readers of our research, Juan King explained the "real life" of low-income movers like himself:

You see situations—family, children—on TV and everything is ideal. So they have movers. They call Atlas Van Lines to come in, and Atlas comes in and these big hawking guys come out of the truck. They're packing up stuff and then they orderly organize it, and then you write on the box what room it's going in, and these people load up the truck. And [the family members] get in their car and they meet the truck at their new residence and they just stand there. And the wife stands there and directs traffic: "Oh, that goes there. Put that in the kitchen. Put the sofa over here." And so in real life, it ain't like that (I know that's improper English). It just ain't like that.

To crystallize the difference that time control and access to resources can make when downsizing and moving residence, here are two contrasting cases of relative ease and worry. These stories come from interviews with Burt and Colleen Andrews and with Francesca Turner.

We met the Andrewses, ages 79 and 74, at their upscale retirement community, in a two-bedroom apartment that looked spacious with its high ceilings. Because they needed a more manageable place to live, they had moved "to this lifestyle" from a four-bedroom house where they had lived for more than forty years. In the course of talking about possession divestments, they discussed having shipped things to adult sons who lived some distance away. They mentioned having rented two self-storage units for overflow in the course of downsizing, then consolidating to one unit for long-term storage of things for grandchildren. At the community to which the couple would move, they had attended a move-in fair where such vendors as closet organizers, estate sellers, and moving companies were exhibiting. After the couple moved out of their home and into the apartment, they used one of the recommended businesses for an estate sale back at the house that the new owner was waiting to occupy. The sale went very well. Mr. Andrews said, "You probably get more money by having them do it, even though they get a commission from doing it." His wife said, "We probably wouldn't have priced things the way they did. . . . I'm sure they probably priced it better than we could have. You know they probably made more money on it than we would [with a garage sale]." Afterward, the estate seller removed the things that were unsold; otherwise "we'd have had to hire someone to come haul off the stuff." The buyer was able to move in a short time later. Another plus had been the move-in coordinator at the retirement community. Said Mr. Andrews, "She will give people as much help as is necessary," going to their homes and working on floor plans, deciding what furniture will fit. "That's one of the services that this place provides. They will give you a lot of hand-holding in this place. They have accumulated this list of vendors in the area that they have checked out."

Francesca Tanner, in her early sixties, also moved from her house in a two-month episode. She had lived alone, but had a son residing in a distant city. No longer able to afford the expenses of her three-bedroom house, a social worker helped her to identify a church-affiliated, low-income senior building that might suit her. Ms. Tanner could not directly call the facility because it was outside her area code and she lacked a phone calling card, so the social worker had the facility call her. Yes, there was a one-bedroom apartment available and, also lacking a car, she had to find a ride across town to view it. She judged the apartment to be "all right" but they needed her decision about it within twenty-four hours. "I'm thinking that I haven't gotten rid of my house. I got to get rid of my furniture because, as you can see, the furniture that I had in my house, it couldn't fit here in this one-bedroom apartment." The next day she agreed to take the apartment, and had to find another ride back across town to complete the paperwork. The rent would be $370 a month, utilities included. "If I had to pay utilities [separately], I couldn't live here, not with what I get from Social Security." Next problem, how would she pay the first month's rent?

> What I did was, when my money came in for March, I didn't pay the house note. I couldn't pay the house note and pay them here. So I chose to pay the rent here because they have a stipulation that if you don't pay your rent here before the fifth of each month, if that rent is late, their rule is that they can evict you, they will evict you. . . . So I had to choose to pay the rent here, but I still hadn't moved in. I gave them the rent, like the security deposit. So I wasn't able to pay my mortgage. I still hadn't moved in, so what I had to do, I said to myself: How am I going to get rid of all this furniture?

She called one donation agency to send a truck for a pickup, but it never came. Another agency did not pick up in her part of the city. So she started giving things away to her friends and to people they might know: a TV, a loveseat, a refrigerator, an organ. Selling things did not seem to be an option.

> Meanwhile, March went by. Again, I couldn't pay the mortgage on the house, so I had to let that lapse and I had to come over here and pay these people the rent [for April] although I hadn't moved in here. I had to pay the rent. Meanwhile, the mortgage people were sending me threatening letters. . . . I am, like, what am I going to do? So in the meantime, I kept thinking, how am I going to get rid of the rest of the stuff?

After two missed appointments, a veterans organization did come to pick up the major pieces of furniture that remained. Her next immediate problems were moving and what to do with her house. The new building allowed move-ins only Monday through Thursday between 9 a.m. and 2 p.m.—no moves on weekends. Anyone Ms. Tanner knew who could help her to move and drive the truck was working during those hours. Because houses were not selling at the time, she began looking for renters for her house. Finally, she found a couple to rent her house and they would, along with a neighbor, help her move. She set up a date for the move but missed it because in order to rent the moving truck, she had to have a major credit card. On the second try, her pastor let her use his credit card. On the day of the move, the truck rental was delayed and the group got a late start, but ultimately finished up a little before the 2 p.m. deadline.

> Then my house was empty. . . . I left the whole house clean, every room, the basement and all of that. That was it. It was a struggle because the hardest thing was getting rid of the furniture and the truck and getting someone to help me move. . . . That was the hardest thing. That was very hard.

Ms. Tanner later said that she was probably going to let the house go into foreclosure. "I can't afford to pay the mortgage there and pay the rent here. I can't. That's too much."

To sum up, it may be some advantage in downsizing to start with a smaller material convoy, but it is no advantage to lack the time and financial means to manage its uprooting and disposition. For low-income movers, downsizing is just one more way that life is harder. Francesca Tanner's struggle to get to a new home brings to mind what Matthew Desmond, a sociologist who has studied urban housing woes, has observed about poverty: "living it often meant steering through gnarled thickets of interconnected misfortunes and trying not to go crazy."[12]

LOOKING BACK AND LOOKING AHEAD

So people move, settle in, and have the chance to reflect on the entire episode. At the least, they remember it as laborious with periods of fatigue, strain, and frayed nerves. The larger question to ask, now that the relocation is past, is whether they have done the right thing? Was it worth all the trouble? It is well to remember that not all of these transitions had been voluntary, some having been forced by circumstance and some by family pressure. And by the time we spoke with people, months after they moved, their replies to any evaluative questions had probably already been used on others. We asked all of our households whether "things had turned out as you hoped they would?" Direct answers to the question were largely (90 percent) positive: "yes," "pretty much," "better than expected." Negative answers tended to faultfinding with the new place. When asked how things fit in the new place, the majority felt that things fit fine ("just right"), but a smaller number admitted to still having too much ("we're still downsizing").

Looking back more broadly on the management of their posses-sions, people still second-guessed their decisions about this or that item: a vanity, a trunk, a quilt, a platter, kitchen utensils, ice skates, tools. They had overdisposed and underdisposed. At the same time, while explaining their possession handling, our participants also reminded us about the constraints they had been under. Having committed to move, they said that they only had so much space in the new place and only had so much time to accomplish the down-sizing. As a practical matter, things had to be dealt with presently and in large quantities. Patricia Phail's verdict was: "I am very com-fortable on what we kept and what we didn't keep and what we got rid of. I am very comfortable."

Aside from the contents of the material convoy, how did people feel about the relocation of their own persons for which the down-sizing had cleared the way? One emotion was general relief that the episode was over.

> When I signed the papers releasing myself from the house it was like a burden lifted off of me. I felt lighter. It's something you can't really explain. Just when you've been going through something and you get through it, the burden feels like it's lifted off of you. (Alice Frawley)

In another variation, widowed persons found themselves freed from a memory-laden setting (from an absent presence) where they had made a life with their late spouse. Before moving, Dale Swapp tried to decorate for Christmas as his recently deceased wife would have done, "but that didn't go so well. That was pretty tough. I knew I couldn't do what she would have loved me to have done. . . . So that was a pretty tough period of time." Once moved, Ruth Ann Barber bought all new furniture after selling the pieces that she and her late husband had collected: "I moved away from my husband! You know? He doesn't live here, so I don't—. See, over there, every step I took, you know, he was following me. So I felt so-o-o-o much better when I got over here."

In our sample for the Midwest Study there was also a set of people who felt relieved to have traded up to better living conditions.

- "I was glad to get in [this apartment] and be settled in. And again, the rent thing, that was a relief. . . . That rental where I was staying was taking all of my money." (Martha Farnsworth)
- [By moving:] "We got rid of the mice, the roaches." (Hubert Odum)
- "I didn't feel too safe over there [a bigger building]. I feel more safe over here than I did over there." (Sandra Graves)
- "[This building] is precious to me. I have never, never in my life lived in a building this new." (Juan King)
- "I just remember the first night that I stayed here. It was just peaceful. It was peaceful." (Celia Buckles)

As has been said before, encounters with possessions are encounters with the self. In retrospect, some people reflected that "it was time" to have downsized and moved because they could no longer have managed the demands of their old place with the bodily limitations they now had.[13] We have also observed that the experience could reconstitute the self as agentic, as empowered.[14] Having come through a whole-house shakeout, downsizers are left with a set of stories, a portfolio of anecdotes that sums to something more than tales of this or that item. Possessions have a storytelling value.[15] In this case, possession management during disbandment, especially in recollecting satisfactory dispositions, can be deployed for the presentation of oneself as having acted responsibly. Stories about the fate of things, or even stories about the failure to place things, are ways to represent oneself as conscientious and dutiful. An affirmation of the present self as accomplished and careful can be seen as a positive adaptation to narrowing life domains.[16] Individuals can make the claim that they have chosen to put themselves on a new footing with a smaller set of possessions and that the outcome is satisfactory. Yes, the household is reduced, but things were taken care of, and I have come safely through the move. Marjorie Curtis made this point exactly when we asked her whether, in giving up things, she had lost a bit of herself. "If I did," she replied, "it's been replaced with, uh, a feeling of safety. Um, and, the feeling that I was able to do it all myself—that's a great ego builder."

A face-forward resilience shined out of certain conversations. Martha Farnsworth gained a new identity from the material discipline of living in a smaller place. "So I have to stop adding anything here. I have to remember that, and that is the key word, too, in aging. You are not in acquisitive mode any more, you are in a getting-rid-of mode. You are not acquiring, you are disposing; you should always be disposing, not acquiring." Others felt set for the future. "I have thought since," June Crawford said, "that one good thing about this is—this is the last time I'll ever have to move." Turning to her husband she asked, "I would not want to move again, right?" "Right!" he replied. Alice Frawley had the same thought: "I told the people when I moved in here they're going to have to roll me out or carry me out, because it would have to be really bad for me to move! I said, 'Y'all are stuck with me!'" A 94-year-old woman I interviewed for the Ageing as Future project invited me to step into the galley kitchen of her one-bedroom apartment at an assisted living building. She told me to open an overhead cupboard. There, in a large space with room for lots of dishes, rested just four dinner plates. "That's all I need now," she said with a smile and an air of satisfaction.

Finally, a few widows discovered the pleasure of living alone, of making their own choices and organizing their time. One of them, Debra Stinson, was in her eighties when her husband entered his final illness and that was when their daughter also came to live with them. After he died, mother and daughter lived together, but then they reluctantly gave up the house, with Debra moving to a studio apartment and her daughter moving to a separate apartment in town. We asked what it was like, having gone through all this loss. Her extended reply:

> It has been a really good relief for me. I mean, I hate it for my daughter. I mean, I wouldn't tell her that, but it has been good for me to be able to have my own place and keep it like I want. I was worried about it, and like I said, I do get lonesome. I get lonesome for her real bad, but like I said, I had never lived by myself before.
>
> This is the first time I have ever had an apartment or ANYTHING by myself! Because I lived with my parents until I got married, which was the way back then. And I lived with them until I got married, and then I lived with my husband. And then I had children when he was in the army, and even when he'd go out on maneuvers or something, I had the children there at home. Then when we moved over to Turner Street he was still living, and when he got sick [my daughter] moved in. So I had her, and I'm really glad I had her when he passed away. I didn't have to come home to an empty home like a lot of people do.
>
> I didn't know how I was going to take living by myself. But you know, I go to bed when I want to at night, and I get up when I want to in the morning. . . . I listen to whatever I want to on the TV. And to tell you the honest truth, my husband controlled the thing—what do you call it? [Interviewer: The remote?] Yeah. He controlled that. And when he would go and be away at night for a while, I couldn't make up my mind what I wanted to watch, when I could watch anything. *I couldn't make up my mind what I wanted to watch!*
>
> When I moved here, I had the same problem! Because [before] I would either let my daughter or granddaughter decide what we were going to watch. I just said "Well, you all decide, you know I don't care." And you know when I moved here I thought, "I can watch anything I want, but what do I want to watch?" I'd just go through the channels. [Laughter] It was a total different experience, but a good one.

So there she was, now 87 years old; she had lost her husband, she missed her daughter, and she had had to let go of possessions in the move. There she was, sitting there on the couch, holding the remote and having a fine time.

CONCLUSION

The people we met told us that downsizing for a residential move in later life is hard work, tiring and trying, a big job. The press of reduced space and limited time nevertheless eases the release of possessions, and their surrender brings a curtain down on certain roles and identities that the things had supported and symbolized. If people miss things, what they miss is a part of themselves. It is a mistake to suppose that some elders have an easier time of it because they are not well off and their material convoys are modest. In the shifting about and disposition of possessions, people's lack of time and resources make the logistics of a relocation that much harder to handle. Looking back, however, almost all the households we visited were content with what they had done and where they were now, having accomplished a transition that many had long known was awaiting them.[17]

Wanting to end our interviews on a happy note, we asked people whether they had gotten any new things since they had arrived at their present homes. There had indeed been some restocking of the material convoy—mostly ordinary goods such as furnishings, appliances, and clothing. Consumption resumed for Frances Lucas: "Unfortunately, I had promised myself that I would not shop anymore or buy anything—especially clothes. Yesterday, I bought clothes for my birthday, which I didn't need, but I did it anyway." For her birthday, Jill Crosby got a plant that now sat in her bay window: "It's the first I've had in probably ten years." Finally, Belva Carter, asked if she felt downsizing as a loss, said: "No, uh-uh, no. I just feel like I'm gaining more all the time. I look to the future, this adventure. I mean, new things. And I want to get new things."

9

ADVICE

The world is well supplied with authorities on how to manage possessions. Modern guilt about overconsumption and over-stuffed homes has made home organizing and clutter control a mainstay of popular media and self-help books. Instructions for taming one's material convoy are available for any stage of life, including the specific circumstance of downsizing in later life for eventual residential relocation. Such guidance is carried by advice manuals, blogs, newspaper and magazine features, and broadcast programs. I know because I have added a few ideas to these streams.

These sources offer all sorts of help. For example, the chore of sifting through paper is a common feature of downsizing (chapter 7). As it happens, the Cooperative Extension System of the U.S. federal government has a most useful publication on managing household records, "Organize Important Papers."[1] This article covers what to gather, what to keep (and for how long), and what to discard—a road map to putting one's affairs in order. Self-help tips in the books and blogs of senior move managers are always worth attention. Move managers are skilled at recirculating large quantities of material goods and work with networks of providers for specific solutions (e.g., pet adoption, photo album consolidation, hazardous waste disposal). Their how-to advice is remarkably consistent, but they differ in the kinds of pep talks they give and the motivational balance that they strike between reassurance and tough love.[2]

The availability of downsizing advice, however, does not mean that it is used. We asked our participants whether they had consulted books, websites, or television programs in planning their transitions, but people reported little take-up from such sources. Preparing for and executing a move is something that people feel they already know how to do. It is a stubbornly DIY affair whose challenges will not be apparent until the activity begins. Older adults find that these relocations differ from the moves they made at age 25 or age 45, not only because of the downsizing imperative but also because of the now older bodies undertaking the move.

Adding to the advice already out there, what follows are some conclusions drawn specifically from the angle of our research. Our participants had ideas for peers in the same situation, and I, too, have things to suggest: to older adults, to family members and friends, and to professionals in the field.

PEER TO PEER

The people with whom we talked had advice for others who face downsizing and relocation. Their recommendations, offered at the end of interviews, came with some amount of self-congratulation for having accomplished the transition. There was advice about choosing a destination. There was advice about dealing with realtors, building managers, and moving companies (keep an eye on them). Giving, selling, and donating all had dos and don'ts (see chapters 4, 5, and 6). Our interviewees had tips to offer, for example, about boxes—packing them, labeling them, and their size (small is better because "when you get to 85 you don't want a big box"). "Pod" storage containers had their enthusiasts. People should get enough sleep and work in the morning "because you're fresher."

For general guidance, the two main strains were "don't accumulate" and "start early," which both amount to a recommendation that older adults be disciplined in their habits of housing possessions. Yet, as some of our participants recognized, it is probably not human nature to be so disciplined:

> Well, I did write on my Christmas cards to my older friends, "Start now!" Maybe there are people who start years ahead of when they move, but I didn't. . . . What I would advise people is not to let it accumulate in the first place. But I think everybody does—if you have the space. (LeNora Russel)

Sylvia Reynolds said: "Everyone knows moving is the worst job in the world. Downsizing, if it can be any worse, is very worse. . . . I guess my best advice to anybody would be: Start getting rid of stuff way in advance—avoid living in clutter." Once a move is in view, the admonition to start early, give yourself enough time, and "do it while you can" implies that there is a point when it would be too late to manage events well: "So that would be my advice: Don't wait till the last minute. Do it when you are still able to handle things and tell everybody else what you want to do with your things" (Brenda Valkos). Lorraine Morse said the same when asked what she would say to others:

> That's a senior? A senior? Do it while they can. While they can make the decision, while they physically can do it, and they have the mental ability to think through processes. And I see too many [people] moving in here who waited way too long and they are confused. They can't think through things. They usually in many cases have a partner that is ill, not always, but there's usually one of a couple, and they've just waited too long. SO they need to be young.

Chapter 1 identified downsizing as a cognitive, emotional, and social task, and our movers had recommendations along all three lines. The cognitive counsel was pointed: organize, make lists, make time lines, plan ahead, measure and map the new space, and proceed methodically "one day at a time, one room at a time; maybe down to just your dresser drawers in that whole room." For emotional self-management, there was encouragement to adopt a positive attitude: "You can do it," "It'll be OK." In prospect it can seem overwhelming, but "take it one step at a time, one decision at a time." Tamp down your sentimentality about things, think small, and heed the fit heuristic: "It's very peaceful when you realize you can live with a lot less and still be happy and comfortable." Downsizing, as our participants saw it, will have social requirements. Do rely on family members and others and get help "because you will need it." Isabel Arnold said, "Don't try to do it by yourself, you know. Receive help, seek help, be willing to talk it through." What Gerald Saltzman said in chapter 4 bears restating: "Well, if you're older or are limited in any way, you're going to need help, and you're just going to have to somehow find help. . . . And don't be shy about seeking help and getting it, even if you have to pay for it."

With his parting advice, Martin Hawk recapped the entire typical sequence of divestment strategies (chapter 4) while stressing the exigency of the undertaking: "Get rid of as much as you can, by any means possible. Give it to your daughter, give it to friends and family, family and friends, donate it or sell it, donate it, recycle it, and as a last resort, just dump it. But get rid of stuff."

TO OLDER ADULTS: THINGS AND TIME

I underline the participants' caution not to delay downsizing to an advanced age, arriving at the project lacking the stamina of body and mind to do the job well. Before the purging, though—in one's early retirement years—I would encourage a phase of embracing possessions and testing their roles in the material convoy. Awaken what Sophie Woodward has called the "dormant" things and explore their possibilities.[3] Objects claim space, but they are equally a claim on time—to use them or enjoy them requires minutes, hours, days. The scarcity of time that marks middle age fades away in retirement, so those items that had been kept for "someday" can now have your attention. In U.S. culture, retirees must continually account for themselves in terms of what they are "doing" nowadays, so here is something to do.[4] What about those books, those tools, those gadgets, that box of family history, those photo albums, those shelves of music, that yarn, that gardening equipment, those back-of-the-closet and back-of-the-attic whatnots, and what about those someday things that had been put aside for fixing? So many possessions in a household have been awaiting the kind of leisure that retirement affords, so show them your love. If now is not the time to reintroduce these things to your life, then there is your answer as to their importance to the material convoy.

The time available to explore and rediscover things is a paradox. If retirement time is abundant, the remaining length of a (healthy) lifetime is uncertain and doubly uncertain within a marriage. Older adults suspect that there will inevitably come a time when they cannot live independently—it is the "known unknown" of later life.[5] Aware of this or even in anticipation of this, Americans tend to form ideas about where they might live next, even though they may have a strong preference to stay put.[6] Bill Ahlstrom recalled the decision to return to the area where he and his wife had lived before they retired to a community some nine hours' drive away. He said that "it was mostly [my wife] seeing the writing on the wall, that if anything happened to me she would be alone." Even people who had already made a postretirement move still realized that there might be another move in their future. This recognition that the future is limited ("the writing on the wall") should make a large convoy—its material "thereness"—feel all the more unsettling. And observing this from the sidelines unsettles family members, too.

Against all our participants' advice, the one good reason to hold off on downsizing until a move is imminent is that the new place will guide the divesting (chapter 3). Once the size and nature of the destination is known, that puts a limit on what will fit and what sorts and quantities of possessions would be appropriate to bring, such as big furniture, yard implements, clothing. Putting off downsizing may also activate the only motivation to which some people respond—a deadline. On the other hand, divesting over an extended period far in advance of a possible move affords more control over time-consuming dispositions, something also stressed by advice manuals about downsizing (chapter 2). If cherished possessions or heirlooms need to be conducted safely into the future, their gifting can await the right time or the ability of recipients to take the things in. With a long lead time, suitable recipients could be groomed. When selling things of value, it takes patience to find worthy buyers and get good prices as transactional processes play out. The careful and considered review of your things not only protects objects toward which you feel a need to act responsibly but also guards your privacy.[7] There may be household contents—for example, diaries or photographs—that should not be open to the view of others during a hurry-up disbandment or later clean-out by heirs. The same goes for computer contents and browsing history. A newspaper headline such as "Sex Toys in the Attic" should be prompt enough to start taking care of things that should never be held up to inspection by one's relatives during the sorting into piles.[8]

If there is not some voluntary divestment in advance of a potential move, then you should resign yourself to about two or three months of pretty hard work as the deadline looms. A spouse, helpers, and money can ease the project, but only so much. Years of tidy housekeeping kept the place squared away, but start the sorting and the pent-up disorder of the material convoy will rush out and make a mess as the weeks wind down. Those thousands of items in multiple rooms came into the household one at a time, but they will need to go out in batches, sped along by the fit, me/not-me, utility, offer-claim, and gender-kin decisional heuristics (chapter 4). Beware of attempts to find "good homes" for too many things—homes that are good enough will do. Under the time constraints of mobilizing for a move, there must be efficiency. Attempts to optimize gifts and sales will only slow the work. Some belongings can be placed in just the right setting, but most others will land here or there by chance or by the kindness of claimants. Our participants tended to forgive themselves for not doing better.

There are dear things that will not, cannot make the trip to the new place, and their divestment will be felt as a loss (chapter 8). Kevin Hetherington wrote of the "absent presence" of objects, how their departure is never complete because their trace effects remain in the void they leave behind.[9] Rather than regard them as gone, the absent presence of special things can be cultivated. "Those tiles over there," said Grace Brown, "they were Mom and Dad's, they had them all around the kitchen." Now she was to content with "just a few." Dale Swapp's late wife was known for her collections, which Mr. Swapp felt he had to release. But he kept some sample items in a display case, thus keeping her present, too. There is no way to shed possessions without making ghosts, but ghosts can be kept close. Even just one thing can be granted the power to represent a whole universe within a shadow box or small tin shrine.

TO OTHERS: MAKE IT CONCEIVABLE

I have been in countless conversations with people who regret that they cannot convince spouses or parents to dispose of household contents in anticipation of the future. "She won't part with a thing!" This is the later-life variation on the possession dismay that drives the better housekeeping advice from home organizers. Getting people started on any kind of behavior change is a major challenge of our era. If there is a magic switch to flip that would motivate folks to lose weight, quit smoking, exercise, limit screen time, and save more for retirement—the world would dearly love to know about it.

Inertia toward the material convoy—leaving it be—makes perfect sense (chapter 2). It requires little effort, aside from ignoring the threat of the convoy's "thereness." Against an uncertain future, belongings promise continuity of the self and even possible selves. Divestment is a lot of work, and besides, unless one has an exact destination in mind, it's not time just yet to get rid of too many Christmas decorations.

If family members and friends want to get things rolling—and such efforts must always be accompanied by offers to help—I have some ideas but no guarantees. First, try a cautionary tale. Whereas older adults do not seek much advice about downsizing, what does impress them is a negative role model. We heard cautionary tales about having assisted parents, parents-in-law, aunts and uncles, and friends clean out, close up, and move. Burt Andrews, for one, had his examples for us: "We've been through this with family members." An aunt in Virginia entered a nursing home: "We had to go out there and dismantle her house." His mother-in-law lived in Oregon, and "we had to move her from one apartment to another and then to an assisted living facility, and downsize her. So we had been through this long distance." Perhaps such scare stories will appeal to an elder's self-interest if they reach the realization that a smaller convoy actually increases one's freedom, enlarging rather than diminishing one's options. If ever a move loomed, fewer things would widen the choice of places into which the things would fit and would facilitate a rapid move if health or circumstances changed.

Second, play the "gift" card and appeal to the interests of others (chapter 5). Most stories about having downsized a friend or relative conclude with the lesson that Mr. Andrews drew: "That's one of the reasons why we decided we're going to do it ourselves while we're capable and not have to have our kids travel 800 miles in a hurry to do it." Tam Perry has written that taking care of this can be an emotional gift: to a spouse, now or as preparation for a widowed future; and to kin members' peace of mind and freedom from responsibility and to ease their potential care burden.[10] Our participants certainly said as much: "I do not want to leave this house with 47 years of accumulation for my kids to have to go through." "It would be a help to my sons eventually." "We don't want our kids to just be overwhelmed." Said Patricia Connell: "We did this for our children. We cleaned out both my husband's parents' house and my mother and dad's house after they passed, and we didn't want them to have to do that. So this is another present that we're giving them."

Third, and back to self-interest, go hardball and play the embarrassment card. It's not only that mortifying items could come to light in the sorting, it's that one's domestic neglectfulness could be on view. New Yorker cartoonist Roz Chast is an unsparing observer of life's neuroses. Her graphic memoir, *Can't We Talk about Something More Pleasant?*, recalls her experience of seeing her parents through the end of their lives.[11] In one chapter, she turns her pen and camera on the apartment that they vacated after forty-eight years and the bewildering accumulation of things left behind. She includes pages of cringe-worthy photos of overstuffed rooms and unexplainable multiples of objects: "Museum of old Shick shavers." "So-o-o-o-o many pencils!!!!!!" "Why is there a drawer of jar lids?" Roz Chast wrings dark humor from all of this, but it's hard to imagine anyone who would want possession shaming as an enduring legacy in family lore: "Ah, Grandpa! Remember all that stuff he had squirreled away?"

Fourth, pay for it, or offer to. There are providers whose business it is to facilitate divestment and who succeed to the extent that they can cajole or wheedle the household into releasing things. Their clients are often not the older adults but their children. This is a costly solution and not a path that everyone can follow. Still, paid help may be just the measure that tips the downsizing project from "never" to conceivable. One of my correspondents, Jodie, wrote of her stubborn mother's dozen large plastic tubs containing news clippings, photos, cards, letters, and such. Jodie hired a young woman who needed extra work to sit with her mother for two days a week and scrapbook the material, talking over each family photo and obituary and sometimes coaxing a disposal. Jodie's mother now "announces to her friends that she is 'getting rid of so much stuff.'" That's an exaggeration, says Jodie, but "it's a start."

One of the most common things that people say about elders and family members and possessions is that "the kids don't want any of the stuff." There can be good reasons for refusals to accept things (chapter 5). Yet once a downsizing has begun in earnest and belongings must be divested, I have another suggestion for relatives or even friends. When things are offered, take them. And take some more. What to do with it, you can figure out later. Such gestures run counter to the advice manuals that warn adult children not to let an elder's convoy visit them and overwhelm them. But I agree with Jean-Sébastien Marcoux that "it is the act of receiving that becomes an act of generosity."[12] Be glad that the household is letting go and do it this favor. Patricia Phail, speaking of her excess religious books and tapes, said, "I didn't want to dump them all in the trash. That would have been really, really hard for me to do, but if I found somebody that had open arms, then it was okay, it was fine." When things are offered, instead of fending them off as "not my taste" and "not my style" and "I don't need it," you can just shut up and take them. Affirm the giver with open arms.

TO THE FIELD: A SHORT LIST

This book has promoted the concept of a material convoy to advance a more comprehensive view of the environment in which aging goes on. Yes, people live in buildings and neighborhoods, and people live amid others, but people also at all times occupy a domestic infrastructure of objects that they have accumulated, now maintain, and may even fear. This convoy counts thousands of items, a great mixture of objects invested with history, emotion, and care. In respect of this investment, we should be sparing in the use of certain words, such as *treasures*, as a shorthand for the constituents of the material convoy. Some possessions are cherished, but most are not, and talk of treasures obscures and distracts from the bulky ordinariness of all the objects that older adults accommodate. Switching from over- to undervaluing possessions, *stuff* is something that people can call their own belongings, but perhaps we should not. Stuff is mere material, indistinct, and slightly bothersome. The word can seem dismissive and trivializes people's complex relationships with their things. Finally, clutter—objects in the wrong place—is not the main problem as the prospect of relocation grows more likely (though clutter can make a home unsafe). Rather than clutter, the volume of possessions is the issue at hand. *Clutter* is a scolding word, besides, and underplays the challenge posed by a material convoy that becomes harder to manage and move.

We should be careful of advice that is too facile. Sort things into piles, people are told, according to the major divestment routes: give, sell, donate, discard. But where do the piles go, and who follows through on their removal? Gifts and do-it-yourself sales are inefficient divestment strategies, not because they are a bad idea but because, under deadline, they are unlikely to dispose of many items relative to the effort required. Nevertheless, people will try these tactics in order to secure good homes for things, confirm their worth, or honor the feelings of others. Mediated sales (estate sales, auctions) are a true batch method and can be encouraged provided that the drawbacks and costs are apparent. Not everyone has sufficient household stock for mediated sales, but they can move the merchandise if the household agrees to cede control. Donation is another batch method that has much to recommend it as long as the ground rules of the organizations (about pickups or the condition of items) are understood. Again, under deadline, the method is pretty convenient and offers some moral satisfaction.

As downsizers work through their possessions, we can also highlight the ways that local communities are ready to cooperate. In consumer studies, writers use the term *conduits* to summarize all of the means by which material can exit households and lives.[13] The term calls up images of pipes, channels, and chutes through which things can flow or be blocked. Conduits are off-ramps for the material convoy, and this book has throughout addressed general categories of these outlets: gifts, sales, and so on. The exact places where things could go and the specific help that is available—these are "community conduits," and they should be publicized widely in order to keep the conceivability of divestment before older adults. Advice manuals typically include a section on resources, and residential facilities will refer their prospects to vendors who can help with the transition. The community at large should also have access to the same kind of pointers but tailored for the locality. Such listings would be a worthwhile information-and-referral service for government agencies, nonprofits, libraries, community groups, or university extension programs. Call it the promotion of "divestment literacy." The project could catalog area businesses that assist relocation; sellers of secondhand goods; donation sites and charities; swaps and flea markets; community groups that mount sales; public services such as shredding events; and waste disposal options, especially for electronics and hazardous material. The management of the material convoy is a household's responsibility, but local communities are standing by with active conduits. Citizens in every place of every age would benefit from knowing about them.

The research reported in this book should serve to open many questions about the management and fate of the material convoy in later life, questions that others can pick up and pursue. With tens of millions of older adults uneasy about the extent of their holdings and the prospect of moving them (chapter 2), this public will welcome insights from further studies conducted in more places and more varied circumstances. One need that I have mentioned multiple times in this book is for survey or assessment techniques that could gauge the size, composition, and handling of the material convoy—at all ages. With such methods we could make comparisons among groups, generations, locales, and eras, as well as track changes within households over time. Population-based conclusions, when paired with the in-depth understanding from qualitative studies, would greatly help push a turn toward wider scholarly interest in the material enactment of the life course.

FAREWELL

Toward the end of Giacomo Puccini's opera *La Bohème*, there is a divestment. The opera follows the lives and loves of young struggling artists in nineteenth-century Paris. They live in the moment; they skate on the rent and dodge their café bills. The last act opens with a scene of horseplay in the artists' garret, but the silliness is interrupted by the sudden arrival of Mimi. She has been sickly all along, but now she is coughing and at death's door. The mood changes swiftly. The friends gather round and resolve to ease her distress— selling earrings to buy medicine, calling the doctor, securing a muff for her cold hands. To help pay for things, one of the group goes out to pawn his overcoat, which has been dear to him. "Shabby old overcoat," he sings, I send you onward. "Now that the happy days have fled, I say farewell to you, my faithful friend. Farewell, farewell." With that, the song concludes with a funereal five-chord progression that descends and rises back up. Shortly afterward, Mimi expires, and the friends are plunged into grief. As this plays out, the entire opera ends by reprising that same five-chord passage, this time stated with finality by the full power of the orchestra. With this single gesture, the composer joins in one theme the dismissal of an overcoat with the closing of a chapter in these lives. Things have changed, the happy days have fled.

Life course change invites both acquisition and divestment. In later life, to continue to live independently and manageably, it is sometimes unavoidably necessary to relocate to smaller quarters with a smaller material convoy. The transition is laborious and difficult, but this book has explored the experiences of people who went through it and lived to tell the tale, sometimes with humor. They took "care" of their things and, in the process, took care of themselves. Setting one's life on a smaller stage could be seen as a step down, but we can choose to see it as a step forward. The last word is Donna Crandall's: "Would I have stayed, if I could? Yes, I would have stayed if I could. But I won't go back. I've got to go on. I can't go back."

Appendix

INTERVIEW PARTICIPANTS
IN THE ELDER AND FAMILY STUDY
AND THE MIDWEST STUDY

Pseudonym	Age	Marital Status
Cynthia Abboud	86	Widowed
Bill Ahlstrom	80	Married
Christine Ahlstrom	77	Married
Burt Andrews	79	Married
Colleen Andrews	74	Married
Isabel Arnold	64	Married
Ruth Ann Barber	82	Widowed
Judith Bauer	69	Widowed
Christine Black	87	Married
Joseph Black	89	Married
Iris Boettcher	88	Widowed
Gayla Bonnet	74	Married
Len Bonnet	72	Married
Nadine Boyd	62	Single
Barbara Briganti	80	Divorced
Grace Brown	65	Divorced
Celia Buckles	73	Widowed
Elizabeth Buresh	66	Married
Belva Carter	83	Divorced
Laverne Cherwinski	86	Widowed
Patricia Connell	82	Married
Carlee Cooper	64	Divorced
William Copple	70	Married
Sheila Cosentino	82	Widowed

(continued)

Pseudonym	Age	Marital Status
Donna Crandall	65	Married
Bradley Crawford	89	Married
June Crawford	90	Married
Jill Crosby	80	Widowed
Andrea Cruz	75	Married
Joseph Cruz	79	Married
Marjorie Curtis	87	Widowed
Roberta Davis	81	Widowed
Cara Deaton	78	Widowed
Georgina Dines	70	Married
James Dines	74	Married
Anita Duvall	71	Married
Ross Duvall	74	Married
Sharon Dvorak	74	Married
Stephen Dvorak	77	Married
Sheira Engel	86	Widowed
Donald Enloe	76	Divorced
Diane Esposito	77	Widowed
Martha Farnsworth	72	Divorced
Wilma Farrell	80	Widowed
Jane Ferguson	85	Widowed
Janis Flatt	78	Widowed
Alice Frawley	66	Divorced
Virgil Frazier	68	Single
Sandra Graves	69	Single
Anne Gunter	88	Widowed
Darlene Hastings	73	Widowed
Martin Hawk	82	Widowed
Cameron Healy	81	Widowed
Marguerite Heinen	84	Widowed
Marian Holroyd	65	Single
Marilyn Howerton	70	Divorced
Audra Huddleston	78	Married
Curtis Huddleston	81	Married
Mary James	87	Widowed
Ginny Johnson	88	Single
Barbara Jones	80	Married
Harold Jones	78	Married
James Kanaga	74	Widowed
Juan King	66	Divorced
Cathleen Koenig	75	Married
Todd Koenig	87	Married

Pseudonym	Age	Marital Status
Lori Kovar	74	Married
Joyce Leseur	85	Widowed
Dale Lilla	84	Married
Frances Lucas	72	Widowed
Betty Mahan	65	Divorced
Sara Manning	84	Widowed
Greg McCarthy	73	Widowed
Camille McCawley	63	Widowed
Josephine Merrill	91	Widowed
Deborah Mohatt	73	Married
Jack Mohatt	73	Married
Lorraine Morse	74	Single
Georgene Mullins	65	Widowed
Dory Myles	80	Widowed
Laura Nardi	76	Married
Ralph Nardi	76	Married
Kathryn Nurski	84	Widowed
Michelle O'Kane	79	Married
Steve O'Kane	83	Married
Hubert Odum	71	Single
Cheryl Palmer	71	Married
Larry Palmer	71	Married
Dionne Peasley	63	Widowed
Jeri Peters	87	Married
Richard Peters	86	Married
David Peterson	87	Single
Patricia Phail	67	Married
Sam Phail	71	Married
Martin Pratt	87	Widowed
Claudia Radford	84	Married
Kenneth Radford	85	Married
Sylvia Reynolds	68	Married
Deborah Richards	75	Divorced
Luke Ries	78	Married
Matthew Rink	82	Married
Nichole Rink	84	Married
Joyce Rosner	82	Widowed
LeNora Russel	66	Divorced
Marty Sable	81	Married
Maureen Sable	77	Married
Abbey Sala	80	Widowed
Gerald Saltzman	78	Widowed

(*continued*)

Pseudonym	Age	Marital Status
Vera Sampson	71	Widowed
Mary Beth Sand	80	Widowed
Hilda Scott	75	Married
Linda Shill	81	Divorced
Edward Sluman	86	Separated
Tia Sparks	60	Widowed
Daryl Staples	71	Married
Gladys Staples	60	Married
Debra Stinson	76	Widowed
Martha Sturek	84	Widowed
Rebecca Sullivan	85	Widowed
Dale Swapp	71	Widowed
Francesca Tanner	61	Divorced
Yvette Timian	74	Widowed
Carolyn Tingey	67	Divorced
Bernadette Tucker	67	Divorced
Marie Udall	78	Divorced
Brenda Valkos	77	Widowed
Bill Wagner	83	Married
Janet Wagner	76	Married
Elden Weale	61	Married
Margaret Weale	65	Married
Margaret Woods	87	Married
Vernon Woods	88	Married
Vera Young	63	Widowed
Wendy Zaharis	85	Widowed

NOTES

INTRODUCTION

1. "Forever," Clare Twomey, accessed January 2, 2020, http://www.claretwomey .com/projects_-_forever.html.

2. "Forever Continues," Clare Twomey, accessed May 10, 2012, http://www.nelson -atkins.org/art/exhibitions/twomey/forevercontinues.cfm.

3. "Forever Continues," Clare Twomey, accessed May 10, 2012, http://www.nelson -atkins.org/art/exhibitions/twomey/forevercontinues.cfm.

4. Gregson, N., *Living with Things: Ridding, Accommodation, Dwelling* (Hereford- shire, UK: Sean Kingston Publishing, 2007).

5. Appadurai, A. (ed.), *The Social Life of Things: Commodities in Cultural Perspective* (Cambridge: Cambridge University Press, 1986).

6. Belk, R. W., "Possessions and the Extended Self," *Journal of Consumer Research* 15 (1988): 139–168.

7. Brown, B., *A Sense of Things* (Chicago: University of Chicago Press, 2004).

8. Miller, D., *Stuff* (Cambridge: Polity Press, 2010).

9. Marcoux, J.-S., "The 'Casser Maison' Ritual: Constructing the Self by Emptying the Home," *Journal of Material Culture* 6 (2001): 213–235.

10. Redfoot, D. L. and Back, K. W., "The Perceptual Presence of the Life Course," *International Journal of Aging and Human Development* 27 (1988): 155–170.

11. Dant, T., *Material Culture in the Social World: Values, Activities, Lifestyles* (Phila- delphia: Open University Press, 1999); Diaz Moore, K. and Ekerdt, D. J., "Age and the Cultivation of Place," *Journal of Aging Studies* 25 (2011): 189–192.

12. Frost, R. O. and Steketee, G., eds., *The Oxford Handbook of Hoarding and Acquir- ing* (New York: Oxford University Press, 2014).

13. Chapin, R. K., Sergeant, J. F., Landry, S. T., Koenig, T., Leiste, M., and Reynolds, K., "Hoarding Cases Involving Older Adults: The Transition from a Private Matter to the Public Sector," *Journal of Gerontological Social Work* 53 (2010): 723–742; Laterman, K., "Helping Those Who Hoard," *New York Times*, July 2, 2017.

14. Timpano, K. R., Muroff, J., and Steketee, G., "A Review of the Diagnosis and Management of Hoarding Disorder," *Current Treatment Options in Psychiatry* 3 (2016): 394–410; Tolin, D., Frost, R. O., and Steketee, G., *Buried in Treasures: Help for Compulsive Acquiring, Saving, and Hoarding*, 2nd ed. (New York: Oxford University Press, 2014).

15. Kroger, J. and Adair, V., "Symbolic Meanings of Valued Personal Objects in Identity Transitions of Late Adulthood," *Identity* 8 (2008): 5–24; Nord, C., "A Day to Be Lived: Elderly People's Possessions for Everyday Life in Assisted Living," *Journal of Aging Studies* 27 (2013): 135–142; Wapner, S., Demick, J., and Redondo, J. P., "Cherished Possessions and Adaptation of Older People to Nursing Homes," *International Journal of Aging and Human Development* 31 (1990): 219–235.

16. Finch, J. and Hayes, L., "Inheritance, Death, and the Concept of the Home," *Sociology* 28 (1994): 417–433; Guillard, V., "Understanding the Process of the Disposition of a Loved One's Possessions Using a Theoretical Framework of Grief," *Consumption Markets & Culture* 20 (2017): 477–496; Johnson, P., *They Left Us Everything: A Memoir* (New York: G.P. Putnam's Sons, 2016); Lovatt, M., "Charity Shops and the Imagined Futures of Objects: How Second-Hand Markets Influence Disposal Decisions When Emptying a Parent's House," *Culture Unbound: Journal of Current Cultural Research* 7 (2015): 13–29.

17. Ekerdt, D. J., Sergeant, J. F., Dingel, M., and Bowen, M. E., "Household Disbandment in Later Life," *Journals of Gerontology Series B: Psychological Sciences and Social Sciences* 59 (2004): S265–S273; Ekerdt, D. J. and Sergeant, J. F., "Family Things: Attending the Household Disbandment of Older Adults," *Journal of Aging Studies* 20 (2006): 193–205.

18. Ekerdt, D. J., Luborsky, M., and Lysack, C., "Safe Passage of Goods and Self During Residential Relocation in Later Life," *Ageing and Society* 32 (2012): 833–850.

19. Ekerdt, D. J. and Baker, L. A., "The Material Convoy After Age 50," *Journals of Gerontology Series B: Psychological Sciences and Social Sciences*, 69 (2014): 442–450.

20. Koss, C. and Ekerdt, D. J., "Residential Reasoning and the Tug of the Fourth Age," *Gerontologist* 57 (2017): 921–929.

21. Weiss, R. S., *Learning from Strangers: The Art and Method of Qualitative Interview Studies* (New York: Free Press, 1995), 125.

22. Financial Crisis Inquiry Commission, *Financial Crisis Inquiry Report* (New York: Public Affairs, 2011).

23. Bosworth, B., "Economic Consequences of the Great Recession: Evidence from the Panel Study of Income Dynamics" (working paper no. 2012-4, Center for Retirement Research at Boston College, February 2012).

24. Deaton, A., "The Financial Crisis and the Well-Being of Americans: 2011 OEP Hicks Lecture," *Oxford Economic Papers* 64 (2012): 1–26.

25. Braun, V. and Clarke, V., "Using Thematic Analysis in Psychology," *Qualitative Research in Psychology* 3 (2006): 77–101; Fereday, J. and Muir-Cochrane, E., "Demonstrating Rigor Using Thematic Analysis: A Hybrid Approach of Inductive and Deductive Coding and Theme Development," *International Journal of Qualitative Methods* 5 (2006): 80–92.

26. Ryan, G. W. and Bernard, H. R., "Data Management and Analysis Methods," in *Handbook of Qualitative Research*, 2nd ed., ed. N. K. Denzin and Y. S. Lincoln, 769–802 (Thousand Oaks, CA: Sage, 2000).

27. Calasanti, T. M. and Slevin, K. F., *Gender, Social Inequalities, and Aging* (Walnut Creek, CA: Rowman Altamira, 2001); Carr, D., *Golden Years? Social Inequality in Later Life* (New York: Russell Sage Foundation, 2019).

1. A CONVOY OF POSSESSIONS ACROSS THE LIFE COURSE

1. Austad, S. N., "Making Sense of Biological Theories of Aging," in *Handbook of Theories of Aging*, 2nd ed., ed. V. L. Bengtson, D. Gans, N. M. Putney, and M. Silverstein, 147–161 (New York: Springer, 2009).

2. Elder, G. H., Johnson, M. K. and Crosnoe, R., "The Emergence and Development of Life Course Theory," in *Handbook of the Life Course*, ed. J. T. Mortimer and M. J. Shanahan, 3–19 (New York: Springer, 2004); Mayer, K. U., "New Directions in Life Course Research," *Annual Review of Sociology* 35 (2009): 413–433.

3. Dannefer, D. and Uhlenberg, P., "Paths of the Life Course: A Typology," in *Handbook of Theories of Aging*, ed. V. L. Bengtson and K. W. Schaie, 306–326 (New York: Springer, 1999).

4. Kahn, R. L. and Antonucci, T. C., "Convoys Over the Life Course: Attachment, Roles, and Social Support," in *Life-Span Development and Behavior*, ed. P. B. Baltes and O. G. Brim, 253–286 (New York: Academic Press, 1980); Plath, D. V., *Long Engagements: Maturity in Modern Japan* (Stanford, CA: Stanford University Press, 1980).

5. Antonucci, T. C., Birditt, K. S., and Ajrouch, K. J., "Convoys of Social Relations: Past, Present and Future," in *Handbook of Life Span Development*, ed. K. L. Fingerman, C. A. Berg, J. Smith, and T. C. Antonucci, 161–182 (New York: Springer, 2011).

6. Antonucci, T. C., Ajrouch, K. J., and Birditt, K. S., "The Convoy Model: Explaining Social Relations from a Multidisciplinary Perspective,"*Gerontologist* 54 (2013): 82–92.

7. Höppner, G. and Urban, M., "Where and How Do Aging Processes Take Place in Everyday Life? Answers from a New Materialist Perspective," *Frontiers in Sociology* 3 (2018): 1–10; Katz, S., ed., *Ageing in Everyday Life: Materialities and Embodiments* (Bristol, UK: Policy Press, 2018); Twigg, J. and Martin, W., eds., *Routledge Handbook of Cultural Gerontology* (London: Routledge, 2015).

8. Ekerdt, D. J., "Possessions as a Material Convoy," in *Routledge Handbook of Cultural Gerontology*, ed. J. Twigg and W. Martin, 313–320 (London: Routledge, 2015).

9. Fingerman, K. L., and Hay, E., "Intergenerational Ambivalence in the Context of the Larger Social Network," in *Intergenerational Ambivalences: New Perspectives on*

Parent-Child Relations in Late Life, ed. K. Pillemer and. K. Luscher, 133–151 (New York: Elsevier/JAI Press, 2004).

10. Noble, G., "Accumulating Being," *International Journal of Cultural Studies* 7 (2004): 233–256.

11. Smith, G. V. and Ekerdt, D. J., "Confronting the Material Convoy in Later Life," *Sociological Inquiry* 81 (2011): 377–391.

12. Carter, H. C., *Storied Possessions: Post-Household Disbandment Older Adult Place-making Through Meaningful Belongings* (PhD diss., University of Missouri, 2018).

13. Dittmar, H., *The Social Psychology of Material Possessions: To Have Is to Be* (New York: St Martin's, 1992); Douglas, M. and Isherwood, B. *The World of Goods: Towards an Anthropology of Consumption*, rev. ed. (London: Routledge, 1996); Gabriel, Y. and Lang, T., *The Unmanageable Consumer: Contemporary Consumption and Its Fragmentation* (Thousand Oaks, CA: Sage, 1995); Hughes, A. and Reimer, S. eds., *Geographies of Commodity Chains* (London: Routledge, 2004); Lunt, P. K. and Livingstone, S. M., *Mass Consumption and Personal Identity* (Philadelphia: Open University Press, 1992); Sassatelli, R. *Consumer Culture: History, Theory, and Politics* (London: Sage, 2007).

14. Gregson, N., *Living with Things: Ridding, Accommodation, Dwelling* (Herefordshire, UK: Sean Kingston Publishing, 2007), 2; Cruz-Cárdenas, J. and Arévalo-Chávez, P., "Consumer Behavior in the Disposal of Products: Forty Years of Research," *Journal of Promotion Management* 24 (2018): 617–636; Miller, D., "The Uses of Value," *Geoforum* 39 (2008): 1122–1132.

15. Dant, T., *Material Culture in the Social World: Values, Activities, Lifestyles* (Philadelphia: Open University Press, 1999).

16. Kleine, S. S. and Baker, S. M., "An Integrative Review of Material Possession Attachment," *Academy of Marketing Science Review* 1 (2004): 1–39; McCracken, G., *Culture and Consumption: New Approaches to the Symbolic Character of Consumer Goods and Activities* (Bloomington: University of Indiana Press, 1988).

17. Ekerdt, D. J., Sergeant, J. F., Dingel, M., and Bowen, M. E., "Household Disbandment in Later Life," *Journals of Gerontology Series B: Psychological Sciences and Social Sciences* 59 (2004): S265–S273.

18. McCracken, *Culture and Consumption*.

19. Gabriel and Lang, *The Unmanageable Consumer*.

20. Belk, R. W., "Possessions and the Extended Self," *Journal of Consumer Research* 15 (1988): 139–168; Csikzentmihalyi, M. and Rochberg-Halton, E., *The Meaning of Things: Domestic Symbols and the Self* (Cambridge: Cambridge University Press, 1981).

21. McCracken, G., "Culture and Consumption Among the Elderly: Three Research Objectives in an Emerging Field," *Ageing & Society* 7 (1987): 214.

22. Markus, H. and Nurius, P., "Possible Selves," *American Psychologist* 41 (1986): 954–969.

23. Mauss, M., *The Gift: The Form and Reason for Exchange in Archaic Societies* (New York: W.W. Norton, 1990).

24. Curasi, C. F., Price, L. L., and Arnould, E. J., "How Individuals' Cherished Possessions Become Families' Inalienable Wealth," *Journal of Consumer Research* 31 (2004):

609–622; Thompson, M., *Rubbish Theory: The Creation and Destruction of Value* (New York: Oxford University Press, 1979); Tobin, S. S., "Cherished Possessions: The Meaning of Things" *Generations* 20, no. 3 (1996): 46–48.

25. Gregson, *Living with Things*.

26. Murphy, K. R. and Gordon, E. M., "New Housing Characteristics in 1955 and Earlier Years." *Monthly Labor Review* (1956): 796–804; U.S. Department of Commerce, *2015 Characteristics of New Housing*, 2015, https://www.census.gov/construction/chars/pdf/c25ann2015.pdf.

27. Harris, A., "U.S. Self-Storage Industry Statistics," *SpareFoot Storage Beat* (updated March 11, 2019), https://www.sparefoot.com/self-storage/news/1432-self-storage-industry-statistics/.

28. Csikszentmihalyi and Rochberg-Halton, *The meaning of things*; Kamptner, N. L., "Personal Possessions and Their Meanings in Old Age," in *The Social Psychology of Aging*, ed. S. Spacapan and S. Oskamp, 165–196 (Newbury Park, CA: Sage, 1989); Richins, M. L., "Valuing Things: The Public and Private Meanings of Possessions," *Journal of Consumer Research* 21 (1994): 504–521; Rubinstein, R. L., "The Significance of Personal Objects to Older People," *Journal of Aging Studies* 1 (1987): 225–238.

29. Belk, "Possessions and the Extended Self"; Csikszentmihalyi and Rochberg-Halton, *The Meaning of Things*; Furby, L., "Possession in Humans: An Exploratory Study of its Meaning and Motivation," *Social Behavior and Personality* 6 (1978): 49–65; Richins, "Valuing Things."

30. Dittmar, *The Social Psychology of Material Possessions*.

31. Belk, "Possessions and the Extended Self," 139; Furby, "Possession in Humans."

32. Kahneman, D., *Thinking, Fast and Slow* (New York: Farrar, Straus and Giroux, 2011).

33. Sartre, J. P., *Being and Nothingness*, trans. H. Barnes (New York: Washington Square Press, 1956), 591.

34. Fromm, E., *To Have or To Be?* (New York: Harper & Row, 1976), 109.

35. Gregson, *Living with Things*, 160.

36. Ekerdt, D.J., "Dispossession: The Tenacity of Things," in *Consumption and Generational Change: The Rise of Consumer Lifestyles and the Transformation of Later Life*, ed. I. R. Jones, P. Higgs, and D. J. Ekerdt, 63–78 (New Brunswick, NJ: Transaction Books, 2009); Lastovicka, J. L. and Fernandez, K.V., "Three Paths to Disposition: The Movement of Meaningful Possessions to Strangers," *Journal of Consumer Research* 31 (2005): 813–823; Roster, C. A., "Letting Go: The Process and Meaning of Dispossession in the Lives of Consumers," *Advances in Consumer Research* 21 (2001): 425–430.

37. Douglas and Isherwood, *The World of Goods*.

38. Morris, B. R., "Reducing Inventory: Divesture of Personal Possessions," *Journal of Women and Aging* 4 (1992): 79–92.

39. Bauman, Z., *Consuming Life* (Malden, MA: Polity Press, 2007); Bourdieu, P. *Distinction: A Social Critique of the Judgement of Taste*, trans. R. Nice (Cambridge, MA: Harvard University Press, 1984); Gosling, S. D., *Snoop: What Your Stuff Says About You* (New York: Basic Books, 2008).

40. Freedonia Group, "Home Organization Products: Demand and Sales Forecasts, Market Share, Market Size, Market Leaders" (study no. 3714, February 2019), https://www.freedoniagroup.com/Home-Organization-Products.html.

41. Lastovicka and Fernandez, "Three Paths to Disposition"; Young, M. M. and Wallendorf, M., "'Ashes to Ashes, Dust to Dust': Conceptualizing Consumer Disposition of Possessions" (paper presented at the American Marketing Association Winter Educators Conference, Chicago, IL, 1989).

42. Johnson, C. L. and Barer, B. M., *Life Beyond 85 Years: The Aura of Survivorship* (New York: Springer, 1997); Morris, "Reducing Inventory."

43. Marsiske, M., Lang, F. R., Baltes, P. B., and Baltes, M. M., "Selective Optimization with Compensation: Life-Span Perspectives on Successful Human Development." In *Compensating for Psychological Deficits and Declines: Managing Losses and Promoting Gains*, ed. R. A. Dixon and. L. Bäckman, 35–79 (Mahway, NJ: Erlbaum, 1995).

44. Gregson, N. and Crewe, L. *Second-Hand Cultures* (Oxford, UK: Berg Publishers, 2003), 202.

45. Elder, Johnson, and Crosnoe, "The Emergence and Development of Life Course Theory."

46. Price, L. L., Arnould, E. J., and Curasi, C. F., "Older Consumers' Disposition of Special Possessions," *Journal of Consumer Research* 27 (2000): 179–201.

47. Shenk, D., Kuwahara, K., and Zablotsky, D., "Older Women's Attachments to Their Home and Possessions," *Journal of Aging Studies* 18 (2004): 157–169.

48. Ekerdt, D. J. and Sergeant, J. F., "Family Things: Attending the Household Disbandment of Older Adults," *Journal of Aging Studies* 20 (2006): 193–205; Price, Arnould, and Curasi, "Older Consumers' Disposition of Special Possessions"; Stum, M. S., "'I Just Want to Be Fair': Interpersonal Justice in Intergenerational Transfers of Nontitled Property," *Family Relations* 48 (1999): 159–166.

49. Roster, "Letting Go."

50. Ekerdt, D. J., "Things and Possessions," in *Ageing in Everyday Life: Materialities and Embodiments*, ed. S. Katz, 29–44 (Bristol, UK: Policy Press, 2018).

51. Gell, A., *Art and Agency: An Anthropological Theory* (Oxford: Oxford University Press, 1998); Joyce, P. and Bennett, T., "Material Powers: Introduction," in *Material Powers: Cultural Studies, History and the Material Turn*, ed. T. Bennett and P. Joyce, 1–22 (New York: Routledge, 2010).

52. Otter, C., "Locating Matter: The Place of Materiality in Urban History," in *Material Powers: Cultural Studies, History and the Material Turn.*, ed. T. Bennett and P. Joyce, 54–75 (New York: Routledge, 2010).

53. Bennett, T. and Joyce, P., eds., *Material Powers: Cultural Studies, History and the Material Turn* (New York: Routledge, 2010); Pickering, A., *The Mangle of Practice: Time, Agency, and Science* (Chicago: University of Chicago Press, 2010).

54. Joyce and Bennet, *Material Powers.*

55. Golant, S. M., *Aging in the Right Place* (Baltimore, MD: Health Professions Press, 2015); Wahl, H.-W., Iwarsson, S., and Oswald, F., "Aging Well and the Environment:

Toward an Integrative Model and Research Agenda for the Future," *Gerontologist* 52 (2012): 306–316.

56. Diaz Moore, K., "Interpreting the "Hidden Program" of a Place: An Example from Dementia Day Care," *Journal of Aging Studies* 18 (2004): 297–320.

57. Oxenhandler, N., "Object Lesson," *New Yorker*, August 7, 1995, 39–41.

58. Ekerdt and Sergeant, "Family Things"; Smith and Ekerdt, "Confronting the Material Convoy in Later Life."

2. WITH AGING, HOW LARGE A CONVOY?

1. Gabriel, Y. and Lang, T., *The Unmanageable Consumer: Contemporary Consumption and Its Fragmentation* (Thousand Oaks, CA: Sage, 1995), 1.

2. Miller, D., "Consumption." In *Handbook of Material Culture.*, ed. C. Tilley, W. Keane, S. Kuchler, M. Rowlands, and P. Spyer, 341–354 (London: Sage, 2006).

3. Cloutier, D., *The Vice of Luxury: Economic Excess in a Consumer Age* (Washington, DC: Georgetown University Press, 2015); Trentmann, F., *Empire of Things: How We Became a World of Consumers, from the Fifteenth Century to the Twenty-First* (New York: HarperCollins, 2016).

4. Sassatelli, R., *Consumer Culture: History, Theory, and Politics* (London: Sage, 2007).

5. Thébaud, S., Kornrich, S., and Ruppanner, L., "Good Housekeeping, Great Expectations: Gender and Housework Norms," *Sociological Methods & Research* (2019): advance publication online.

6. For example, Lucchesi, E. L., "In the Clutter, Reasons to Worry," *New York Times*, January 19, 2019; Semuels, A., "'We Are All Accumulating Mountains of Things': How Online Shopping and Cheap Prices Are Turning Americans Into Hoarders," *Atlantic*, August 21, 2018, https://www.theatlantic.com/technology/archive/2018/08/online-shopping-and-accumulation-of-junk/567985/.

7. Smith, G. V. and Ekerdt, D. J. "Confronting The Material Convoy in Later Life," *Sociological Inquiry* 81 (2011): 377–391.

8. Gauntlett, D., *Media, Gender and Identity: An Introduction* (London: Routledge, 2008); McGee, M., *Self-Help, Inc.: Makeover Culture in American Life* (New York: Oxford University Press, 2005).

9. Simonds, W., *Women and Self-Help Culture: Reading Between the Lines* (New Brunswick, NJ: Rutgers University Press, 1992), 133.

10. Kondo, M., *The Life-Changing Magic of Tidying Up: The Japanese Art of Decluttering and Organizing* (Berkeley, CA: Ten Speed Press, 2014); Wallman, J., *Stuffocation: Why We've Had Enough of Stuff and Need Experience More Than Ever* (New York: Spiegel and Grau, 2015).

11. Cwerner, S. B. and Metcalfe, A., "Storage and Clutter: Discourses and Practices of Order in the Domestic World," *Journal of Design History* 16 (2003): 232.

12. Perry, T. E., "Leaving Home in Later Life: Voluntary Housing Transitions of Older Adults as Gift Giving Practices in the Midwestern United States" (PhD diss., University of Michigan, 2012), ProQuest (AAT 3554198), 157.

13. Menzel, P. and Mann, C. C., *Material World: A Global Family Portrait* (San Francisco: Sierra Club Books, 1994).

14. Landy, M., *Breakdown Inventory* (London: Ridinghouse, 2002).

15. Arnold, J. E., Graesch, A. P., Ragazzini, E., and Ochs, E. *Life at Home in the Twenty-First Century: 32 Families Open Their Doors* (Los Angeles: Cotsen Institute of Archaeology Press, 2012), 25.

16. Arnold et al., *Life at Home in the Twenty-First Century*, 161.

17. Gosling, S. D., Craik, K. H., Martin, N. R., and Pryor, M.R., "The Personal Living Space Cue Inventory: An Analysis and Evaluation," *Environment and Behavior* 37 (2005): 702.

18. Antonucci, T. C., Birditt, K. S., and Ajrouch, K. J. "Convoys of Social Relations: Past, Present and Future," in *Handbook of Life Span Development*, ed. K. L. Fingerman, C. A. Berg, J. Smith, and T. C. Antonucci, 161–182 (New York: Springer, 2011).

19. Arnold et al., *Life at Home in the Twenty-First Century*; Cwerner and Metcalfe, "Storage and Clutter"; Hirschman, E. C., Ruvio, A., and Belk, R. W., "Exploring Space and Place in Marketing Research: Excavating the Garage," *Marketing Theory* 12 (2012): 369–389.

20. Löfgren, O. "It's Simply Too Much! Coping with Domestic Overflow," in *Managing Overflow in Affluent Societies*, ed. B. Czarniawska and O. Löfgren, 101–124 (New York: Routledge, 2012).

21. Korosec-Serfaty, P., "The Home from Attic to Cellar," *Journal of Environmental Psychology* 4 (1984): 304.

22. Korosec-Serfaty, "The Home from Attic to Cellar," 313.

23. Cluver, B. G., "Consumer Clothing Inventory Management" (PhD diss, Oregon State University, 2008), ProQuest (AAT. 3336382); Woodward, S., "The Hidden Lives of Domestic Things: Accumulations in Cupboards, Lofts, and Shelves," in *Intimacies, Critical Consumption and Diverse Economies*, ed. E. Casey and Y. Taylor, 216–231 (London: Palgrave Macmillan, 2015).

24. Gregson, N., *Living with Things: Ridding, Accommodation, Dwelling* (Herefordshire, UK: Sean Kingston Publishing, 2007), 118, 164.

25. Drolet, A., Schwarz, N., and Yoon, C., eds., *The Aging Consumer: Perspectives from Psychology and Economics* (New York: Routledge, 2011).

26. Csikzentmihalyi, M. and Rochberg-Halton, E., *The Meaning of Things: Domestic Symbols and the Self* (Cambridge: Cambridge University Press, 1981), 56.

27. Sherman, E. and Newman, E. S., "The meaning of Cherished Personal Possessions for the Elderly,"*Journal of Aging and Human Development* 8 (1977–78): 188.

28. Price, L. L., Arnould, E. J., and Curasi, C. F. "Older Consumers' Disposition of Special Possessions," *Journal of Consumer Research* 27 (2000): 179–201.

29. McCracken, G. "Culture Consumption Among the Elderly: Three Research Objectives in an Emerging Field," *Ageing and Society* 7 (1987): 203–224.

30. Csikszentmihalyi and Rochberg-Halton, *The Meaning of Things*, 95.

31. Carstensen, L. L., " Social and Emotional Patterns in Adulthood: Support for Socioemotional Selectivity Theory," *Psychology and Aging* 7 (1992): 331–338; Carstensen, L. L., Isaacowitz, D. M., and Charles, S. T., "Taking Time Seriously: A Theory of Socioemotional Selectivity," *American Psychologist* 54 (1999): 165–181.

32. Drolet, A., Lau-Gesk, L., Williams, P., and Jeong, H. G., "Socio-emotional Selectivity Theory: Implications for Consumer Research," in *The Aging Consumer: Perspectives from Psychology and Economics*, ed. A. Drolet, N. Schwarz, and C. Yoon, 51–72 (New York: Routledge, 2011).

33. Fung, H. H., Carstensen, L. L., and Lutz, A. M., "Influence of Time On Social Preferences: Implications for Life-Span Development," *Psychology and Aging* 14 (1990): 595–604.

34. Riley, M., Foner, A., and Waring, J. "Sociology of Age," in *Handbook of Sociology*, ed. N. J. Smelzer, 243–290 (Newbury Park, CA: Sage, 1988).

35. Ekerdt, D. J., Luborsky, M., and Lysack, C., "Safe Passage of Goods and Self During Residential Relocation in Later Life," *Ageing and Society* 32 (2012): 833–850.

36. Jones, I. R., Higgs, P., and Ekerdt, D. J., eds., *Consumption and Generational Change: The Rise of Consumer Lifestyles and the Transformation of Later Life* (New Brunswick, NJ: Transaction Books, 2008).

37. Kleine, S. S. and Baker, S. M., " An Integrative Review of Material Possession Attachment," *Academy of Marketing Science Review* 1 (2004): 1–39.

38. Ekerdt, D. J. and Baker, L. A., "The Material Convoy After Age 50," *Journals of Gerontology Series B: Psychological Sciences and Social Sciences* 69 (2014): 442–450.

39. Cole, T. R., *The Journey of Life: A Cultural History of Aging in America* (New York: Cambridge University Press, 1992).

40. Bucks, B. K., Kennickell, A. B., Mach, T. L., and Moore, K. B. "Changes in U.S. Family Finances from 2004 to 2007: Evidence from the Survey of Consumer Finances," *Federal Reserve Bulletin* (February 2009): A1–A55; Cornwell, B., Laumann, E. O., and Schumm, L. P., "The Social Connectedness of Older Adults: A National Profile," *American Sociological Review* 73 (2008): 185–203; Ferraro, K. F. and Morton, P. M., "What Do We Mean by Accumulation? Advancing Conceptual Precision for a Core Idea in Gerontology," *Journals of Gerontology Series B: Psychological Sciences and Social Sciences* 73 (2018): 269–278.

41. Fernandez-Villaverde, J. and Krueger, D., "Consumption Over the Life Cycle: Facts from Consumer Expenditure Survey Data," *Review of Economics and Statistics* 89 (2007): 552–565; Foster, A. C. "Consumer Expenditures Vary by Age," *Beyond the Numbers: Prices and Spending* 4, no. 14, U.S. Bureau of Labor Statistics, December 2015, https://www.bls.gov/opub/btn/volume-4/consumer-expenditures-vary-by-age.htm.

42. Ajrouch, K. J., Blandon, A. Y., and Antonucci, T. C., "Social Networks Among Men and Women: The Effects of Age and Socioeconomic Status," *Journals of Gerontology Series B: Psychological Sciences and Social Sciences* 60 (2005): S311–S317; Cornwell, Laumann, and Schumm, "The Social Connectedness of Older Adults."

43. Banks, J., Blundell, R., Oldfield, Z., and Smith, J. P., "Housing Price Volatility and Downsizing in Later Life," in *Research Findings in the Economics of Aging*, ed. D. A. Wise, 337–379 (Chicago: University of Chicago Press, 2010).

44. Carstensen, L. L. "The Influence of a Sense of Time on Human Development," *Science* 312 (2006): 1913–1915; Ekerdt, Luborsky, and Lysack, "Safe Passage of Goods and Self During Residential Relocation in Later Life"; Marshall, V. W., "Age and Awareness of Finitude in Developmental Gerontology," *Omega: Journal of Death and Dying* 6 (1975): 113–129.

45. Luborsky, M. R., Lysack, C. L., and Van Nuil, J., "Refashioning One's Place in Time: Stories of Household Downsizing in Later Life," *Journal of Aging Studies* 25 (2011): 243–252.

46. Gal, D., "A Psychological Law of Inertia and the Illusion of Loss Aversion," *Judgment and Decision Making* 1 (2006): 23–32.

47. Ekerdt and Baker, "The Material Convoy After Age 50."

48. Ekerdt, D. J. and Addington, A. "Possession divestment by sales in later life." *Journal of Aging Studies* 34 (2015): 21–28.

49. Ekerdt, D. J., Addington, A., and Hayter, B. "Distributing Possessions: Personal Property Can Become a Social Matter," *Generations* 35, no. 3 (2011): 34–40.

50. Details are in Ekerdt and Baker, "The Material Convoy After Age 50."

51. Ranada, Å. L. and Hagberg, J.-E., "All the Things I Have—Handling One's Material Room in Old Age," *Journal of Aging Studies* 31 (2014): 110–118.

52. AARP, *These Four Walls: Americans 45+ Talk About Home and Community* (Washington, DC: AARP, May 2003).

53. U.S. Census Bureau, "American Fact Finder," United States Census Bureau (website), https://factfinder.census.gov/faces/tableservices/jsf/pages/productview.xhtml.

54. U.S. Census Bureau, *Projected 5-Year Age Groups and Sex Composition: Main Projections Series for the United States, 2017–2060* (Washington, DC: U.S. Census, 2018).

55. Schau, H. J., Gilly, M. C., and Wolfinbarger, M., "Consumer Identity Renaissance: The Resurgence of Identity-Inspired Consumption in Retirement," *Journal of Consumer Research* 36 (2009): 255–276.

56. Gilleard, C. and Higgs, P., *Contexts of Ageing: Class, Cohort and Community* (Malden, MA: Polity Press, 2005); Katz, S., *Cultural Aging: Life Courses, Lifestyle, and Senior Worlds* (Orchard Park, NY: Broadview Press, 2005).

3. MOVING CALLS THE QUESTION

1. Finch, J. and Hayes, L., " Inheritance, Death, and the Concept of the Home," *Sociology* 28 (1994): 417–433.; Guillard, V., "Understanding the Process of the Disposition of a Loved One's Possessions Using A Theoretical Framework of Grief," *Consumption Markets & Culture* 20 (2017): 477–496; Johnson, P., *They Left Us Everything: A Memoir* (New York: G. P. Putnam's Sons, 2016); Lovatt, M., "Charity Shops and the Imagined Futures of Objects: How Second-Hand Markets Influence Disposal Decisions When

Emptying a Parent's House," *Culture Unbound: Journal of Current Cultural Research* 7 (2015): 13–29.

2. Sergeant, J. F., Ekerdt, D. J., and Chapin, R., "Measurement of Late-Life Residential Relocation: Why Are Rates for Such a Manifest Event So Varied?," *Journals of Gerontology Series B: Psychological Sciences and Social Sciences* 63 (2008): S92–S98.

3. Smith, E. K., "Residential Satisfaction, Psychological Well-Being, and Personality Traits: Effects on Relocation among Older Adults" (PhD diss., University of Kansas, 2014), ProQuest (AAT 3665053).

4. Haverstick, K. and Zhivan, N. A., *Older Americans on the Go: How Often, Where, and Why?*, Boston College Center for Retirement Research (2009), 9–18.

5. See also Banks, J., Blundell, R., Oldfield, Z., and Smith, J. P., "Housing Price Volatility and Downsizing in Later Life," in *Research Findings in the Economics of Aging*, ed. D. A. Wise, 337–379 (Chicago: University of Chicago Press, 2010).

6. Joint Center for Housing Studies of Harvard University, *Demographic Change and the Remodeling Outlook* (2017).

7. MetLife Mature Market Institute and National Association of Home Builders, *Housing Trends Update for the 55+ Market: New Insights from the American Housing Survey* (Westport, CT: MetLife, 2011).

8. Banks et al., "Housing Price Volatility and Downsizing in Later Life."

9. Joint Center for Housing Studies of Harvard University, *Housing America's Older Adults: Meeting The Needs of an Aging Population* (2014).

10. Banks et al., "Housing Price Volatility and Downsizing in Later Life."

11. Keenan, T. A., *Home and Community Preferences of the 45+ Population* (Washington, DC: AARP Research and Strategic Analysis, 2010).

12. Vasunilashorn, S., Steinman, B. A., Liebig, P. S., and Pynoos, J., "Aging in Place: Evolution of a Research Topic Whose Time Has Come," *Journal of Aging Research* (2012): article ID 120952.

13. Centers for Disease Control and Prevention, "Healthy Places Terminology," Centers for Disease Control and Prevention (website), https://www.cdc.gov/healthyplaces /terminology.htm.

14. Koss, C. and Ekerdt, D. J., "Residential Reasoning and the Tug of the Fourth Age," *Gerontologist* 57 (2017): 921–929.

15. Speare, A. and Meyer, J. W., "Types of Elderly Residential Mobility and Their Determinants," *Journal of Gerontology* 43 (1988): S74–S81; Wiseman, R. F., "Why Older People Move: Theoretical Issues," *Research on Aging* 2 (1980): 141–154.

16. Litwak, E. and Longino, C. F., Jr., "Migration Patterns Among the Elderly: Developmental Perspective," *Gerontologist* 27 (1987): 266–274.

17. Bradley, D. E. and Longino, C. F., "Geographic Mobility and Aging in Place," in *International Handbook of Population Aging*, ed. P. Uhlenberg, 319–339. New York: Springer, 2009; Evandrou, M., Falkingham, J., and Green, M., "Migration in Later Life: Evidence from the British Household Panel Study," *Population Trends* 141 (2010): 77–94; Weeks, L., Keefe, J., and Macdonald, D., "Factors Predicting Relocation Among Older Adults," *Journal of Housing for the Elderly* 26 (2012): 355–371.

18. Lawton, M. P. and Nahemow, L., "Ecology and the Aging Process," in *The Psychology of Adult Development and Aging*, ed. C. Eisdorfer and M. P. Lawton, 619–674 (Washington, DC: American Psychological Association, 1973).

19. Kahana, E., Lovegreen, L., Kahana, B., and Kahana, M., " Person, Environment, and Person-Environment Fit as Influences on Residential Satisfaction of Elders," *Environment and Behavior* 35 (2003): 434–453.

20. Diaz Moore, K., "An Ecological Framework of Place: Situating Environmental Gerontology Within a Life Course Perspective," *International Journal of Aging and Human Development* 79 (2014): 183–209; Rowles, G. D. and Watkins, J. F., "History, Habit, Heart and Hearth: On Making Spaces Into Places," in *Aging Independently: Living Arrangements and Mobility*, ed. K. W. Shaie, H.-W. Wahl, H. Mollenkopf, and F. Oswald, 77–96 (New York: Springer, 2003); Wahl, H. W. and Oswald, F., "Environmental Perspectives on Ageing," in *The SAGE Handbook of Social Gerontology*, ed. D. Dannefer and C. Philipson, 111–124 (London: Sage, 2010).

21. Golant, S. M., *Aging in the Right Place* (Baltimore, MD: Health Professions Press, 2015).

22. Perry, T. E., Andersen, T. C., and Kaplan, D. B., "Relocation Remembered: Perspectives on Senior Transitions in the Living Environment," *Gerontologist* 54 (2014): 75–81; Scheidt, R. J., and Windley, P. G., "Environmental Gerontology: Progress in the Post-Lawton Era," in *Handbook of the Psychology of Aging*, 6th ed., ed. J. E. Birren and K. W. Schaie, 105–125 (Amsterdam: Elsevier, 2006); Wahl, H.-W., Iwarsson, S., and Oswald, F., "Aging Well and the Environment: Toward an Integrative Model and Research Agenda for the Future," *Gerontologist* 52 (2012): 306–316.

23. Haverstick and Zhivan, *Older Americans on the Go*.

24. Sergeant, J. F. and Ekerdt, D. J., "Motives for Residential Mobility in Later Life: Post-Move Perspectives of Elders and Family Members," *International Journal of Aging and Human Development* 66 (2008): 131–154.

25. Golant, S. M., *Aging in the Right Place.*

26. Granbom, M., Himmelsbach, I., Haak, M., Löfqvist, C., Oswald, F., and Iwarsson, S., "Residential Normalcy and Environmental Experiences of Very Old People: Changes in Residential Reasoning over Time," *Journal of Aging Studies* 29 (2014): 9–19.

27. Koss and Ekerdt, "Residential Reasoning and the Tug of the Fourth Age."

28. Baltes, P. B. and Smith, J., "New Frontiers in the Future of Aging: From Successful Aging of the Young Old to the Dilemmas of the Fourth Age," *Gerontology* 49 (2003): 123–135; Blaikie, A., *Ageing and Popular Culture* (New York: Cambridge University Press, 1999); Lloyd, L., "The Fourth Age," in *Routledge Handbook of Cultural Gerontology*, ed. J. Twigg and W. Martin, 261–268. London: Routledge, 2015.

29. Diehl, M. K. and Wahl, H.-W., "Awareness of Age-Related Change: Examination of a (Mostly) Unexplored Concept," *Journal of Gerontology: Psychological Sciences and Social Sciences* 65B (2010): 340–350.

30. Higgs, P. and Gilleard, C., *Rethinking Old Age: Theorising the Fourth Age* (London: Palgrave, 2015), 14.

31. Ekerdt, D. J. and Sergeant, J. F., "Family Things: Attending the Household Disbandment of Older Adults," *Journal of Aging Studies* 20 (2006): 193–205; Sergeant and Ekerdt, "Motives for Residential Mobility in Later Life."

32. Stum, M. S., "Families and Inheritance Decisions: Examining Non-titled Property Transfers," *Journal of Family and Economic Issues* 21 (2000): 177–202.

33. Sergeant, Ekerdt, and Chapin, "Measurement of Late-Life Residential Relocation."

34. Wahl, H. W. and Lang, F. R., "Aging in Context Across the Adult Life Course: Integrating Physical and Social Environmental Research Perspectives," *Annual Review of Gerontology and Geriatrics* 23 (2003): 1–33.

35. National Association of Realtors Research Group, *2019 Profile of Home Staging*, National Association of Realtors, March 2019, https://www.nar.realtor/sites/default /files/documents/2019-profile-of-home-staging-03-14-2019.pdf.

36. McCracken, G., *Culture and Consumption: New Approaches to the Symbolic Character of Consumer Goods and Activities* (Bloomington: University of Indiana Press, 1988), 87.

37. Redfoot, D. L. and Back, K. W., "The Perceptual Presence of the Life Course," *International Journal of Aging and Human Development* 27 (1988): 155–170.

38. Rowles, G. D. and Chaudhury, H., eds., *Home and Identity in Late Life: International Perspectives* (New York: Springer, 2005); Rowles, G. D. and Bernard, M. A., eds., *Environmental Gerontology: Making Meaningful Places in Old Age* (New York: Springer, 2013).

4. CONTOURS OF HOUSEHOLD DISBANDMENT

1. Korosec-Serfaty, P., "The Home from Attic to Cellar," *Journal of Environmental Psychology* 4 (1984): 304.

2. Perry, T. E., "Leaving Home in Later Life: Voluntary Housing Transitions of Older Adults as Gift Giving Practices in the Midwestern United States" (PhD diss., University of Michigan, 2012), ProQuest (AAT 3554198), 171–172.

3. Gregson, N., *Living with Things: Ridding, Accommodation, Dwelling* (Herefordshire, UK: Sean Kingston Publishing, 2007), 164.

4. Curasi, C. F., Price, L. L., and Arnould, E. J., "How Individuals' Cherished Possessions Become Families' Inalienable Wealth," *Journal of Consumer Research* 31 (2004): 609–622.

5. Ekerdt, D. J., Luborsky, M., and Lysack, C., "Safe Passage of Goods and Self During Residential Relocation in Later Life," *Ageing and Society* 32 (2012): 833–850.

6. Belk, R. W., "Collectors and Collecting," in *Handbook of Material Culture*, ed. C. Tilley, W. Keane, S. Kuchler, M. Rowlands, and P. Spyer, 534–535 (London: Sage Publications, 2006); Pearce, S., *Collecting in Contemporary Practice* (London: Sage, 1997).

7. Gregson, N., *Living with Things.*

8. Gigerenzer, G. and Todd, P. M., *Simple Heuristics That Make Us Smart* (New York: Oxford University Press, 1999), 5; Todd, P. M. and Gigerenzer, G., "Précis of

Simple Heuristics That Make Us Smart," *Behavioral and Brain Sciences* 23 (2000): 727–780.

9. Simon, H. A., "Invariants of Human Behavior," *Annual Review of Psychology* 41 (1990): 1–19.

10. Kondo, M., *The Life-Changing Magic of Tidying Up: The Japanese Art of Decluttering and Organizing* (Berkeley, CA: Ten Speed Press, 2014).

11. Kalymun, M., "The Prevalence of Factors Influencing Decisions Among Elderly Women Concerning Household Possessions During Relocation," *Journal of Housing for the Elderly* 3 (1985): 81–99.

12. Furby, L., "Possession in Humans: An Exploratory Study of Its Meaning and Motivation," *Social Behavior and Personality* 6 (1978): 49–65.

13. Dittmar, H., "Material and Consumer Identities," in *Handbook of Identity Theory and Research*, vol. 2, ed. S. J. Schwartz, K. Luyckx, and V. L. Vignoles, 745–769. New York: Springer Science+Business Media, 2011; Kleine, S. S., Kleine, R. E., and Allen, C. T., "How Is a Possession "Me" or "Not Me"? Characterizing Types and an Antecedent of Material Possession Attachment," *Journal of Consumer Research* 22 (1995): 327–343; Mittal, B., "I, Me, and Mine—How Products Become Consumers' Extended Selves," *Journal of Consumer Behaviour* 5 (2006): 550–562.

14. Fish, S., "Moving On" (*Opinionator* blog), *New York Times*, May 27, 2013.

15. Markus, H. and Nurius, P., "Possible Selves," *American Psychologist* 41 (1986): 954–969.

16. Ekerdt, D. J., Sergeant, J. F., Dingel, M., and Bowen, M. E., "Household Disbandment In Later Life," *Journals of Gerontology Series B: Psychological Sciences and Social Sciences* 59 (2004): S265–S273; Ekerdt, D. J. and Sergeant, J. F., "Family Things: Attending the Household Disbandment of Older Adults," *Journal of Aging Studies* 20 (2006): 193–205.

17. Rowles, G. D. and Chaudhury, H., eds., *Home and Identity in Late Life: International Perspective* (New York: Springer, 2005); Rowles, G. D. and Bernard, M. A., eds., *Environmental Gerontology: Making Meaningful Places in Old Age* (New York: Springer, 2013).

18. Luborsky, M. R., Lysack, C. L., and Van Nuil, J., "Refashioning One's Place in Time: Stories of Household Downsizing in Later Life," *Journal of Aging Studies* 25 (2011): 243–252.

19. Addington, A. and Ekerdt, D. J., "The Reproduction of Gender Norms Through Downsizing in Later Life Residential Relocation," *Research on Aging* 36 (2014): 3–21.

20. Janning, M., *The Stuff of Family Life: How Our Homes Reflect Our Lives* (Lanham, MD: Rowman & Littlefield, 2017); Kinchin, J. "Interiors: Nineteenth-Century Essays on the 'Masculine' and the 'Feminine' Room," in *The Gendered Object*, ed. P. Kirkham, 12–30. Manchester, UK: Manchester University Press, 1996.

21. Ekerdt and Sergeant, "Family Things."

22. Liang, J., Krause, N. M., and Bennett, J., "Social Exchange and Well-Being: Is Giving Better Than Receiving?," *Psychology and Aging* 16 (2001): 511–523.

23. Aneshensel, C. S., Pearlin, L. I., Mullan, J. T., Zarit, S. H., and Whitlatch, C. J. *Profiles in Caregiving: The Unexpected Career* (San Diego: Academic Press, 1995).

5. GIFTS TO OTHERS

1. Carrier, J. G., "Exchange," in *Handbook of Material Culture*, ed. C. Tilley, W. Keane, S. Kuchler, M. Rowlands, and P. Spyer, 373–383 (London: Sage Publications, 2006); Otnes, C. and Beltramini, R. F., eds., *Gift Giving: A Research Anthology* (Bowling Green, OH: Bowling Green State University Popular Press, 1996).

2. Angel, J. L., Mudrazija, S., and Binstock, R., "Aging, Inheritance, and Gift-Giving," in *Handbook of Aging and the Social Sciences*, 7th ed., ed. R. H. Binstock and L. K. George, 163–173 (Burlington, MA: Academic Press); Finch, J. and Mason, J., *Passing On: Kinship and Inheritance in England* (London: Routledge, 2013); Remle, R. C., "The Midlife Financial Squeeze: Intergenerational Transfers of Financial Resources Within Aging Families," in *Handbook of Sociology of Aging*, ed. R. A. Settersten and J. L. Angel, 179–192 (New York: Springer Science + Business Media, 2011).

3. Price, L. L., Arnould, E. J., and Curasi, C. F. "Older Consumers' Disposition of Special Possessions," *Journal of Consumer Research* 27 (2000): 179–201.

4. Ruth, J. A., Otnes, C. C., and Brunel, F. F., "Gift Receipt and the Reformulation of Interpersonal Relationships," *Journal of Consumer Research* 25 (1999): 385–402.

5. Hunter, E. G. and Rowles, G. D., "Leaving a Legacy: Toward a Typology," *Journal of Aging Studies* 19 (2005): 327–247; Marcoux, J.-S., "The 'Casser Maison' Ritual: Constructing the Self by Emptying the Home," *Journal of Material Culture* 6 (2001): 213–235; Marx, J. I., Solomon, J. C., and Miller, L. Q., "Gift Wrapping Ourselves: The Final Gift Exchange," *Journal of Gerontology: Social Sciences* 59B (2004): S274–S280.

6. Ekerdt, D. J., Luborsky, M., and Lysack, C., "Safe Passage of Goods and Self During Residential Relocation in Later Life," *Ageing and Society* 32 (2012): 833–850.

7. Roster, C. A., "Letting Go: The Process and Meaning of Dispossession in the Lives of Consumers," *Advances in Consumer Research* 21 (2001): 425–430.

8. Addington, A. and Ekerdt, D. J., "The Reproduction of Gender Norms Through Downsizing in Later Life Residential Relocation," *Research on Aging* 36 (2014): 3–21; Gregson, N., Metcalfe, A., and Crewe, L., "Moving Things Along: The Conduits and Practices of Divestment in Consumption," *Transactions of the Institute of British Geographers* 32 (2007b): 187–200; Price, Arnould, and Curasi, "Older Consumers' Disposition of Special Possessions."

9. Kirkham, P., ed., *The Gendered Object* (Manchester, UK: Manchester University Press, 1996).

10. Addington and Ekerdt, "The Reproduction of Gender Norms Through Downsizing in Later Life Residential Relocation."

11. Finch and Mason, *Passing On*.

12. Marcoux, "The 'Casser Maison' Ritual."

13. Curasi, C. F., Price, L. L., and Arnould, E. J., "How Individuals' Cherished Possessions Become Families' Inalienable Wealth," *Journal of Consumer Research* 31 (2004): 609–622; Weiner, A. B., *Inalienable Possessions: The Paradox of Keeping-While-Giving* (Berkeley: University of California Press, 1992).

14. Price, Arnould, and Curasi,"Older Consumers' Disposition of Special Posses-sions"; Stum, M. S., "'I Just Want to Be Fair': Interpersonal Justice in Intergenerational Transfers of Non-titled Property," *Family Relations* 48 (1999): 159–166.

15. This term is adapted from Morris, B. R., "Reducing Inventory: Divesture of Per-sonal Possessions," *Journal of Women and Aging* 4 (1992): 79–92.

16. Marcoux, "The 'Casser Maison' Ritual"; Marx, Solomon, and Miller, "Gift Wrap-ping Ourselves."

17. Marx, Solomon, and Miller, "Gift Wrapping Ourselves."

18. Marcoux, "The 'Casser Maison' Ritual," 222.

19. Curasi, C. F., Price, L. L., and Arnould, E. J., "The Aging Consumer and Inter-generational Transmission of Cherished Possessions," in *The Aging Consumer: Perspec-tives from Psychology and Economics*, ed. A. Drolet, N. Schwarz, and C. Yoon, 149–172 (New York: Routledge, 2010).

20. Marcoux, "The 'Casser Maison' Ritual," 229.

6. SELLING POSSESSIONS

1. Ekerdt, D. J. and Addington, A., "Possession Divestment by Sales in Later Life," *Journal of Aging Studies* 34 (2015): 21–28.

2. Smith, G. V. and Ekerdt, D. J., "Confronting the Material Convoy in Later Life," *Sociological Inquiry* 81 (2011): 377–391.

3. Caramanica, J., "Reality TV's New Wave: Trash Picking with a Smile," *New York Times*, January 8, 2011; Clouse, A. "Narratives of Value and the *Antiques Roadshow*: "A Game of Recognitions," *Journal of Popular Culture* 41 (2008): 3–20; Denegri-Knott, J. and Molesworth, M., "Love it. Buy it. Sell it": Consumer Desire and the Social Drama of eBay," *Journal of Consumer Culture* 10 (2010): 56–79.

4. Appadurai, A., ed., *The Social Life of Things: Commodities in Cultural Perspective* (Cambridge: Cambridge University Press, 1986).

5. Kopytoff, I., "The Cultural Biography of Things: Commodification as a Process," in *The Social Life of Things: Commodities in Cultural Perspective*, ed. A. Appadurai, 64–94. Cambridge: Cambridge University Press, 1986.

6. Gregson, N., Metcalfe, A., and Crewe, L., "Moving Things Along: The Conduits and Practices of Divestment in Consumption," *Transactions of the Institute of British Geogra-phers* 32 (2007b): 187–200; Herrmann, G. M., "Gift or Commodity: What Changes Hands in the U.S. Garage Sale," *American Ethnologist* 24 (1997): 910–930; Lastovicka, J. L. and Fernandez, K.V., "Three Paths to Disposition: The Movement of Meaningful Posses-sions to Strangers," *Journal of Consumer Research* 31 (2005): 813–823.

7. Herrmann, "Gift or Commodity."

8. Ekerdt and Addington, "Possession Divestment by Sales in Later Life."

9. Herrmann, "Gift or Commodity," 916–917.

10. Kahneman, D., *Thinking, Fast and Slow* (New York: Farrar, Straus and Giroux, 2011).

11. Roster, C. A., "Letting Go: The Process and Meaning of Dispossession in the Lives of Consumers," *Advances in Consumer Research* 21 (2001): 425–430.

12. Gregson, N., *Living with Things: Ridding, Accommodation, Dwelling* (Herefordshire, UK: Sean Kingston Publishing, 2007).

13. Herrmann, "Gift or Commodity"; Lastovicka and Fernandez, "Three Paths to Disposition"; McCracken, G., *Culture and Consumption: New Approaches to the Symbolic Character of Consumer Goods and Activities* (Bloomington: University of Indiana Press, 1988); Roster, "Letting Go."

14. Appelgren, S. and Bohlin, A., "Growing in Motion: The Circulation of Used Things on Second-Hand Markets," *Culture Unbound: Journal of Current Cultural Research* 7 (2015): 143–168.

15. Cheetham, F., "Out of Control? An Ethnographic Analysis of the Disposal of Collectable Objects Through Auction," *Journal of Consumer Behaviour* 8 (2009): 318.

16. Lastovicka and Fernandez, "Three Paths to Disposition."

17. Gregson, N., Metcalfe, A., and Crewe, L., "Identity, Mobility and the Throwaway Society," *Environment and Planning D: Society and Space* 25 (2007a): 682–700; Laitala, K. "Consumers' Clothing Disposal Behaviour: A Synthesis of Research Results," *International Journal of Consumer Studies* 38 (2014): 444–457.

18. Zelizer, V. A., *The Social Meaning of Money* (Princeton, NJ: Princeton University Press, 1997).

19. Miller, D., "The Uses of Value," *Geoforum* 39 (2008): 1122–1132.

7. DONATIONS AND DISCARDS

1. Gregson, N., Metcalfe, A., and Crewe, L., "Identity, Mobility and the Throwaway Society," *Environment and Planning D: Society and Space* 25 (2007a): 682–700; Lucas, G., "Disposability and Dispossession in the Twentieth Century," *Journal of Material Culture* 7 (2002): 5–22.

2. Gregson, N. and Crewe, L., *Second-Hand Cultures* (Oxford: Berg Publishers, 2003); Parsons, E., and Maclaran, P., "'Unpacking Disposal': Introduction to the Special Issue," *Journal of Consumer Behaviour* 8 (2009): 301–304.

3. Brooks, A., *Clothing Poverty: The Hidden World of Fast Fashion and Second-Hand Clothes* (London: Zed Books, 2015); Norris, L., "Shoddy Rags and Relief Blankets: Perceptions of Textile Recycling in North India," in *Economies of Recycling: The Global Transformation of Materials, Values and Social Relations.*, ed. C. Alexander and J. Reno, 35–38 (London: Zed Books, 2012); Rivoli, P., *The Travels of a T-Shirt in the Global Economy: An Economist Examines the Markets, Power, and Politics of World Trade*, 2nd ed. (Hoboken, NJ: John Wiley & Sons, 2014).

4. Alexander, C. and Reno, J., eds., *Economies of Recycling: The Global Transformation of Materials, Values and Social Relations* (London: Zed Books, 2012).

5. Appelgren, S. and Bohlin, A., "Growing in Motion: The Circulation of Used Things on Second-Hand Markets," *Culture Unbound: Journal of Current Cultural Re-*

search 7 (2015): 143–168; Gregson and Crewe, *Second-Hand Cultures*; Gregson, N., Metcalfe, A., and Crewe, L., "Moving Things Along: The Conduits and Practices of Divestment in Consumption," *Transactions of the Institute of British Geographers* 32 (2007b): 187–200; Hetherington, K., "Second-Handedness: Consumption, Disposal and Absent Presence," *Environment and Planning D: Society and Space* 22 (2004): 157–173.

6. U.S. Environmental Protection Agency, *Moving Out, Moving In: Making Environmental Choices When You Move* (EPA-530-K-04-002) (Washington, DC: U.S. Environmental Protection Agency, 2004).

7. Strasser, S., *Waste and Want: A Social History of Trash* (New York: Metropolitan Books, 1999), 5.

8. Lieber, R., "Decluttering? Here's What Not to Shed," *New York Times*, February 24, 2018.

9. McCracken, G., *Culture and Consumption: New Approaches to the Symbolic Character of Consumer Goods and Activities* (Bloomington: University of Indiana Press, 1988); Roster, C. A., "Letting Go: The Process and Meaning of Dispossession in the Lives of Consumers," *Advances in Consumer Research* 21 (2001): 425–430.

10. Hetherington, "Second-Handedness," 169.

11. Roster, "Letting Go," 429.

12. Hirschman, E. C., Ruvio, A., and Belk, R. W., "Exploring Space and Place in Marketing Research: Excavating the Garage," *Marketing Theory* 12 (2012): 381.

13. Gregson, N., *Living with Things: Ridding, Accommodation, Dwelling* (Herefordshire, UK: Sean Kingston Publishing, 2007); Hetherington, "Second-Handedness."

8. EMOTION AND EVALUATION

1. Green, O. and Ayalon, L., "'Home Is Where My Couch Is': The Role of Possessions in the Process of Moving and Adjusting to Continuing Care Retirement Communities," *Qualitative Health Research* 29, no. 4 (2019): 577–588.

2. Perry, T. E., "Leaving Home in Later Life: Voluntary Housing Transitions of Older Adults as Gift Giving Practices in the Midwestern United States" (PhD diss., University of Michigan, 2012), ProQuest (AAT 3554198), 179.

3. Price, L. L., Arnould, E. J., and Curasi, C. F., "Older Consumers' Disposition of Special Possessions," *Journal of Consumer Research* 27 (2000): 186.

4. Hetherington, K., "Second-Handedness: Consumption, Disposal and Absent Presence," *Environment and Planning D: Society and Space* 22 (2004): 157–173.

5. Hetherington, "Second-Handedness," 168.

6. Perry, "Leaving Home in Later Life," 159–160.

7. Belk, R. W., "Possessions and the Extended Self," *Journal of Consumer Research* 15 (1988): 139–168.

8. Sergeant, J. F. and Ekerdt, D. J., "Motives for Residential Mobility in Later Life: Post-Move Perspectives of Elders and Family Members," *International Journal of Aging and Human Development* 66 (2008): 131–154.

9. Ariely, D. and Wertenbroch, K., "Procrastination, Deadlines, and Performance: Self-Control by Precommitment," *Psychological Science* 13 (2002): 219–224.

10. Folkman, S., "Stress: Appraisal and Coping," in *Encyclopedia of Behavioral Medicine*, ed. M. Gellman and J. R. Turner, 1913–1915 (New York: Springer, 2013).

11. Freund, P. E. S., "The Expressive Body: A Common Ground for the Sociology of Emotions and Health and Illness," *Sociology of Health & Illness* 12 (1990): 452–477.

12. Desmond, M., *Evicted: Poverty and Profit in the American City* (New York: Crown Publishers, 2016), 285–286.

13. Luborsky, M. R., Lysack, C. L., and Van Nuil, J., "Refashioning One's Place in Time: Stories of Household Downsizing in Later Life," *Journal of Aging Studies* 25 (2011): 243–252.

14. Ekerdt, D. J., Luborsky, M., and Lysack, C., "Safe Passage of Goods and Self During Residential Relocation in Later Life," *Ageing and Society* 32 (2012): 833–850.

15. Kleine, S. S. and Baker, S. M., "An Integrative Review of Material Possession Attachment," *Academy of Marketing Science Review* 1 (2004): 1–39.

16. Marsiske, M., Lang, F. R., Baltes, P. B., and Baltes, M. M., "Selective Optimization with Compensation: Life-Span Perspectives on Successful Human Development," in *Compensating for Psychological Deficits and Declines: Managing Losses and Promoting Gains*, ed. R. A. Dixon and. L. Bäckman, 35–79 (Mahway, NJ: Erlbaum, 1995).

17. Koss, C. and Ekerdt, D. J., "Residential Reasoning and the Tug of the Fourth Age," *Gerontologist* 57 (2017): 921–929.

9. ADVICE

1. U.S. Department of Agriculture, Cooperative Extension, "Organize Important Papers," Financial Security for All, May 30, 2019, https://articles.extension.org/pages /11750/organize-important-papers.

2. Smith, G. V. and Ekerdt, D. J., "Confronting the Material Convoy in Later Life," *Sociological Inquiry* 81 (2011): 377–391.

3. Woodward, S., "The Hidden Lives of Domestic Things: Accumulations in Cupboards, Lofts, and Shelves," in *Intimacies, Critical Consumption and Diverse Economies*, ed. E. Casey and Y. Taylor, 216–231 (New York: Palgrave Macmillan, 2015).

4. Ekerdt, D., "In Defense of the Not-So-Busy Retirement," *Wall Street Journal*, April 23, 2018.

5. Ekerdt, D. J., Koss, C. S., Li, A., Münch, A., Lessenich, S., and Fung, H. H., "Is Longevity a Value for Older Adults?," *Journal of Aging Studies* 43 (2017): 46–52.

6. Koss, C. and Ekerdt, D. J., "Residential Reasoning and the Tug of the Fourth Age," *Gerontologist* 57 (2017): 921–929.

7. Magnusson, M., *The Gentle Art of Swedish Death Cleaning: How to Free Yourself and Your Family from a Lifetime of Clutter* (New York: Scribner, 2017).

8. Wadler, J., "Sex Toys in the Attic" (*Booming* blog), *New York Times*, November 9, 2013.

9. Hetherington, K. "Second-Handedness: Consumption, Disposal and Absent Presence," *Environment and Planning D: Society and Space* 22 (2004): 157–173.

10. Perry, T. E., "Moving as a Gift: Relocation in Older Adulthood," *Journal of Aging Studies* 31 (2014): 1–9.

11. Chast, R., *Can't We Talk about Something More Pleasant? A Memoir* (New York: Bloomsbury Publishing, 2014).

12. Marcoux, J.-S., "The 'Casser Maison' Ritual: Constructing the Self by Emptying the Home," *Journal of Material Culture* 6 (2001): 213–235.

13. Gregson, N., Metcalfe, A., and Crewe, L., "Moving Things Along: The Conduits and Practices of Divestment in Consumption," *Transactions of the Institute of British Geographers* 32 (2007): 187–200; Hetherington, "Second-Handedness."

REFERENCES

AARP. *These Four Walls: Americans 45+ Talk About Home and Community.* Washington, DC: AARP, May 2003.

Addington, A., and Ekerdt, D. J. "The Reproduction of Gender Norms Through Downsizing in Later Life Residential Relocation." *Research on Aging* 36 (2014): 3–21.

Ajrouch, K. J., Blandon, A. Y., and Antonucci, T. C. "Social Networks Among Men and Women: The Effects of Age and Socioeconomic Status." *Journals of Gerontology Series B: Psychological Sciences and Social Sciences* 60 (2005): S311–S317

Alexander, C., and Reno, J., eds. *Economies of Recycling: The Global Transformation of Materials, Values and Social Relations.* London: Zed Books, 2012.

Aneshensel, C. S., Pearlin, L. I., Mullan, J. T., Zarit, S. H., and Whitlatch, C. J. *Profiles in Caregiving: The Unexpected Career.* San Diego: Academic Press, 1995.

Angel, J. L., Mudrazija, S., and Binstock, R. "Aging, Inheritance, and Gift-Giving." In *Handbook of Aging and the Social Sciences*, 7th ed., ed. R. H. Binstock and L. K. George, 163–173. Burlington, MA: Academic Press.

Antonucci, T. C., Ajrouch, K. J., and Birditt, K. S. "The Convoy Model: Explaining Social Relations from a Multidisciplinary Perspective." *Gerontologist* 54 (2013): 82–92.

Antonucci, T. C., Birditt, K. S., and Ajrouch, K. J. "Convoys of Social Relations: Past, Present and Future." In *Handbook of Life Span Development*, ed. K. L. Fingerman, C. A. Berg, J. Smith, and T. C. Antonucci, 161–182. New York: Springer, 2011.

Appadurai, A., ed. *The Social Life of Things: Commodities in Cultural Perspective.* Cambridge: Cambridge University Press, 1986.

Appelgren, S., and Bohlin, A. "Growing in Motion: The Circulation of Used Things on Second-Hand Markets." *Culture Unbound: Journal of Current Cultural Research* 7 (2015): 143–168.

Ariely, D., and Wertenbroch, K. "Procrastination, Deadlines, and Performance: Self-Control by Precommitment." *Psychological Science* 13 (2002): 219–224.

Arnold, J. E., Graesch, A. P., Ragazzini, E., and Ochs, E. *Life at Home in the Twenty-First Century: 32 Families Open Their Doors*. Los Angeles: Cotsen Institute of Archaeology Press, 2012.

Austad, S. N. "Making Sense of Biological Theories of Aging." In *Handbook of Theories of Aging*, 2nd ed., ed. V. L. Bengtson, D. Gans, N. M. Putney, and M. Silverstein, 147–161. New York: Springer, 2009.

Baltes, P. B. "On the Incomplete Architecture of Human Ontogeny: Selection, Optimization, And Compensation as Foundation of Developmental Theory." *American Psychologist* 52 (1997): 366–380.

Baltes, P. B., and Smith, J. "New Frontiers in the Future of Aging: From Successful Aging of the Young Old to the Dilemmas of the Fourth Age." *Gerontology* 49 (2003): 123–135.

Banks, J., Blundell, R., Oldfield, Z., and Smith, J. P. "Housing Price Volatility and Downsizing in Later Life." In *Research Findings in the Economics of Aging*, ed. D. A. Wise, 337–379. Chicago: University of Chicago Press, 2010.

Bauman, Z. *Consuming Life*. Malden, MA: Polity Press, 2007.

Belk, R. W. "Possessions and the Extended Self." *Journal of Consumer Research* 15 (1988): 139–168.

———. "Collectors and Collecting." In *Handbook of Material Culture*, ed. C. Tilley, W. Keane, S. Kuchler, M. Rowlands, and P. Spyer, 534–535. London: Sage Publications, 2006.

Bennett, T., and Joyce, P. eds. *Material Powers: Cultural Studies, History and the Material Turn*. New York: Routledge, 2010.

Blaikie, A. *Ageing and Popular Culture*. New York: Cambridge University Press, 1999.

Bosworth, B. *Economic Consequences of the Great Recession: Evidence from the Panel Study of Income Dynamics*. Working paper no. 2012-4, Center for Retirement Research at Boston College, February 2012.

Bourdieu, P. *Distinction: A Social Critique of the Judgement of Taste*, trans. R. Nice, Cambridge, MA: Harvard University Press, 1984.

Bradley, D. E., and Longino, C. F. "Geographic Mobility and Aging in Place." In *International Handbook of Population Aging*, ed. P. Uhlenberg, 319–339. New York: Springer, 2009.

Braun, V., and Clarke, V. "Using Thematic Analysis in Psychology." *Qualitative Research in Psychology* 3 (2006): 77–101.

Brooks, A. *Clothing Poverty: The Hidden World of Fast Fashion and Second-Hand Clothes*. London: Zed Books, 2015.

Brown, B. *A Sense of Things*. Chicago: University of Chicago Press, 2004.

Bucks, B. K., Kennickell, A. B., Mach, T. L., and Moore, K. B. "Changes in U.S. Family Finances from 2004 To 2007: Evidence from the Survey of Consumer Finances." *Federal Reserve Bulletin* (February 2009): A1–A55.

Calasanti, T. M., and Slevin, K. F. *Gender, Social Inequalities, and Aging*. Walnut Creek, CA: Rowman Altamira, 2001.

Caramanica, J. "Reality TV's New Wave: Trash Picking with a Smile." *New York Times*, January 8, 2011.

Carr, D. *Golden Years?: Social Inequality in Later Life*. New York: Russell Sage Foundation, 2019.

Carrier, J. G. "Exchange." In *Handbook of Material Culture*, ed. C. Tilley, W. Keane, S. Kuchler, M. Rowlands, and P. Spyer, 373–383. London: Sage Publications, 2006.

Carstensen, L. L. "Social and Emotional Patterns in Adulthood: Support for Socioemotional Selectivity Theory." *Psychology and Aging* 7 (1992): 331–338.

———. "The Influence of a Sense of Time on Human Development." *Science* 312 (2006): 1913–1915.

Carstensen, L. L., Isaacowitz, D. M., and Charles, S. T. "Taking Time Seriously: A Theory of Socioemotional Selectivity." *American Psychologist* 54 (1999): 165–181.

Carter, H. C. "Storied Possessions: Post-Household Disbandment Older Adult Placemaking Through Meaningful Belongings." PhD diss., University of Missouri, 2018.

Centers for Disease Control and Prevention. "Healthy Places Terminology." Centers for Disease Control and Prevention (website). https://www.cdc.gov/healthyplaces/terminology.htm.

Chapin, R. K., Sergeant, J. F., Landry, S. T., Koenig, T., Leiste, M., and Reynolds, K. "Hoarding Cases Involving Older Adults: The Transition from a Private Matter to the Public Sector." *Journal of Gerontological Social Work* 53 (2010): 723–742.

Chast, R. *Can't We Talk About Something More Pleasant? A Memoir*. New York: Bloomsbury Publishing, 2014.

Cheetham, F. "Out of Control? An Ethnographic Analysis of the Disposal of Collectable Objects Through Auction." *Journal of Consumer Behaviour* 8 (2009): 316–326.

Clouse, A. "Narratives of Value and the *Antiques Roadshow*: "A Game of Recognitions." *Journal of Popular Culture* 41 (2008): 3–20.

Cloutier, D. *The Vice of Luxury: Economic Excess in a Consumer Age*. Washington, DC: Georgetown University Press, 2015.

Cluver, B. G. "Consumer Clothing Inventory Management." PhD diss., Oregon State University, 2008. ProQuest (AAT 3336382).

Cole, T. R. *The Journey of Life: A Cultural History of Aging in America*. New York: Cambridge University Press, 1992.

Cornwell, B., Laumann, E. O., and Schumm, L. P. "The Social Connectedness of Older Adults: A National Profile." *American Sociological Review* 73 (2008): 185–203.

Cruz-Cárdenas, J., and Arévalo-Chávez, P. "Consumer Behavior in the Disposal of Products: Forty Years of Research." *Journal of Promotion Management* 24 (2018): 617–636.

Csikzentmihalyi, M., and Rochberg-Halton, E. *The Meaning of Things: Domestic Symbols and the Self*. Cambridge: Cambridge University Press, 1981.

Curasi, C. F., Price, L. L., and Arnould, E. J. "How Individuals' Cherished Possessions Become Families' Inalienable Wealth." *Journal of Consumer Research* 31 (2004): 609–622.

———. "The Aging Consumer and Intergenerational Transmission of Cherished Possessions." In *The Aging Consumer: Perspectives from Psychology and Economics*, ed. A. Drolet, N. Schwarz and C. Yoon, 149–172. New York: Routledge, 2010.

Cwerner, S. B., and Metcalfe, A. "Storage and Clutter: Discourses and Practices of Order in the Domestic World." *Journal of Design History* 16 (2003): 229–239.

Dannefer, D., and Uhlenberg, P. "Paths of the Life Course: A Typology." In *Handbook of Theories of Aging*, ed. V. L. Bengtson and K. W. Schaie, 306–326. New York: Springer, 1999.

Dant, T. *Material Culture in the Social World: Values, Activities, Lifestyles*. Philadelphia: Open University Press, 1999.

Deaton, A. "The Financial Crisis and the Well-Being of Americans: 2011." OEP Hicks Lecture. *Oxford Economic Papers* 64 (2012): 1–26.

Denegri-Knott, J., and Molesworth, M. "Love It. Buy It. Sell It": Consumer Desire and the Social Drama of eBay." *Journal of Consumer Culture* 10 (2010): 56–79.

Desmond, M. *Evicted: Poverty and Profit in the American City*. New York: Crown Publishers, 2016.

Diaz Moore, K. "Interpreting the "Hidden Program" of a Place: An Example from Dementia Day Care." *Journal of Aging Studies* 18 (2004): 297–320.

———. "An Ecological Framework of Place: Situating Environmental Gerontology Within a Life Course Perspective." *International Journal of Aging and Human Development* 79 (2014): 183–209.

Diaz Moore, K., and Ekerdt, D. J. "Age and the Cultivation of Place." *Journal of Aging Studies* 25 (2011): 189–192.

Diehl, M. K., and Wahl, H.-W. "Awareness of Age-Related Change: Examination of a (Mostly) Unexplored Concept." *Journal of Gerontology: Psychological Sciences and Social Sciences* 65B (2010): 340–350.

Dittmar, H. *The Social Psychology of Material Possessions: To Have Is to Be*. New York: St Martin's, 1992.

———. "Material and Consumer Identities." In *Handbook of Identity Theory and Research*, vol. 2, ed. S. J. Schwartz, K. Luyckx, and V. L. Vignoles, 745–769. New York: Springer Science+Business Media, 2011.

Douglas, M., and Isherwood, B. *The World of Goods: Towards an Anthropology of Consumption*, rev. ed. London: Routledge, 1996.

Drolet, A., Lau-Gesk, L., Williams, P., and Jeong, H. G. "Socio-emotional Selectivity Theory: Implications for Consumer Research." In *The Aging Consumer: Perspectives from Psychology and Economics*, ed. A. Drolet, N. Schwarz, and C. Yoon, 51–72. New York: Routledge, 2011.

Drolet, A., Schwarz, N., and Yoon, C., eds. *The Aging Consumer: Perspectives from Psychology and Economics*. New York: Routledge, 2011.

Ekerdt, D. J. "Dispossession: The Tenacity of Things." In *Consumption and Generational Change: The Rise of Consumer Lifestyles and the Transformation of Later Life*, ed. I. R. Jones, P. Higgs, and D. J. Ekerdt, 63–78. New Brunswick, NJ: Transaction Books, 2009.

———. "Possessions as a Material Convoy." In *Routledge Handbook of Cultural Gerontology*, ed. J. Twigg and W. Martin, 313–320. London: Routledge, 2015.

———. "In Defense of the Not-So-Busy Retirement." *Wall Street Journal*, April 23, 2018: R1–R2.

———. "Things and Possessions." In *Ageing in Everyday Life: Materialities and Embodiments*, ed. S. Katz, 29–44. Bristol, UK: Policy Press, 2018.

Ekerdt, D. J., and Addington, A. "Possession Divestment by Sales in Later Life." *Journal of Aging Studies* 34 (2015): 21–28.

Ekerdt, D. J., Addington, A., and Hayter, B. "Distributing Possessions: Personal Property Can Become a Social Matter." *Generations* 35, no.3 (2011): 34–40.

Ekerdt, D. J., and Baker, L. A. "The Material Convoy After Age 50." *Journals of Gerontology Series B: Psychological Sciences and Social Sciences* 69 (2014):442–450.

Ekerdt, D. J., Koss, C. S., Li, A., Münch, A., Lessenich, S., and Fung, H. H. "Is Longevity a Value for Older Adults?" *Journal of Aging Studies* 43 (2017): 46–52.

Ekerdt, D. J., Luborsky, M., and Lysack, C. "Safe Passage of Goods and Self During Residential Relocation in Later Life." *Ageing and Society* 32 (2012): 833–850.

Ekerdt, D. J., and Sergeant, J. F. "Family Things: Attending the Household Disbandment of Older Adults." *Journal of Aging Studies* 20 (2006): 193–205.

Ekerdt, D. J., Sergeant, J. F., Dingel, M., and Bowen, M. E. "Household Disbandment in Later Life." *Journals of Gerontology Series B: Psychological Sciences and Social Sciences* 59 (2004): S265–S273.

Elder, G. H., Johnson, M. K., and Crosnoe, R. "The Emergence and Development of Life Course Theory." In *Handbook of the Life Course*, ed. J. T. Mortimer and M. J. Shanahan, 3–19. New York: Springer, 2004.

Evandrou, M., Falkingham, J., and Green, M. "Migration in Later Life: Evidence from the British Household Panel Study." *Population Trends* 141 (2010): 77–94.

Fereday, J., and Muir-Cochrane, E. "Demonstrating Rigor Using Thematic Analysis: A Hybrid Approach of Inductive and Deductive Coding and Theme Development." *International Journal of Qualitative Methods* 5 (2006): 80–92.

Fernandez-Villaverde, J., and Krueger, D. "Consumption Over the Life Cycle: Facts from Consumer Expenditure Survey Data." *Review of Economics and Statistics* 89 (2007): 552–565.

Ferraro, K. F., and Morton, P. M. "What Do We Mean by Accumulation? Advancing Conceptual Precision for a Core Idea in Gerontology." *Journals of Gerontology Series B: Psychological Sciences and Social Sciences* 73 (2018): 269–278.

Financial Crisis Inquiry Commission. *Financial Crisis Inquiry Report.* New York: Public Affairs, 2011.

Finch, J., and Hayes, L. "Inheritance, Death, and the Concept of the Home." *Sociology* 28 (1994): 417–433.

Finch, J., and Mason, J. *Passing On: Kinship and Inheritance in England.* London: Routledge, 2013.

Fingerman, K. L., and Hay, E. "Intergenerational Ambivalence in the Context of the Larger Social Network." In *Intergenerational Ambivalences: New Perspectives on*

Parent-Child Relations in Late Life, ed. K. Pillemer and. K. Luscher, 133–151. New York: Elsevier/JAI Press, 2004.

Fish, S. "Moving On" (*Opinionator* blog). *New York Times,* May 27, 2013.

Folkman, S. "Stress: Appraisal and Coping." In *Encyclopedia of Behavioral Medicine,* ed. M. Gellman and J. R. Turner, 1913–1915. New York: Springer, 2013.

Foster, A. C. "Consumer Expenditures Vary by Age." *Beyond the Numbers: Prices and Spending* 4, no. 14. U.S. Bureau of Labor Statistics, December 2015, https://www.bls.gov/opub/btn/volume-4/consumer-expenditures-vary-by-age.htm.

Freedonia Group. "Home Organization Products: Demand and Sales Forecasts, Market Share, Market Size, Market Leaders." Study no. 3714, February 2019, https://www.freedoniagroup.com/Home-Organization-Products.html.

Freund, P. E. S. "The Expressive Body: A Common Ground for the Sociology of Emotions and Health and Illness." *Sociology of Health & Illness* 12 (1990): 452–477.

Fromm, E. *To Have or To Be?* New York: Harper & Row, 1976.

Frost, R. O., and Steketee, G., eds. *The Oxford Handbook of Hoarding and Acquiring.* New York: Oxford University Press, 2014.

Fung, H. H., Carstensen, L. L., and Lutz, A. M. "Influence of Time on Social Preferences: Implications for Life-Span Development." *Psychology and Aging* 14 (1990): 595–604.

Furby, L. "Possession in Humans: An Exploratory Study of Its Meaning and Motivation." *Social Behavior and Personality* 6 (1978): 49–65.

Gabriel, Y., and Lang, T. *The Unmanageable Consumer: Contemporary Consumption and Its Fragmentation.* Thousand Oaks, CA: Sage, 1995.

Gal, D. "A Psychological Law of Inertia and the Illusion of Loss Aversion." *Judgment and Decision Making* 1 (2006): 23–32.

Gauntlett, D. *Media, Gender and Identity: An Introduction.* London: Routledge, 2008.

Gell, A. *Art and Agency: An Anthropological Theory.* Oxford: Oxford University Press, 1998.

Gigerenzer, G., and Todd., P. M. *Simple Heuristics That Make Us Smart.* New York: Oxford University Press, 1999.

Gilleard, C. and Higgs, P. *Contexts of Ageing: Class, Cohort and Community.* Malden, MA: Polity Press, 2005.

Golant, S. M. *Aging in the Right Place.* Baltimore, MD: Health Professions Press, 2015.

Gosling, S. D. *Snoop: What Your Stuff Says About You.* New York: Basic Books, 2008.

Gosling, S. D., Craik, K. H., Martin, N. R., and Pryor, M. R. "The Personal Living Space Cue Inventory: An Analysis and Evaluation." *Environment and Behavior* 37 (2005): 683–705.

Granbom, M., Himmelsbach, I., Haak, M., Löfqvist, C., Oswald, F., and Iwarsson, S. "Residential Normalcy and Environmental Experiences of Very Old People: Changes in Residential Reasoning over Time." *Journal of Aging Studies* 29 (2014): 9–19.

Green, O., and Ayalon, L. "'Home Is Where My Couch Is': The Role of Possessions in the Process of Moving and Adjusting to Continuing Care Retirement Communities." *Qualitative Health Research* 29, no. 4 (2019): 577–588.

Gregson, N. *Living with Things: Ridding, Accommodation, Dwelling.* Herefordshire, UK: Sean Kingston Publishing, 2007.

Gregson, N., and Crewe, L. *Second-Hand Cultures.* Oxford: Berg Publishers, 2003.

Gregson, N., Metcalfe, A., and Crewe, L. "Identity, Mobility and the Throwaway Society." *Environment and Planning D: Society and Space* 25 (2007): 682–700.

———. "Moving Things Along: The Conduits and Practices of Divestment in Consumption." *Transactions of the Institute of British Geographers* 32 (2007): 187–200.

Guillard, V. "Understanding the Process of the Disposition of a Loved One's Possessions Using a Theoretical Framework of Grief." *Consumption Markets & Culture* 20 (2017): 477–496.

Harris, A. "U.S. Self-Storage Industry Statistics." *SpareFoot Storage Beat,* updated March 11, 2019, https://www.sparefoot.com/self-storage/news/1432-self-storage-industry-statistics/.

Haverstick, K., and Zhivan, N. A. *Older Americans on the Go: How Often, Where, and Why?* Boston College Center for Retirement Research (2009), 9–18.

Herrmann, G. M. "Gift or Commodity: What Changes Hands in the U.S. Garage Sale." *American Ethnologist* 24 (1997): 910–930.

Hetherington, K. "Second-Handedness: Consumption, Disposal and Absent Presence." *Environment and Planning D: Society and Space* 22 (2004): 157–173.

Higgs, P. and Gilleard, C. *Rethinking Old Age: Theorising the Fourth Age.* London: Palgrave, 2015.

Hirschman, E. C., Ruvio, A., and Belk, R. W. "Exploring Space and Place in Marketing Research: Excavating the Garage." *Marketing Theory* 12 (2012): 369–389.

Hochschild, A. "The Commercial Spirit of Intimate Life and the Abduction of Feminism: Signs from Women's Advice Books." *Theory, Culture & Society* 11 (1994): 1–24.

Höppner, G., and Urban, M. "Where and How Do Aging Processes Take Place in Everyday Life? Answers from a New Materialist Perspective." *Frontiers in Sociology* 3 (2018): 1–10.

Hughes, A., and Reimer, S. eds., *Geographies of Commodity Chains.* London: Routledge, 2004.

Hunter, E. G., and Rowles, G. D. "Leaving a Legacy: Toward a Typology." *Journal of Aging Studies* 19 (2005): 327–247.

Janning, M. *The Stuff of Family Life: How Our Homes Reflect Our Lives.* Lanham, MD: Rowman & Littlefield, 2017.

Johnson, C. L., and Barer, B. M. *Life Beyond 85 Years: The Aura of Survivorship.* New York: Springer, 1997.

Johnson, P. *They Left Us Everything: A Memoir.* New York: G. P. Putnam's Sons, 2016.

Joint Center for Housing Studies of Harvard University. *Housing America's Older Adults: Meeting the Needs of an Aging Population.* 2014.

———. *Demographic Change and the Remodeling Outlook.* 2017.

Jones, I. R., Higgs, P., and Ekerdt, D. J., eds. *Consumption and Generational Change: The Rise of Consumer Lifestyles and the Transformation of Later Life.* New Brunswick, NJ: Transaction Books, 2008.

Joyce, P., and Bennett, T. "Material Powers: Introduction." In *Material Powers: Cultural Studies, History and the Material Turn*, ed. T. Bennett and P. Joyce, 1–22. New York: Routledge, 2010.

Kahana, E., Lovegreen, L., Kahana, B., and Kahana, M. "Person, Environment, and Person-Environment Fit as Influences on Residential Satisfaction of Elders." *Environment and Behavior* 35 (2003): 434–453.

Kahn, R. L., and Antonucci, T. C. "Convoys Over the Life Course: Attachment, Roles, and Social Support." In *Life-Span Development and Behavior*, ed. P. B. Baltes and O. G. Brim, 253–286. New York: Academic Press, 1980.

Kahneman, D. *Thinking, Fast and Slow*. New York: Farrar, Straus and Giroux, 2011.

Kalymun, M. "The Prevalence of Factors Influencing Decisions Among Elderly Women Concerning Household Possessions During Relocation." *Journal of Housing for the Elderly* 3 (1985): 81–99.

Kamptner, N. L. "Personal Possessions and Their Meanings in Old Age." In *The Social Psychology of Aging*, ed. S. Spacapan and S. Oskamp, 165–196. Newbury Park, CA: Sage, 1989.

Katz, S. *Cultural Aging: Life Courses, Lifestyle, and Senior Worlds*. Orchard Park, NY: Broadview Press, 2005.

Katz, S., ed., *Ageing in Everyday Life: Materialities and Embodiments*. Bristol, UK: Policy Press, 2018.

Keenan, T. A. *Home and Community Preferences of the 45+ Population*. Washington, DC: AARP Research and Strategic Analysis, 2010.

Kinchin, J. "Interiors: Nineteenth-Century Essays on the 'Masculine' and the 'Feminine' Room." In *The Gendered Object*, ed. P. Kirkham, 12–30. Manchester, UK: Manchester University Press, 1996.

Kirkham, P., ed. *The Gendered Object*. Manchester, UK: Manchester University Press, 1996.

Kleine, S. S., and Baker, S. M. "An Integrative Review of Material Possession Attachment." *Academy of Marketing Science Review* 1 (2004): 1–39.

Kleine, S. S., Kleine, R. E., and Allen, C. T. "How Is a Possession "Me" or "Not Me"? Characterizing Types and an Antecedent of Material Possession Attachment." *Journal of Consumer Research* 22 (1995): 327–343.

Kondo, M. *The Life-Changing Magic of Tidying Up: The Japanese Art of Decluttering and Organizing*. Berkeley, CA: Ten Speed Press, 2014.

Kopytoff, I. "The Cultural Biography of Things: Commodification as a Process." In *The Social Life of Things: Commodities in Cultural Perspective*, ed. A. Appadurai, 64–94. Cambridge: Cambridge University Press, 1986.

Korosec-Serfaty, P. "The Home from Attic to Cellar." *Journal of Environmental Psychology* 4 (1984): 303–321.

Koss, C., and Ekerdt, D. J. "Residential Reasoning and the Tug of the Fourth Age." *Gerontologist* 57 (2017): 921–929.

Kroger, J., and Adair, V. "Symbolic Meanings of Valued Personal Objects in Identity Transitions of Late Adulthood." *Identity* 8 (2008): 5–24.

Laitala, K. "Consumers' Clothing Disposal Behaviour: A Synthesis of Research Results." *International Journal of Consumer Studies* 38 (2014): 444–457.

Landy, M. *Breakdown Inventory.* London: Ridinghouse, 2002.

Lastovicka, J. L., and Fernandez, K. V. "Three Paths to Disposition: The Movement of Meaningful Possessions to Strangers." *Journal of Consumer Research* 31 (2005): 813–823.

Laterman, K. "Helping Those Who Hoard." *New York Times*, July 2, 2017.

Lawton, M. P., and Nahemow, L. "Ecology and the Aging Process." In *The Psychology of Adult Development and Aging*, ed. C. Eisdorfer and M. P. Lawton, 619–674. Washington, DC: American Psychological Association, 1973.

Liang, J., Krause, N. M., and Bennett, J. "Social Exchange and Well-Being: Is Giving Better Than Receiving?" *Psychology and Aging* 16 (2001): 511–523.

Lieber, R. "Decluttering? Here's What Not to Shed." *New York Times*, February 24, 2018.

Litwak, E., and Longino, C. F., Jr. "Migration Patterns Among the Elderly: Developmental Perspective." *Gerontologist* 27 (1987): 266–274.

Lloyd, L. "The Fourth Age." In *Routledge Handbook of Cultural Gerontology*, ed. J. Twigg and W. Martin, 261–268. London: Routledge, 2015.

Löfgren, O. "It's Simply Too Much! Coping with Domestic Overflow." In *Managing Overflow in Affluent Societies*, ed. B. Czarniawska and O. Löfgren, 101–124. New York, Routledge, 2012.

Lovatt, M. "Charity Shops and the Imagined Futures of Objects: How Second-Hand Markets Influence Disposal Decisions When Emptying a Parent's House." *Culture Unbound: Journal of Current Cultural Research* 7 (2015): 13–29.

Luborsky, M. R., Lysack, C. L., and Van Nuil, J. "Refashioning One's Place in Time. Stories of Household Downsizing in Later Life." *Journal of Aging Studies* 25 (2011): 243–252.

Lucas, G. "Disposability and Dispossession in the Twentieth Century." *Journal of Material Culture* 7 (2002): 5–22.

Lucchesi, E. L. "In the Clutter, Reasons to Worry." *New York Times*, January 19, 2019.

Lunt, P. K., and Livingstone, S. M. *Mass Consumption and Personal Identity.* Philadelphia: Open University Press, 1992.

Magnusson, M. *The Gentle Art of Swedish Death Cleaning: How to Free Yourself and Your Family from a Lifetime of Clutter.* New York: Scribner, 2017.

Marcoux, J.-S. "The 'Casser Maison' Ritual: Constructing the Self by Emptying the Home." *Journal of Material Culture* 6 (2001): 213–235.

Markus, H., and Nurius, P. "Possible Selves." *American Psychologist* 41 (1986): 954–969.

Marshall, V. W. "Age and Awareness of Finitude in Developmental Gerontology." *Omega: Journal of Death and Dying* 6 (1975): 113–129.

Marsiske, M., Lang, F. R., Baltes, P. B., and Baltes, M. M. "Selective Optimization with Compensation: Life-Span Perspectives on Successful Human Development." In *Compensating for Psychological Deficits and Declines: Managing Losses and Promoting Gains*, ed. R. A. Dixon and. L. Bäckman, 35–79. Mahway, NJ: Erlbaum, 1995.

Marx, J. I., Solomon, J. C., and Miller, L. Q. "Gift Wrapping Ourselves: The Final Gift Exchange." *Journal of Gerontology: Social Sciences* 59B (2004): S274–S280.

Mauss, M. *The Gift: The Form and Reason for Exchange in Archaic Societies*. New York: W. W. Norton, 1990.

Mayer, K. U. "New Directions in Life Course Research." *Annual Review of Sociology* 35 (2009): 413–433.

McCracken, G. "Culture and Consumption Among the Elderly: Three Research Objectives in an Emerging Field." *Ageing & Society* 7 (1987): 203–224.

———. *Culture and Consumption: New Approaches to the Symbolic Character of Consumer Goods and Activities*. Bloomington: University of Indiana Press, 1988.

McGee, M. *Self-Help, Inc.: Makeover Culture in American Life*. New York: Oxford University Press, 2005.

Menzel, P., and Mann, C. C. *Material World: A Global Family Portrait*. San Francisco: Sierra Club Books, 1994.

MetLife Mature Market Institute and National Association of Home Builders. *Housing Trends Update for the 55+ Market: New Insights from the American Housing Survey*. Westport, CT: MetLife, 2011.

Miller, D. "Consumption." In *Handbook of Material Culture*, ed. C. Tilley, W. Keane, S. Kuchler, M. Rowlands, and P. Spyer, 341–354. London: Sage, 2006.

———. "The Uses of Value." *Geoforum* 39 (2008): 1122–1132.

———. *Stuff*. Cambridge: Polity Press, 2010.

———. *Consumption and Its Consequences*. Cambridge: Polity Press, 2012.

Mittal, B. "I, Me, and Mine—How Products Become Consumers' Extended Selves." *Journal of Consumer Behaviour* 5 (2006): 550–562.

Morris, B. R. "Reducing Inventory: Divesture of Personal Possessions." *Journal of Women and Aging* 4 (1992): 79–92.

Murphy, K. R., and Gordon, E. M. "New Housing Characteristics in 1955 and Earlier Years." *Monthly Labor Review* (1956): 796–804.

National Association of Realtors Research Group, *2019 Profile of Home Staging*, National Association of Realtors, March 2019, https://www.nar.realtor/sites/default/files/documents/2019-profile-of-home-staging-03-14-2019.pdf.

Noble, G. "Accumulating Being." *International Journal of Cultural Studies* 7 (2004): 233–256.

Nord, C. "A Day to Be Lived: Elderly Peoples' Possessions for Everyday Life in Assisted Living." *Journal of Aging Studies* 27 (2013): 135–142.

Norris, L. "Shoddy Rags and Relief Blankets: Perceptions of Textile Recycling in North India." In *Economies of Recycling: The Global Transformation of Materials, Values and Social Relations*, ed. C. Alexander and J. Reno, 35–38. London: Zed Books, 2012.

Otnes, C., and Beltramini, R. F., eds., *Gift Giving: A Research Anthology*. Bowling Green, OH: Bowling Green State University Popular Press, 1996.

Otter, C. "Locating Matter: The Place of Materiality in Urban History." In *Material Powers: Cultural Studies, History and the Material Turn*, ed. T. Bennett and P. Joyce, 54–75. New York: Routledge, 2010.

Oxenhandler, N. "Object Lesson." *New Yorker*, August 7, 1995, 39–41.

Parsons, E., and Maclaran, P. "'Unpacking Disposal': Introduction to the Special Issue." *Journal of Consumer Behaviour* 8 (2009): 301–304.

Pearce, S. *Collecting in Contemporary Practice*. London: Sage, 1997.

Perry, T. E. "Leaving Home in Later Life: Voluntary Housing Transitions of Older Adults as Gift Giving Practices in the Midwestern United States." PhD diss., University of Michigan, 2012. ProQuest (AAT 3554198).

———. "Moving as a Gift: Relocation in Older Adulthood." *Journal of Aging Studies* 31 (2014): 1–9.

Perry, T. E., Andersen, T. C., and Kaplan, D. B. "Relocation Remembered: Perspectives on Senior Transitions in the Living Environment." *Gerontologist* 54 (2014): 75–81.

Pickering, A. *The Mangle of Practice: Time, Agency, and Science*. Chicago: University of Chicago Press, 2010.

Plath, D. V. *Long Engagements: Maturity in Modern Japan*. Stanford, CA: Stanford University Press, 1980.

Price, L. L., Arnould, E. J., and Curasi, C. F. "Older Consumers' Disposition of Special Possessions." *Journal of Consumer Research* 27 (2000): 179–201.

Ranada, Å. L., and Hagberg, J.-E. "All the Things I Have—Handling One's Material Room in Old Age." *Journal of Aging Studies* 31 (2014): 110–118.

Redfoot, D. L., and Back, K. W. "The Perceptual Presence of the Life Course." *International Journal of Aging and Human Development* 27 (1988): 155–170.

Remle, R. C. "The Midlife Financial Squeeze: Intergenerational Transfers of Financial Resources Within Aging Families." In *Handbook of Sociology of Aging*, ed. R. A. Settersten and J. L. Angel, 179–192. New York: Springer Science + Business Media, 2011.

Richins, M. L. "Valuing Things: The Public and Private Meanings of Possessions." *Journal of Consumer Research* 21 (1994): 504–521.

Riley, M., Foner, A., and Waring, J. "Sociology of Age." In *Handbook of Sociology*, ed. N. J. Smelzer, 243–290. Newbury Park, CA: Sage, 1988.

Rivoli, P. *The Travels of a T-Shirt in the Global Economy: An Economist Examines the Markets, Power, and Politics of World Trade*, 2nd ed. Hoboken, NJ: John Wiley & Sons, 2014.

Roster, C. A. "Letting Go: The Process and Meaning of Dispossession in the Lives of Consumers." *Advances in Consumer Research* 21 (2001): 425–430.

Rowles, G. D., and Bernard, M. A., eds. *Environmental Gerontology: Making Meaningful Places in Old Age*. New York: Springer, 2013.

Rowles, G. D., and Chaudhury, H., eds. *Home and Identity in Late Life: International Perspectives*. New York: Springer, 2005.

Rowles, G. D., and Watkins, J. F. "History, Habit, Heart and Hearth: On Making Spaces into Places." In *Aging Independently: Living Arrangements and Mobility*, ed. K. W. Shaie, H.-W. Wahl, H. Mollenkopf, and F. Oswald, 77–96. New York: Springer, 2003.

Rubinstein, R. L. "The Significance of Personal Objects to Older People." *Journal of Aging Studies* 1 (1987): 225–238.

Ruth, J. A., Otnes, C. C., and Brunel, F. F. "Gift Receipt and the Reformulation of Interpersonal Relationships." *Journal of Consumer Research* 25 (1999): 385–402.

Ryan, G. W., and Bernard, H. R. "Data Management and Analysis Methods." In *Handbook of Qualitative Research*, 2nd ed., ed. N. K. Denzin and Y. S. Lincoln, 769–802. Thousand Oaks, CA: Sage, 2000.

Sartre, J. P. *Being and Nothingness*, trans. H. Barnes. New York: Washington Square Press, 1956.

Sassatelli, R. *Consumer Culture: History, Theory, and Politics*. London: Sage, 2007.

Schau, H. J., Gilly, M. C., and Wolfinbarger, M. "Consumer Identity Renaissance: The Resurgence of Identity-Inspired Consumption in Retirement." *Journal of Consumer Research* 36 (2009): 255–276.

Scheidt, R. J., and Windley, P. G. "Environmental Gerontology: Progress in the Post-Lawton Era." In *Handbook of the Psychology of Aging*, 6th ed., ed. J. E. Birren and K. W. Schaie, 105–125. Amsterdam: Elsevier, 2006.

Semuels, A. "'We Are All Accumulating Mountains of Things': How Online Shopping and Cheap Prices Are Turning Americans into Hoarders." *Atlantic*, August 21, 2018, https://www.theatlantic.com/technology/archive/2018/08/online-shopping-and-accumulation-of-junk/567985/.

Sergeant, J. F., and Ekerdt, D. J. "Motives for Residential Mobility in Later Life: Post-Move Perspectives of Elders and Family Members." *International Journal of Aging and Human Development* 66 (2008): 131–154.

Sergeant, J. F., Ekerdt, D. J., and Chapin, R. "Measurement of Late-Life Residential Relocation: Why Are Rates for Such a Manifest Event So Varied?" *Journals of Gerontology Series B: Psychological Sciences and Social Sciences* 63 (2008): S92–S98.

———. "Older Adults' Expectations to Move: Do They Predict Actual Community-Based or Nursing Facility Moves Within 2 Years?" *Journal of Aging and Health* 22 (2010): 1029–1053.

Shenk, D., Kuwahara, K, and Zablotsky, D. "Older Women's Attachments to Their Home and Possessions." *Journal of Aging Studies* 18 (2004): 157–169.

Sherman, E., and Newman, E. S. "The Meaning of Cherished Personal Possessions for the Elderly." *Journal of Aging and Human Development* 8 (1977–78): 181–192.

Silverman, D. *Interpreting Qualitative Data: Methods for Analysing Talk, Text, and Interaction*, 2nd ed. London: Sage, 2001.

Simon, H. A. "Invariants of Human Behavior." *Annual Review of Psychology* 41 (1990): 1–19.

Simonds, W. *Women and Self-Help Culture: Reading Between the Lines*. New Brunswick, NJ: Rutgers University Press, 1992.

Smith, E. K. "Residential Satisfaction, Psychological Well-Being, and Personality Traits: Effects on Relocation among Older Adults." PhD diss., University of Kansas, 2014. ProQuest (AAT 3665053).

Smith, G. V., and Ekerdt, D. J. "Confronting the Material Convoy in Later Life." *Sociological Inquiry* 81 (2011): 377–391.

Speare, A., and Meyer, J. W. "Types of Elderly Residential Mobility and Their Determinants." *Journal of Gerontology* 43 (1988): S74–S81.

Strasser, S. *Waste and Want: A Social History of Trash*. New York: Metropolitan Books, 1999.

Stum, M. S. "'I Just Want to Be Fair': Interpersonal Justice in Intergenerational Transfers of Non-titled Property." *Family Relations* 48 (1999): 159–166.

——. "Families and Inheritance Decisions: Examining Non-titled Property Transfers." *Journal of Family and Economic Issues* 21 (2000): 177–202.

Thébaud, S., Kornrich, S., and Ruppanner, L. "Good Housekeeping, Great Expectations: Gender and Housework Norms." *Sociological Methods & Research* (2019): advance publication online.

Thompson, M. *Rubbish Theory: The Creation and Destruction of Value.* New York: Oxford University Press, 1979.

Timpano, K. R., Muroff, J., and Steketee, G. "A Review of the Diagnosis and Management of Hoarding Disorder." *Current Treatment Options in Psychiatry* 3 (2016): 394–410.

Tobin, S. S. "Cherished Possessions: The Meaning of Things." *Generations* 20, no. 3 (1996): 46–48.

Todd, P. M., and Gigerenzer, G. "Précis of *Simple Heuristics That Make Us Smart.*" *Behavioral and Brain Sciences* 23 (2000): 727–780.

Tolin, D., Frost, R. O., and Steketee, G. *Buried in Treasures: Help for Compulsive Acquiring, Saving, and Hoarding,* 2nd ed. New York: Oxford University Press, 2014.

Trentmann, F. *Empire of Things: How We Became a World of Consumers, from the Fifteenth Century to the Twenty-First.* New York: HarperCollins, 2016.

Twigg, J., and Martin, W., eds., *Routledge Handbook of Cultural Gerontology.* London: Routledge, 2015.

U.S. Census Bureau. "American Fact Finder." United States Census Bureau (website). https://factfinder.census.gov/faces/tableservices/jsf/pages/productview.xhtml.

——. *Projected 5-Year Age Groups and Sex Composition: Main Projections Series for the United States, 2017–2060.* Washington, DC: U.S. Census, 2018.

U.S. Department of Agriculture, Cooperative Extension. "Organize Important Papers." Financial Security for All. May 30, 2019. https://articles.extension.org/pages/11750 /organize-important-papers.

U.S. Department of Commerce. *2015 Characteristics of New Housing.* U.S. Department of Housing and Urban Development, 2015, https://www.census.gov/construction /chars/pdf/c25ann2015.pdf.

U.S. Environmental Protection Agency. *Moving Out, Moving In: Making Environmental Choices When You Move* (EPA-530-K-04-002). Washington, DC: U.S. Environmental Protection Agency, 2004.

Vasunilashorn, S., Steinman, B. A., Liebig, P. S., and Pynoos, J. "Aging in Place: Evolution of a Research Topic Whose Time Has Come." *Journal of Aging Research* (2012): article ID 120952.

Wadler, J. "Sex Toys in the Attic" (*Booming* blog). *New York Times,* November 9, 2013.

Wahl, H.-W., Iwarsson, S., and Oswald, F. "Aging Well and the Environment: Toward an Integrative Model and Research Agenda for the Future." *Gerontologist* 52 (2012): 306–316.

Wahl, H. W., and Lang, F. R. "Aging in Context Across the Adult Life Course: Integrating Physical and Social Environmental Research Perspectives." *Annual Review of Gerontology and Geriatrics* 23 (2003): 1–33.

Wahl, H. W., and Oswald, F. "Environmental Perspectives on Ageing." In *The SAGE Handbook of Social Gerontology*, ed. D. Dannefer and C. Philipson, 111–124. London: Sage, 2010.

Wallman, J. *Stuffocation: Why We've Had Enough of Stuff and Need Experience More Than Ever.* New York: Spiegel & Grau, 2015.

Wapner, S., Demick, J., and Redondo, J. P. "Cherished Possessions and Adaptation of Older People to Nursing Homes." *International Journal of Aging and Human Development* 31 (1990): 219–235.

Weeks, L., Keefe, J., and Macdonald, D. "Factors Predicting Relocation Among Older Adults." *Journal of Housing for the Elderly* 26 (2012): 355–371.

Weiner, A. B. *Inalienable Possessions: The Paradox of Keeping-While-Giving.* Berkeley: University of California Press, 1992.

Weiss, R. S. *Learning from Strangers: The Art and Method of Qualitative Interview Studies.* New York: Free Press, 1995.

Wiseman, R. F. "Why Older People Move: Theoretical Issues." *Research on Aging* 2 (1980): 141–154.

Woodward, S. "The Hidden Lives of Domestic Things: Accumulations in Cupboards, Lofts, and Shelves." In *Intimacies, Critical Consumption and Diverse Economies*, ed. E. Casey and Y. Taylor, 216–231. New York: Palgrave Macmillan, 2015.

Young, M. M., and Wallendorf, M. "'Ashes to Ashes, Dust to Dust': Conceptualizing Consumer Disposition of Possessions." Paper presented at the American Marketing Association Winter Educators Conference, Chicago, 1989.

Zelizer, V. A. *The Social Meaning of Money.* Princeton, NJ: Princeton University Press, 1997.

INDEX

Page references in italics refer to the locations where terms are defined.

AARP, 73–74
actor-network theory, 39, 40
Addington, Aislinn, 134
aging, 54–58; fourth age in, 79;
    residential relocations and, 69, 70
aging in place, 74
ancestors, responsibility to, 29–30
Antonucci, Toni, 21
archives, 177
Arnould, Eric, 129
auction sales, 164–165
Ayalon, Liat, 189

baby boom generation, 58
Back, Kurt, 7, 90
Belk, Russell, 4, 32, 193
belongings, 6
birdbaths, 132, 191
books, 105–106, 131; donating, 170, 172,
    177; missing, 192; pleasure derived
    from, 27; selling, 162

Carter, Jimmy, 172
charities, donating possessions to, 170–176

Chast, Roz, 217–218
cherished-object studies, 54–55
cherished possessions, 96–97
children: adoptions of, 24; in
    disbandment context, 120–126;
    disbandment decisions ceded to, 117;
    gender-specific gifts to, 135–136; gifts
    refused by, 146
china. *See* dishes and dining items
claims, fairness and equity in, 138–139
clothes, 106; donating, 172; historical, 177
clutter, 44–47, 219
Cluver, Brigitte, 53
cohorts, 57–58; Health and Retirement
    Study of, 60–67
collections, 97–100; "archiving," 144;
    keeping sample items from, 216; of
    photographs, 143; value of, 27
conduits, 220
consumer commodities, 151–152
consumption, 43–44; by cohorts, 57–58;
    recycling and, 179–180
convoy model of social relations, 21; of
    material support, 22

convoys. *See* material convoys

couples, 116

Craigslist, 89, 113, 162

Csikszentmihalyi, Mihaly, 31, 54, 56

Curasi, Carolyn, 129, 149

Dant, Tim, 25–26

de-accumulation, 82–83

deadline stress, 193–197

deceased spouses, possessions of, 108–109

decommoditization, 151

Detroit, 15–16

disbanding, 7

disbandments, 92, 127; as cognitive task, 93–95; contexts of, 115–126; decisional heuristics in, 101–109; duration of, 88–90; sequence of strategies for, 112–115; sorting in, 95–101

discarding possessions, 169–170, 178–182, 188; two-stage process for, 185–186

dishes and dining items (china), 26–27, 121; declining use of, 107–108; as gifts, 135, 136; pricing of, 161

disposing possessions, 7, 178–180; two-stage process for, 185–186

dispossession, 7

divesting, 7; work of, 38

divestment rituals, 85

documents, 183–185; management of, 210

donating, 169–170, 187–188, 220; flow of possessions leading to, 170–172; intentional placements, 176–178; reasons for, 172–176; in sequence of strategies, 112, 113

Douglas, Mary, 33

downsizing, 7; in anticipation of life changes, 34–35; as parental responsibility, 46; sequence of events in, 82–88; social class and, 198–204; sources of advice on, 210–211

Elder and Family Study, 11–12; collections mentioned in, 98–99; duration of disbandments in, 88; family context for disbandments in, 120, 123; "family things" in, 142; on reasons for moving, 76–77; sale of houses in, 87; sales of possessions in, 152; on work of moving, 194

elderly people. *See* older people

electronics, 104

emotions: in detachment from sold possessions, 163–165; following divesting possessions, 190–193; in moving, 189–190, 193–195; reflecting on moving, 204–209

endowment effect, 32, 161

entertaining, 106–108

environmental gerontology, 39, 75, 91

estate (tag) sales, 158–160, 220; emotions in, 164; pricing in, 160–162; staying away from, 165

exchange theory of aging, 123

fairness and equity in gifting and inheritance, 140–141

family: in context for disbandments, 120–126; "family things," 142, 149; gender and, in gift giving heuristic, 133–136; gifts refused by, 144–148; giving possessions to, 112–113; resistance to de-accumulation by, 83

Fish, Stanley, 106

fishing equipment, 131

fit heuristic, 102–104, 191–192, 197

floor plans, 102

forebears, responsibility to, 29–30

Forever (museum exhibit), 1–3

foster care, 24

fourth age (in life stages), 79, 82

Fromm, Erich, 32

Furby, Lita, 32

furniture, 96; fit heuristic for, 102–104; restocking of, 209; sales of, 156; selling on Craigslist, 162

future, possessions tied to vision of, 28–29

Gabriel, Yiannis, 43

garage sales, 156–157, 160

gender: in giving heuristic, 133–136; space and responsibilities divided by, 116, 117

gifts, 128–129, 148–149, 218–219; ambiguous placements of, 142–144; offers of, and claims for, 137–141; placing decisions for, 129–133; refusals of, 144–148; in sequence of strategies, 112; social reciprocity in, 29

Gosling, Samuel, 48–49

Great Recession, 15, 16

Green, Ohad, 189

Gregson, Nicky, 4, 33, 53, 95–97

Habitat for Humanity, 172, 175

Hagberg, Jan-Erik, 65

Haverstick, Kelly, 71, 76

Health and Retirement Study (HRS), 60, on mobility rates, 70–71; moves anticipated in, 83–84; on reasons for moving, 73–74; results of, 61–67; sales of possessions in, 152–153

health issues: as context in disbandments, 117–118; in reasons for moving, 78, 80–81

Herrmann, Gretchen, 154, 160

Hetherington, Kevin, 185, 215–216

heuristics, 127; deadlines as, 195–197; in disbandments, 101–102; fit, 102–104; gender in, in gift giving, 133–136; household utility, 104; me/not-me, 104–109

hoarding, 10

hobbies, 110

home organization products, 34, 52

home ownership, 72

homes, 9. See also houses

homoctesis (gifting by gender), 134

household disbandment, 92. See also disbandments

household management manuals, 45–46

households: clutter in, 44–45; infrastructure of, 39, 40; possessions in, 47–52

household utility heuristic, 104

houseplants, 132

houses, 9; anticipatory changes in, 80; moving, 69–70; prices of, 15–16; selling, 84–87, 168; size of, 31, 71–73; staging of, 85–86

inalienable things, 142–144

infrastructure of possessions, 39, 40

intentional placements, 176–178

Internal Revenue Service, 176

Isherwood, Baron, 33

junk, 182

Kahn, Robert, 21

Kalymun, Mary, 102

Kamptner, Laura, 31

Kansas City, 15–16

kin. See family

Kondo, Marie, 102

Korosec-Serfaty, Perla, 53

Koss, Catheryn, 79

Kvist, Sannah, 47

La Bohème (opera, Puccini), 221–222

Landy, Michael, 47

Lang, Tim, 43

Lawton, Powell, 75

life changes, 34–35

life course perspective, 20–21; linked lives in, 36

linked lives, 36

lists (inventories), 94

Litwak, Eugene, 75

Longino, Charles, 75

maintenance of material convoys, 35–38

management of possessions, 63–65

Marcoux, Jean-Sébastien, 7, 137, 147–149, 218

marital status, 115–117

Markus, Hazel, 109

Marx, Jonathan, 147

material convoys, 22, 24–25; items in overlapping convoys, 142; maintenance of, 35–38; material agency of, 38–40; restocking of, 209; shedding objects from, 32–35; social class and size of, 198–199; socioemotional selectivity theory applied to, 57

materialism, 34

McCracken, Grant, 28, 85

men: as widowers, 117

me/not-me heuristic, 104–109

Menzel, Peter, 47

Midwest Study, 12, 95; collections mentioned in, 98–99; couples in, 116; duration of disbandments in, 88; family as context for disbandments in, 120; housing price data in, 15–16; on reasons for moving, 77; residential relocating in, 72–73; "safe passage" placement in, 130; sale of houses in, 87; sale of possessions in, 156; trading up in, 206

Miller, Daniel, 6, 43, 167

minimalism, 44

missing possessions, 190–193

mobility rates, 70–71

money: as objective of sales, 165–168; transfers of, 129

mortality: family denials of, 83; moving as confrontation with, 90

move managers, 119–120, 210–211

moving, 69–70; deadline stress in, 193–197; demographic data on, 70–73; environmental responsibilities in, 179; items left behind in, 186–187; moving day, 189–190; reasons for, 73–82; reflecting on, 204–209; sequence of events in, 82–88; social class and, 198–204

museums, 177

Nahemow, Lucille, 75

National Association of Senior Move Managers, 119

Nurius, Paula, 109

objects, 6

older people, 54–58; accumulation pattern for, 59–60; household management manuals for, 45–46

Oxenhandler, Noelle, 40

paper, 183–185; management of, 210

Perry, Tam, 46, 95, 190, 193, 217

photographs, 143

pianos, 146, 192

pleasure in possessions, 27

possessions, 6; acquisition of, 25–26; cherished, 96–97; clutter distinguished from, 44–45; collections, 97–100; discarding, 169–170; donating, 170–172; duration of disbandments of, 88–90; human agency in construction of, 39; infrastructure of, 40; management of, 63–65; pleasure in, 27; reasons for shedding, 32–35; restocking of, 209; selling, 150–152; social roles tied to, 22–23; theories of meanings of, 31–32; tied to vision of future, 28–29; utility of, 26; value of, 26–27; volume of, 61–63

Price, Linda, 55, 129, 190

pricing of items for sales, 160–162

properties, 6

Puccini, Giacomo, 221–222

Ranada, Åsa, 65

recycling, 179, 180

Redfoot, Donald, 7, 90

relocation: disbandments for, 92; possessions as obstacles to, 65–67
residential care, 10
residential reasoning, 79
retirement: as context in disbandments, 118; range of ages for, 74–75; time available in, 213–214
Richins, Marsha, 31
Rochberg-Halton, Eugene, 31, 54, 56
Roster, Catherine, 130, 186
Rubinstein, Robert, 31
rummage sales, 173

"safe passage" placement, 130–132, 176
Sartre, Jean-Paul, 32
self: in detachment from sold possessions, 163–165; in me/not-me heuristic, 104–109; possessions as extensions of, 32; possible future selves, 109–111
self-storage industry, 31, 100–101
selling possessions, 150–151, 167–168; as consumer commodities, 151–152; detachment from, 163–165; pricing for, 160–162; procedures for, 155–160; proceeds from, 166, 168; sellers of, 152–155
senior move managers, 119–120, 210–211
Sergeant, Julie, 70, 76–77, 83, 120
Shenk, Dena, 36
shredding (of documents), 184–185
Simon, Herbert, 101
Smith, Gabriella, 45
social class, 198–204
social convoys, 21; age differences in, 58; future selves in, 109; material convoys distinguished from, 22; measurements of, 49
social networks, 22
social roles: changes in, 34; possessions tied to, 22–23
socioemotional selectivity theory, 57
sorting, 95–101; trash as category in, 181

staging of houses, 85–86
storage: home organization products for, 34, 52; rented storage facilities, 100–101; space for, 31
storytelling, in sales, 163–164
Strasser, Susan, 181
stress in moving, 193–197
stuff, 6, 113–115, 219; donating, 177–178

tag sales. *See* estate (tag) sales
taxes: deductions for donations, 176; shredding of old documents for, 184–185
theft, 33
things, 6
thrift stores, 172, 173
trash, 178–182
treasures, 219
Twomey, Clare, 1–4

unemployment, 16
upkeep of material convoy, 37
utility of possessions, 26; in household utility heuristic, 104

value of possessions, 26–27
volume of possessions, 61–63

wedding dresses, 28, 175, 177
Weiss, Robert, 14
wheelchair ramps, 156
Whiteread, Rachel, 191
widowhood, 115–117; emotions in, 193, 205–208; possessions of deceased husbands, 108–109
wine glasses, 33–34
women's shelters, 175–176
Woodward, Sophie, 53, 213

yard sales, 156–157, 161

Zelizer, Viviana, 167
Zhivan, Natalia, 71, 76